CW01512935

A Handbook on Jeremiah

Textual Criticism and the Translator
Volume 2

Edited by Harold P. Scanlin

Published for the United Bible Societies,
New York, New York
by Eisenbrauns,
Winona Lake, Indiana

A Handbook
on Jeremiah

by

Jan de Waard

Eisenbrauns
Winona Lake, Indiana
2003

© 2003 by Eisenbrauns.
All rights reserved.
Printed in the United States of America.

Library of Congress Cataloging-in-Publication Data

Waard, Jan de.
  A Handbook on Jeremiah / by Jan de Waard ; edited by Harold P. Scanlin.
    p.   cm. — (Textual criticism and the translator ; v. 2)
  ISBN 1-57506-057-4
  1. Bible. O.T. Jeremiah—Criticism, Textual.   2. Bible. O.T. Jeremiah—
Translating.   I. Scanlin, Harold P.   II. Title.   III. Series.
  BS1525.52.W33   2003
  224′.20446—dc22

                                                    2003014680

The paper used in this publication meets the minimum requirements of the American
National Standard for Information Sciences—Permanence of Paper for Printed Library
Materials, ANSI Z39.48-1984.♾

CONTENTS

PREFACE

The United Bible Societies, a global fellowship of 135 national Bible Societies, is currently engaged in over 700 Bible translation projects throughout the world. It is the Bible Societies' policy to base their translations on the best available editions of the ancient texts. UBS and its member societies have taken an active role in producing critical editions by calling upon leading textual scholars, specializing in both Old Testament and New Testament, to prepare these editions.

For the New Testament, the American Bible Society, the British and Foreign Bible Society, the Netherlands Bible Society, and the Württemberg Bible Society, under the inspiration and leadership of Dr. Eugene A. Nida, brought together an international team of New Testament textual scholars: Kurt Aland, Matthew Black, Bruce Metzger, and Allen Wikgren, later joined by Barbara Aland, Johannes Karavidopoulos, and Carlo Martini. The result was the publication of the United Bible Societies' *Greek New Testament* (1966), now in its fourth edition (1993), which has served an entire generation of Bible translators. A perusal of the prefaces to most modern Bible translations reveals that this edition has formed the basis for their work.

In 1969 the Hebrew Old Testament Text Project was launched, again under the leadership of Dr. Nida, with Dominique Barthélemy, Alexander R. Hulst, Norbert Lohfink, William D. McHardy, H. Peter Rüger, and James A. Sanders serving on the committee. The purpose of the project was thoroughly to analyze about 5,000 textually difficult passages in the Masoretic Text with a view toward offering translators the insights of these leading textual scholars and providing proposals for translation of these difficult passages. This project produced a five-volume *Preliminary and Interim Report*, and under the pen of the committee's chairman, Dr. Dominique Barthélemy, the first three volumes of the final report, *Critique textuelle de l'Ancien Testament*, have been published.

Based in a significant measure on the groundbreaking work of Barthélemy and the rest of the Hebrew Old Testament Text Project, the decision was made that the time had come to produce a new edition of *Biblia Hebraica*, to supersede the *Stuttgartensia* edition, which itself was a revision of Kahle's third edition of *Biblia Hebraica*. The first fascicle of this new edition, *The Megillot*, will be published in 2004.

vii

All these publications have taken their place as basic tools for original language Bible study, text-critical studies, exegesis, and Bible translation. Nevertheless, the United Bible Societies felt that it would be important to offer Bible translators additional help if they were to make the best use of these fundamental works. Accordingly, we have launched this series, "Textual Criticism and the Translator," to provide translators with additional help in applying the results of these textual studies in their work. We are convinced that many others will benefit from these studies, and we are pleased to launch this series under the publishing auspices of Eisenbrauns, thereby reaching a wider audience.

This is the second volume in the series, *A Handbook on Jeremiah*, produced by Dr. Jan de Waard, who combines a high level of competence in Old Testament textual studies and experience as a translator and translation consultant for the United Bible Societies. Through this special combination of skills, he combines careful textual analysis with practical recommendations for exegesis and translation.

Future volumes are being planned to offer similar treatments of other Old Testament books, as well as an English edition of the introductions to the three published Final Report volumes by Dominique Barthélemy. These extensive introductions, totaling over 400 pages in the original French edition, provide a comprehensive guide to the whole subject of Old Testament textual criticism and its implications for Bible translation. It is hoped that other volumes will deal with the text of the New Testament.

This series, which we hope will serve to encourage textual studies by both Bible translators and exegetes, would not have been possible without the vision of Dr. Eugene A. Nida, who recognized the vital importance of source texts based on the best of scholarship. Special appreciation and thanks is also expressed for the monumental work of the late Dominique Barthélemy (1921–2002) which forms the foundation of the present volume.

Harold P. Scanlin
Series Editor

LIST OF ABBREVIATIONS

Aq	Aquila, quoted according to the Septuagint edition of Göttingen
BDB	Brown, Driver, and Briggs, *A Hebrew and English Lexicon of the Old Testament*
BH2	*Biblia Hebraica* (ed. R. Kittel; 1913)
BH3	*Biblia Hebraica* (ed. R. Kittel; 1937)
BHS	*Biblia Hebraica Stuttgartensia* (4th edition, 1990)
Bib	*Biblica*
BJ	La Bible de Jérusalem (1973)
BP	La Bible: Ancien Testament (Bibliothèque de la Pléiade, 1956–59)
BR	M. Buber and F. Rosenzweig, *Bücher der Kündung* (1985)
BWAT	Beiträge zur Wissenschaft vom Alten Testament
BZ	*Biblische Zeitschrift*
C	De Heilige Schrift, in opdracht van "Petrus Canisius" (1990)
CBQ	*Catholic Biblical Quarterly*
CEV	Holy Bible, Contemporary English Version (1995)
Chouraqui	André Chouraqui, *La Bible* (1985)
CSEL	*Corpus Scriptorum Ecclesiasticorum Latinorum*
CTAT	D. Barthélemy, *Critique Textuelle de l'Ancien Testament*
DCH	David J. A. Clines (ed.), *The Dictionary of Classical Hebrew*
DJD	Discoveries in the Judaean Desert
ErIsr	*Eretz-Israel*
EÜ	Einheitsübersetzung der Heiligen Schrift: Das Alte Testament (1974)
FC	La Bible en français courant (1986)
G	The Septuagint, quoted according to the edition of Göttingen
GN	Die Gute Nachricht: Die Bibel in heutigem Deutsch (1982)
GNB	Good News Bible (1978)
GrN	Groot Nieuws Bijbel: Vertaling in omgangstaal (1983)
GrNa	Groot Nieuws Bijbel met aantekeningen (1998)
HALAT	W. Baumgartner et al., *Hebräisches und aramäisches Lexikon zum Alten Testament*
HUB	*The Hebrew University Bible: The Book of Jeremiah* (1997)
HUCA	*Hebrew Union College Annual*
I(nt)B	Interpreter's Bible
JQR	*Jewish Quarterly Review*
JSS	*Journal of Semitic Studies*
JTS	*Journal of Theological Studies*

ix

KJV   The King James Version
LB   The Living Bible (1985)
LV   De Bijbel naar de Leidse Vertaling (1899–1912)
M   The Masoretic Text, quoted according to the Leningrad Codex (Facsimile Edition, 1998)
MGWJ   Monatsschrift für Geschichte und Wissenschaft des Judentums
Moffatt   James Moffatt, *A New Translation of the Bible* (1935)
NAB   The New American Bible (1970)
NAV   Die nuwe Afrikaans Vertaling (1983)
NEB   The New English Bible: The Old Testament (1970)
NIV   The New International Version (1988)
NJB   The New Jerusalem Bible (1985)
NJV   The New Jewish Version of the Jewish Publication Society (1985)
NRSV   The New Revised Standard Version (1989)
NV   Nieuwe Vertaling (1953)
π'   All columns of the Hexapla
PEQ   *Palestine Exploration Quarterly*
2Q   Jeremiah texts from the second cave of Qumran, quoted according to Discoveries in the Judaean Desert of Jordan III
4Qa and c   Jeremiah texts from the fourth cave of Qumran, quoted according to DJD XV
RB   *Revue biblique*
REB   The Revised English Bible (1989)
RGrN   Groot Nieuws Bijbel (Revised 1996)
RL   Revidierter Luther Text (Revised Luther Version; 1984)
RSV   Revised Standard Version (1952)
S   Syriac Peshitta Version, quoted according to Codex Ambrosianus
SEB   Stuttgarter Erklärungsbibel (1992)
StV   Staten Vertaling (States General Translation; 1618–19)
SR   Nouvelle version Segond révisée (1978)
Syh   Syro-Hexapla, quoted according to Codex Syro-hexaplaris Ambrosianus
Sym   Symmachus, quoted according to the Septuagint edition of Göttingen
T   Targum, cited according to the Sperber edition
Th   Theodotion, quoted according to the Septuagint edition of Göttingen
TILC   Traduzione interconfessionale in lingua corrente (1989)
TOB   Traduction oecuménique de la Bible (1988)
V   Vulgate, quoted according to the edition of San Girolamo
Vet Lat   Vetus Latina, cited according to the edition of Sabatier
VT   *Vetus Testamentum*
W   Willibrord Vertaling (1975)
ZA   *Zeitschrift für Assyriologie*
ZAW   *Zeitschrift für die alttestamentliche Wissenschaft*
ZDPV   *Zeitschrift des deutschen Palästina-Vereins*

WORKS CITED

Abulwalid Merwan ibn Ganaḥ. *Kitâb al-Lu maᶜ.* Edited by J. Derenbourg (BEHE.H66). Paris, 1886.

_____ . *Kitâb al-Uṣul.* Edited in A. Neubauer, *The Book of Hebrew Roots.* Oxford, 1875.

Albright, W. F. "A Catalogue of Early Hebrew Lyric Poems." *HUCA* 28 (1950–51) 1–39.

Anderlind, L. "Ackerbau und Thierzucht in Syrien, insbesondere in Palästina." *ZDPV* 9 (1886) 1–73.

Baillet, M., J. T. Milik, and R. de Vaux. *Les 'Petites Grottes' de Qumran.* DJD III. Oxford: Clarendon, 1962.

Barr, J. *Comparative Philology and the Text of the Old Testament.* Oxford: Clarendon, 1968.

Barthélemy, D. *Critique textuelle de l'Ancien Testament 2.* Fribourg: Editions Universitaires / Göttingen: Vandenhoeck & Ruprecht, 1986.

Bauer, H., and P. Leander. *Historische Grammatik der hebräischen Sprache des Alten Testamentes.* Halle: Max Niemeyer, 1922.

Bochart, S. *Hierozoicon.* Edited by J. Leusden. Leiden, 1692.

_____ . *Opera omnia I,* 1–318. Edited by J. Leusden. Leiden, 1692.

Bogaert, P.-M. *Le livre de Jérémie: Le prophète et son milieu, les oracles et leur transmission.* Leuven: Peeters, 1981.

Böttcher, F. *Proben alttestamentlicher Schrifterklärung.* Leipzig: Weidmann, 1833.

Bright, J. *Jeremiah.* Garden City, N.Y.: Doubleday, 1965.

Brockington, L. H. *The Hebrew Text of the Old Testament: The Readings Adopted by the Translators of the New English Bible.* Oxford: Oxford University Press, 1973.

Brown, F., S. R. Driver, and C. A. Briggs. *A Hebrew and English Lexicon of the Old Testament.* Oxford: Clarendon, 1968.

Buxtorf, J. *Lexicon chaldaicum, talmudicum et rabbinicum.* Basel: Ludovicus König, 1639.

Cappel, L. *Commentarii et notae criticae in V.T.* Amsterdam: P. & J. Blaeu, 1684.

Carroll, R. P. *Jeremiah.* Philadelphia: Westminster Press, 1986.

Castle, E. *Lexicon heptaglotton.* London, 1686.

Dahood, M. "Two Textual Notes on Jeremia." *CBQ* 23 (1961) 462–64.

_____ . "Philological Notes on Jer 18:14–15." *ZAW* 74 (1962) 207–9.

_____ . "Hebrew-Ugaritic Lexicography IV." *Bib* 47 (1966) 403–19.

_____ . "The Word-pair ᶜakal // kalah in Jeremiah xxx 16." *VT* 27 (1977) 482.

Delitzsch, F. *Die Lese- und Schreibfehler im Alten Testament.* Berlin, 1920.

Diaz Esteban, F. *Sefer 'Oklah We-'Oklah*. Madrid: Consejo Superior de Investigaciones Científicas, 1975.

Doederlein, J. C. "Zu den Hexaplen des Origenes." *RBML* 1 (1777) 217–56.

Driver, G. R. "Linguistic and Textual Problems: Jeremiah." *JQR* 28 (1937–38) 97–129.

_____. "Difficult Words in the Hebrew Prophets." Pp. 52–72 in *Studies in Old Testament Prophecy*. Edited by H. H. Rowley. Edinburgh: T. & T. Clark, 1950.

_____. "Birds in the Old Testament." *PEQ* 87 (1955) 5–20; 129–40.

_____. "Review of Köhler/Baumgartner *Supplementum ad Lexicon Veteris Testamenti Libros*." *JSS* 4 (1959) 147–49.

_____. "Abbreviations in the Massoretic Text." *Textus* 1 (1960) 112–31.

_____. "Once Again Abbreviations." *Textus* 4 (1963) 76–94.

Duhm, B. *Das Buch Jeremia*. Tübingen and Leipzig: Mohr (Siebeck), 1901.

Ehrlich, A. B. *Randglossen zur hebräischen Bibel, Vierter Band: Jesaia, Jeremia*. Leipzig: Hinrichs, 1912.

Emerton, J. A. "Notes on Jeremiah 12,9 and on Some Suggestions of J. D. Michaelis about the Hebrew words *naha*, *'aebra* and *jada'*." *ZAW* 81 (1969) 182–91.

Ewald, H. *Ausführliches Lehrbuch der hebräischen Sprache des Alten Bundes*. Göttingen: Dieterich, 1863.

Field, F. *Origenis Hexaplorum quae supersunt*. Hildesheim: Georg Olms, 1964.

Frank, R. M. "The Jeremias of Pethion Ibn Ayyub al-Sahhâr." *CBQ* 21 (1959) 136–70.

Freedman, D. N., and J. R. Lundbom. "Haplography in Jeremiah 1–20." *ErIsr* 26 (1999) 28–38.

Freedman, H. *Jeremiah*. London: Soncino, 1949. Rev. A. J. Rosenberg. New York: Judaica, 1985.

Gesenius, W. *Thesaurus philologicus criticus linguae hebraicae et chaldaicae V.T. I–III*. Leipzig, 1829–58.

Gesenius, W., E. Kautzsch, and A. E. Cowley. *Gesenius' Hebrew Grammar*. Oxford: Clarendon, 1910.

Giesebrecht, F. *Das Buch Jeremia*. Göttingen: Vandenhoeck & Ruprecht, 1907.

Ginsburg, C. D. *The Massorah Compiled from Manuscripts: Alphabetically and Lexically Arranged*. Vols. I–IV. London, 1880–1905.

Grätz, H. "Exegetische Studien zum Propheten Jeremia." *MGWJ* 32 (1883) 49–63, 97–116, 146–60, 193–208, 289–96, 337–46, 385–98, 481–96.

Holladay, W. L. *Jeremiah 1*. Philadelphia: Fortress Press, 1986.

_____. *Jeremiah 2*. Minneapolis: Fortress Press, 1989.

Houbigant, C. F. *Biblia Hebraica cum notis criticis et versione latina ad notas criticas facta*. . . . Paris: Apud A. C. Briasson & L. Durand, 1753.

Ibn Ezra, A. *Sephat Jether . . . zur Verteidigung R. Saadia's gegen . . . Dunasch ben Librat*. Edited by G. Uppmann. Frankfurt, 1843.

Janzen, J. G. *Studies in the Text of Jeremiah*. Cambridge: Harvard University Press, 1973.

Jean, C. F., and J. Hoftijzer. *Dictionnaire des inscriptions sémitiques de l'ouest*. Leiden: E. J. Brill, 1965.

Jones, D. R. *Jeremiah*. Grand Rapids: William B. Eerdmans, 1992.

Joüon, P. *Grammaire de l'hébreu biblique*. Rome: Pontifical Biblical Institute, 1947.

Joüon, P., and T. Muraoka. *A Grammar of Biblical Hebrew.* Vols. 1–2. Rome: Pontifical Biblical Institute, 1993.

Kennicott, B. *Dissertatio secunda super ratione textus hebraici.* Edited by G. A. Teller. Leipzig, 1765.

_____. *Dissertatio generalis in V.T. hebraicum.* Oxford, 1780.

Kimchi, D. *Sepher Mikhlol.* . . . Edited by Isaac ben Aaron Rittenberg. Lyck, 1862.

Kimchi, J. *Sepher ha-Galuj.* Edited by H. J. Mathews. Berlin, 1887.

Köhler, L. "Beobachtungen am hebräischen und griechischen Text von Jeremia Kap. 1– 9." *ZAW* 29 (1909) 1–39.

König, E. *Historisch-komparative Syntax der hebräischen Sprache.* Leipzig: J. C. Hinrichs, 1897.

_____. *Hebräisches und aramäisches Wörterbuch zum Alten Testament.* Vaduz, Lichtenstein: Sändig Reprints, 1986.

Kokovzov, P. *Mi-Sifre ha-Balshanut ha-ʿIvrit bime habenayim.* St. Petersburg, 1916.

Komlosh, Y. "The Targum Yirmiyahu." *Bar-Ilan* 7–8 (1969) 38–48.

Landsberger, F. "The House of the People." *HUCA* 22 (1949) 149–55.

Levy, J. *Chaldäisches Wörterbuch über die Targumim.* Leipzig: Baumgärtner, 1868.

Lilienthal, T. C. *Commentatio critica sistens duorum codicum manuscriptorum . . . notitiam.* Königsberg, 1770.

McKane, W. *Jeremiah I and II.* Edinburgh: T. & T. Clark, 1986 and 1996.

Meyer, I. *Jeremia und die falschen Propheten.* Freiburg: Universitätsverlag / Göttingen: Vandenhoeck & Ruprecht, 1977.

Michaelis, J. D. *Supplementa ad lexica hebraica I–VI.* Edited by T. C. Tychsen. Göttingen, 1792.

Min, Y.-J. *The Minuses and Pluses of the LXX Translation of Jeremiah as Compared with the Massoretic Text.* Ph.D. dissertation. Jerusalem, 1977.

Montfaucon, B. de. *Hexaplorum Origenis quae supersunt.* Paris: Ludovicum Guerin et al., 1769–70.

Moran, W. L. "Ugaritic sîsûma and Hebrew sîs." *Bib* 39 (1958) 69–71.

Movers, F. C. *De utriusque recensione vaticiniorum Ieremiae graecae alexandrinae et hebraicae masoreticae indole et origine.* . . . Hamburg, 1837.

Nötscher, F. *Das Buch Jeremias.* Bonn: Hanstein, 1934.

Noldius, C. *Concordantiae particularum ebraeo-chaldaicarum.* . . . Edited by I. G. Tympius. Jena, 1734.

Ognibeni, B. *La seconda parte del Sefer ʾoklah weʾoklah.* Madrid: Instituto de Filología del CSIC / Fribourg: Universitätsverlag, 1995.

Perles, F. *Analekten zur Textkritik des Alten Testaments.* Munich, 1895. Reprinted Leipzig: Gustav Engel, 1922.

Ranke, E. *Par palimpsestorum wirceburgensium.* Vienna, 1871.

Reuchlin, J. *De rudimentis hebraicis libri III.* Pforzheim, 1506.

Reventlow, H. *Liturgie und prophetisches Ich bei Jeremia.* Gütersloh: Gerd Mohn, 1963.

Reymond, P. *Dictionnaire d'Hébreu et d'Araméen Bibliques.* Paris: Du Cerf—Société Biblique Française, 1991.

Richter, G. "Untersuchungen zu den Geschlechtsregistern der Chronik." *ZAW* 34 (1914) 107–41.

Rossi, J. B. de. *Variae lectiones veteris testamenti librorum.* Parma: Ex Regio Typographeo, 1784–88.

Rudolph, W. *Jeremia.* Tübingen: J. C. B. Mohr (Paul Siebeck), 1968.

Saadya. Fragments of *Kutub al-Lughah,* edited by S. L. Skoss: "A Study of Inflection in Hebrew from Saadia Gaon's Grammatical Work 'Kutub al-Lughah.'" *JQR* 33 (1942–43) 171–212.

Sabatier, P. *Bibliorum sacrorum latinae versiones antiquae seu Vetus Italica.* Reims: Apud Reginaldum Florentain, 1743.

Sarsowsky, A. "Notizen zu einigen biblischen, geographischen und ethnographischen Namen." *ZAW* 32 (1912) 146–51.

Schenker, A. Nebukadnezzars Metamorphose vom Unterjocher zum Gottesknecht." *RB* 89 (1982) 498–527.

Schleusner, J. F. *Novus thesaurus philologico-criticus sive lexicon in LXX et reliquos interpretes graecos ac scriptores apocryphos VT.* Leipzig: Weidmann, 1820–21.

Schmuttermayr, G. "Beobachtungen zu Jer 5,13." *BZ* n.s. 9 (1965) 215–32.

Schwally, F. "Die Reden des Buches Jeremia gegen die Heiden." *ZAW* 8 (1888) 177–217.

Segal, M. Z. "Beayot millim." *Lešonénu* 10 (1939) 150–56.

Selms, A. van. *Jeremia I–III.* Nijkerk: G. F. Callenbach, 1972–89. [II, 1989; III, 1984]

Simons, J. *The Geographical and Topographical Texts of the Old Testament.* Leiden, 1959.

Smyth, H. W. *Greek Grammar.* Cambridge: Harvard University Press, 1984.

Soden, W. von. "Der neubabylonische Funktionär 'simmagir' und der Feuertod des Shamash-shum-ukin." *ZA* 62 (1972) 84–90.

Soggin, J. A. "Einige Bemerkungen über Jeremias 2,34." *VT* 8 (1958) 433–35.

Sperber, A. *The Bible in Aramaic.* Leiden: E. J. Brill, 1959–73.

Spohn, G. L. *Jeremias vates e versione judaeorum alexandrinorum.* . . . Leipzig, 1824.

Stade, B. "Deuterozacharja." *ZAW* 1 (1881) 1–96.

_____. "Miscellen 8." *ZAW* 5 (1885) 175–78.

_____. "Das vermeintliche aramäisch-assyrische Aequivalent der מלכת השמים Jr 7,44." *ZAW* 6 (1886) 289–339.

Talmon, S. "Amen as an Introductory Oath Formula." *Textus* 7 (1969) 124–29.

Thackeray, H. St. J. *A Grammar of the Old Testament in Greek.* Cambridge: Cambridge University Press, 1909.

Thomas, D. W. "A Note on *welo yadaʿu* in Jeremiah 14:18." *JTS* 39 (1938) 273–74.

Thompson, J. A. *The Book of Jeremiah.* Grand Rapids: William B. Eerdmans, 1980.

Tov, E. *The Dead Sea Scrolls on Microfiche.* Leiden: E. J. Brill, 1993.

Ulrich, E. *Qumran Cave 4 ·X: The Prophets.* DJD 15. Oxford: Clarendon Press, 1997.

Venema, H. *Commentarius ad librum prophetiarum Jeremiae.* Leeuwarden, 1765.

Volz, P. "Studien zum Text des Jeremia." *BWAT* 25 (1920).

_____. *Der Prophet Jeremia.* Leipzig: A. Deichertsche Verlagsbuchhandlung D. Werner Scholl, 1928.

Waltke, B. K., and M. O'Connor. *An Introduction to Biblical Hebrew Syntax.* Winona Lake, Ind.: Eisenbrauns, 1990.

Weber, R., and R. Gryson. *Biblia Sacra iuxta Vulgatam Versionem.* Stuttgart: Deutsche Bibelgesellschaft, 1994.

Weil, G. E. *Massorah gedolah iuxta codicem Leningradensem B 19 a. I: Catalogi.* Rome: Pontifical Biblical Institute, 1971.

Wernberg-Møller, P. "The Pronoun אתמה and Jeremiah's Pun." *VT* 6 (1956) 315–16.

_____. "Observations on the Hebrew Participle." *ZAW* 71 (1959) 54–67.

Wichelhaus, J. *De Ieremiae versione alexandrina.* Halle, 1847.

Yeivin, I. *Geniza Bible Fragments with Babylonian Massorah and Vocalization I–V.* Jerusalem, 1973.

Ziegler, J. *Beiträge zur Jeremias-Septuaginta.* Göttingen: Vandenhoeck & Ruprecht, 1958.

_____. *Septuaginta XV: Ieremias, Baruch, Threni, Epistula Ieremiae.* Göttingen: Vandenhoeck & Ruprecht, 1976.

INTRODUCTION

The principles and procedures for the treatment of the textual cases in this volume are exactly the same as those described in the introduction to the first volume of the series: *A Handbook on Isaiah* (Winona Lake, Ind.: Eisenbrauns, 1997) 1–3. Only the statistics would look rather different.

In the case of Jeremiah, more than twenty textual cases have been added by Dominique Barthélemy to the original number selected for treatment in the *Preliminary and Interim Report on the Hebrew Old Testament Text Project IV* (New York: United Bible Societies, 1979) 174–331. Most of these, although of undeniable textual importance, were not considered to be of translational relevance. Moreover, of the cases the *Preliminary Report* and the *Final Report* (CTAT 2) have in common, more than forty were eliminated for the same reason. Occasionally, the motivations for doing so were quite specific. In more than five instances, no textual, or even translational, problem could be detected at all. In two cases all textual options were allowed in translation, depriving the case therefore of its interest. Four times the problem was purely interpretational and, in addition, all translations consulted seemed to follow in different ways the same interpretation. In more than ten other instances, translations appeared to be entirely determined by the requirements of the receptor language with regard to participant structure and pronominal assimilation.

As in the Isaiah handbook, all those cases have been omitted in which NEB stands alone among modern versions with a particular textual option which, furthermore, has been "corrected" in REB. The same policy has been applied in one single parallel phenomenon involving RSV and NRSV.

The publication of *The Book of Jeremiah* in the *Hebrew University Bible* (1997) came at a very welcome moment, and the author has received much benefit from this magnificent edition. Revisions of some functional equivalence translations such as GN and GrN appeared during the interval between the two handbooks, but they are only quoted where different from the editions they intend to replace. More systematically compared now are the complete new Bible of CEV, and, on the Jewish side, the Bible of André Chouraqui.

The greatest problems interpreters and translators of Jeremiah face are connected with the important divergencies between the texts of M and G. The differences mainly are of two kinds: (a) the fact that the text of G is shorter than that of M, and (b) the circumstance that the oracles against the nations which in M are located at the end of the book (chaps. 46–51) follow in G 25.13. In addition, the order of the oracles is different in both texts. These phenomena have been widely discussed in the remote past, and even more intensely in the recent past. The present publication will only rarely add new aspects to the discussion. Its unique aim is to draw conclusions from the scholarly debate for the translator and the practice of translation.

The Greek text of Jeremiah is considerably shorter than the Masoretic one. The following details can already be found in the commentary of Giesebrecht (p. xxv): 2700 words of M are lacking in G whereas G has approximately one hundred words which cannot be found in M. According to the computerized counts of Y.-J. Min (159), the first figure has to be changed to 3097 or approximately 1/7 of M. Among the ancient versions, this shortness is only characteristic of G, since V, S, and T generally follow M. It would therefore be possible to assume that G is an abridged version of M and that the omissions could partly be explained by stylistic rework which had taken place within the Greek text tradition and partly by a scribal error of homoioarcton (the same beginning) or homoioteleuton (the same ending). However, such assumptions could only be made before the Qumran discoveries. Since then, twelve fragments of Jeremiah have been found gathered under the symbol of 4QJer-a which are dated 200 BC and which reflect M, as well as three fragments labeled 4QJer-b from the Hasmonean period. Two of these are rather large, covering 9.22–10.21 and 43.2–10, labeled 4QJer-d in the final edition of DJD, and they represent a text type as reflected in G. The small fragment of 50.4–6, 4QJer-e in the final edition, sides, on the other hand, with M against G. The Qumran text of Jeremiah has inspired Gerald Janzen to examine again the problems of relationships between M and G. From his conclusions (127–28) the following statements can be quoted:

(1) M can be characterized by much secondary expansion. Part of the expansion consists of considerable explicit information in the form of full names and titles and explicit verbal subjects and objects. Some of the expansions consist of interpolations from parallel and related passages which denote sometimes considerable glossing and harmonization. These interpolations also concern Old Testament passages outside Jeremiah. Moreover, M is characterized by large doublets.Therefore, M seems to be a revised text.

(2) In contrast, G seems to contain only a small amount of secondary expansion. Especially where it does not show variation, it seems to have preserved a text which is superior to M and faithful to the Hebrew Vorlage at home in Alexandria.

I would like to note a few items in relation to the first of these transparent conclusions. The part of the expansions dealing with explicit information could, at least in functional equivalence translations, be dealt with translationally regardless of the Hebrew Vorlage. The other part not. Holladay (2.3) has correctly observed that the expansions described in the second part are typical of the prose sections, not of the poetic ones. The example from 28.1 as it has been discussed in the handbook may illustrate this.

As can be seen from the presentation, we have difficulties. We face in M a conflated text which has been contaminated by data from the beginning of the preceding two chapters, Jeremiah 26–27. The committee considered that text as typical of the second redaction and the text of G as primitive. But since it related the variant to the literary and not to the textual level of the text, M received an A evaluation which means for the translator, the text to be rendered. On the other side, translators may have to follow G for reasons of discourse cohesion. This may still be a relatively simple dilemma which NIV solves in a more or less deceptive manner. It remains true, however, that following G cannot easily be described in one sentence of a common language footnote. And in fact a hybrid behavior with regard to base texts can be noted.

However, it cannot sufficiently be stressed that although the shorter text of G may frequently be due to a Hebrew Vorlage shorter than M, each textual variant has to be assessed anew, as correctly stated by Freedman and Lundbom (37). That it is sometimes difficult to decide an issue is shown by the case discussed in 50.2.

Here G could have a minus caused by textual accident, but it is likewise possible that M has a plus in the form of a literary amplification. The fact that the literary initiative was taken on the level of the proto-Masoretic text made it possible for the committee to credit M with A and B evaluations, but this does not really help translators in interconfessional projects with Orthodox participation. Sometimes the issue is clear as in the case of 23.10 the first line of which is lacking in G. However, the first line starts in M with מְנָאֲפִים, "for adulterers" and the second line with כִּי מִפְּנֵי, "for because of" and Meyer (117, note 1) is certainly correct in stating that the first line of M has accidentally been omitted in G through homoioarcton (an identical beginning). Cases of apparent homoioteleuton and haplography (Janzen, 117–19) can also be cited.

It will also be clear that a number of these minuses and pluses seriously change the narrative as such. For example, in 52.15 of the total of 21 words in M, G renders only the 3d, 4th and 5th word, and of the first 2 words in the next verse G has nothing corresponding to it. A literal English translation of M in verses 15 and 16 would run as follows: "Nebuzaradan the captain of the guard carried into exile some of the poorest of the people and the rest of the people who were left in the city and the deserters who had defected to the king of Babylon, together with the rest of the artisans. But Nebuzaradan the captain of the guard left some of the poorest people of the land to be vinedressers and tillers of the soil." However, G only has the following information: "But the captain of the guard left the remnant of the people to be vinedressers and farmers." It is my strong conviction that no short annotation for a general readership can be made which explains well enough where and why M and G are different. Yet this is exactly what should be done if we continue to insist that all semantically significant variations should be footnoted.

To take another example: of the 22 words of Jer 40.4b and 5a of M, starting with וְאִם in 4 and ending with יָשׁוּב in 5a, G only renders 3 words: εἰ δὲ μή ἀπότρεχε, "if not, go away" (47.4b–5a). The first 3 words εἰ δὲ μή seem to resume the first 6 Hebrew words whereas ἀπότρεχε gives the impression of being a translation of the last Hebrew word of verse 4: לָךְ. Maybe G simply is an allusive abbreviation of M (so Barthélemy, 736), but it remains a fact that the two narrative parts are totally different. G reads in a literal English translation only: "But if not, go away" whereas M reads: "And if you don't want to come with me to Babylon, you need not. See, the whole land is before you: go wherever seems good and right to you. But he still did not turn back (or: still did not answer)." Again one faces a situation which cannot easily be described in a short annotation. It may be possible to deal with this textual feature approximately in a formal correspondence translation, but in a functional equivalence translation it becomes virtually impossible. It does not make much sense to reproduce one translation in the footnotes of another, and bringing into focus divergencies between the versions and M without explaining them makes the general reader only more perplexed.

I have selected the preceding case for another reason as well. Since Cappel, scholars have been paying attention to the fact that the first three words of 5a in M were lacking in G and they have sometimes excluded these words from M as a corrupted gloss. But methodologically it seems totally unjustifiable to look at the absence of three words in G and not to consider the absence of fifteen preceding ones.

This whole discussion about the shorter text of G should not make us forget that G also presents a few pluses. For example, 2.28 M in literal English translation reads only: "Yes, as many as your cities are your gods, O Judah," but G adds: "and as many as the streets of Jerusalem have they sacrificed to Baal" which presumably means: "and as many altars for Baal as Jerusalem has streets." Cornill, Rudolph, Janzen and Holladay consider this plus of G as original, whereas McKane rejects it. There are valid arguments for both hypotheses especially since the expanded text of G corresponds with the Hebrew in 11.13. The HOTTP committee did not discuss this issue for the simple reason that none of the modern translations on which the selection of textual problems was based followed G in this respect. However, when one increases the number of translations to be consulted, one can note that NAB follows G in adding: "And as many as the streets of Jerusalem are the altars you have set up for Baal" and that NJB adds the text in a footnote. It is true that these few pluses of G can more easily be handled in traditional annotations. The decision-making with regard to the question whether the plus or the minus is original, is, however, extremely difficult and often beyond the competence of the average translator.

Translating both M and G would in this case as well make procedures simpler and avoid serious mistakes.

The other major problem concerns the oracles against the nations. In M they are found at the end of the book in chaps. 46 through 51 under the separate heading 46.1, whereas in G they have been inserted after chap. 25.13 from where they cover the Greek text through the Greek chap. 31. Moreover, the order of the oracles is different. M has the order Egypt, Philistia, Moab, Ammon, Edom, Damascus, Kedar, Elam, and Babylon; and G Elam, Egypt, Babylon, Philistia, Edom, Ammon, Kedar, Damascus, and Moab. It is not my intention to dwell on the arguments in favor of one placement and one order or another. Anyone can consult the existing literature at this point. Let me only try to summarize the results of the scholarly debate. The main tendency in recent research is to consider the placement of the oracles in G as original (Rudolph, Rietzschel, McKane, Holladay), but not the sequence of the individual oracles. With regard to the last, the main tendency is to judge the sequence of M as being original, mainly because of its chronological and geographical nature (Streane, Peake, Rudolph, Weiser, Rietzschel, McKane, Holladay).

It can be argued, of course, that these divergencies can be handled in introductions and footnotes. My harvest of translations doing so has, however, not been particularly rich. Only some translations belonging officially or non-officially to the Study Bible type do so, but in a very summary way. The briefest note can be found at 25.13 in NIV: "After this word, the Septuagint [the Greek translation of the OT] inserts the material found in chaps. 46–51, though rearranged." At the same spot NJB provides this neutral information: "Gk puts these prophecies immediately after ch 25; Hebrew places them at the end of the book," but the reader has to wait till chap. 46 for more precision: "The Hebr. text places the prophecies against the nations at the end of the book, chap. 46–51. In the Gk version, however, they retain their original position and follow their introductory chap. 25, which seems to have been expanded in the light of subsequent events. . . ." In SEB, information of the same nature is only provided at the beginning of chap. 46. More elaborate is TOB which in the introduction to the book signals the placement of the oracles against the nations in the Greek version, commenting: "Cet arrangement représente probablement un état plus ancien du rouleau, . . ." and which in a more substantive footnote at 25.13 remarks: "C'est ici que s'insère en gr. la série des oracles contre les nations (46–51) et dans un ordre plus logique qui semble moins primitif que celui d'hébr., les vv 15–38 venant en conclusion de cet ensemble. Les ch. 26–45 et 52 d'hébr. forment alors la deuxième partie du livre en gr." Even more detailed are the observations in "Die Bibel mit Erklärungen," published in Berlin, DDR, 1989, which do not deserve citation because of the rare use of this edition. The other editions have been cited because they frequently function as models which in many cases means: they are copied. The information in TOB is somewhat more elaborate which can be explained by the fact that this is the only ecumenical translation with Orthodox participation. However, even there the annotations are insufficient.

Bogaert in his Jeremiah research (168–73; 222–38) has convincingly shown that the different arrangements of the two Jeremiah editions have hermeneutical implications for the interpretation of this book since the sequences and emphases are related differently to each other in M and in G. Different arrangements and different emphases imply different meanings and, therefore, different translations. However, these divergencies can hardly be footnoted. Or, one gets such desperate remarks as used in NJB: "Again, in this section, Hebr. and Gk show differences."

A double translation, once according to the Hebrew and once according to the Greek, is not a revolutionary idea as such. It has become almost a regular practice with regard to the book of Esther. In the "Guidelines for Interconfessional Cooperation in Translating the Bible" (New Revised Edition, 1987) the following guideline has been formulated: "In the case of the book of Esther the translation of the complete Greek text will be printed in the deuterocanonical section while the translation of the Hebrew text will be printed among the books of the Hebrew canon."

It is true that the situation of Esther is slightly different in that the two texts have a different canonical status. On the other hand, the case of Jeremiah seems to be far more important. With the two editions of Jeremiah we do not face a *veritas graeca* over against a *veritas hebraica,* but two *veritates hebraicae* between which it sometimes is impossible to choose. It is essential to make this statement, for, although the question is of the utmost importance for cooperation with Orthodox constituencies, it is in no way uniquely generated by such a cooperation. In origin, it is a textual and translational problem asking primarily for a textual and translational answer. It goes without saying that the Greek base text to be translated can only be Ziegler's edition in the Göttingen Septuagint.

The present writer would particularly like to extend his gratitude to the editorial staff of Eisenbrauns for having carefully checked the quotations and bibliography items and for having corrected the English wherever appropriate.

May 1999
Jan de Waard

1

JEREMIAH 1–10

2.16

Textual Decisions

The verbal form of M in this short verse is יִרְעוּךְ, "they will feed on you," a reading which seems to have the support of Aq. According to Syh, Aq has the reading ܢ ܪ̈ܥܘܢ rendered with *confringent* (*tibi*) by Field. However, Ziegler in his apparatus carefully suggests a possible translation *pascent tibi* which may be more likely because of Chrysostom's remark that "some" read ποιμανοῦσιν σε. M certainly is directly supported by S and indirectly by T, because the targumic paraphrase יקטלון גיברך ויבזזון נכסך, "they will kill your strong men and they will plunder your goods," presupposes the reading of M. On the other hand, G reads ἔγνωσάν σε, "they have known you," which presupposes a reading יְדָעוּךְ as also found in one manuscript of Kennicott (403) and in the first hand of five others. The Vulgate, by reading *constupraverunt te*, "they have defiled you," most likely understood the same Vorlage to have an obscene connotation, as Cappel (219) has suggested. Since such a Vorlage clearly is the result of a graphical error, and since M can be handled as an interpretational problem, a B evaluation was given to its reading.

Evaluation of Problems

The particular grammatical object of the verb in M: קָדְקֹד, "skull," of course, creates special problems for the interpretation of the verb. The textual decision, however, is not in favor of the conjecture יְעָרוּךְ, "lay bare," that is, "shaved bald," first proposed by Houbigant, and adopted by NJB: "have shaved your skull," and NAB: "shave the crown of your head." Nor is it in favor of a revocalization יְרֹעֲוּךְ, "break, crush you," as proposed first by Michaelis and most recently again by McKane (37). In fact, the reading of M is protected by a *masorah parva* of the Aleppo Codex indicating its *hapax* character.

However, the meaning "to crush" as an interpretational option was proposed by Nicolai de Lyra and Reuchlin (494) and under their influence it entered into the translations of Luther, KJV, RSV, NRSV: "have broken the crown of your head," and GNB: "have cracked his skull," NEB and REB: "will break your heads."

It must be recognized that here we face a mixed metaphor, one of devouring by grazing, the other of shaving the head. Since such a combination is impossible to maintain in translation (compare the impossible rendering in BR: *weiden den Scheitel dir ab!* "graze bare your skull"), the second metaphor will have to be selected, as in NIV (compare also NJV). The metaphor can then best be taken as a general figure of disgrace, devastation, and mourning and not as a specific figure of military defeat and prisoner-of-war status. So already Moffatt: "strip you to be slaves."

Translation Proposals

NIV is a good model: "have shaved the crown of your head." Translators may want to propose a variant translation such as "have cracked your skull" in a footnote. In addition, they may want to explain the figure as has been done above, referring to such texts as Jer 47.5; 48.37 and Isa 3.17.

2.17

Textual Decisions

The last sentence of the verse in M, בְּעֵת מוֹלִיכֵךְ בַּדָּרֶךְ, "at the time he led you in the way," is also to be found in V, S, T, and in the recensions of G by Origen and Lucian, but it is lacking in the Old Greek. Although the committee considered it probable that the sentence in M was due to redaction II, it rated M with an A, since it regarded it as its task to reconstruct the literary state of which M is the best witness.

Evaluation of Problems

Movers (32) was the first to discover that the sentence under discussion contains eight consonants which recur in the same order in the first four words of the following verse. He therefore suggested that the last three words of the sentence in verse 17 are a dittography of the first four words of verse 18. On these as well as on internal grounds (McKane, 38), the sentence has been considered secondary by most scholars, and BH3 and BHS have proposed its omission. Such proposals did have some impact, mainly on older translations such as LV and Moffatt. Among modern versions based on M, the omission is rare, NEB and NAB being the only English examples which can be quoted. On the other hand, Condamin raised the question whether G does not have a haplographic text. Holladay (52) made a plea for the originality of M on structural and grammatical grounds, and Wichelhaus (112) observed that verse 18 presupposes the presence of the sentence in verse 17.

Translation Proposals

Translations based on M should therefore render the sentence. They may even want to indicate in translation and/or footnote the precise historical reference to the time after the exodus contained in בְּעֵת, as in TOB: *au temps où il était ton guide sur la route*, "in the time, that he was your guide on the way," or in BR: *schon zur Zeit, da er dich gängelte auf dem Weg*, "already in the time that he led you on the way." One should, of course, avoid the negative connotation contained in the German *gängeln* in contemporary language.

2.24

Textual Decisions

This verse starts the description of Israel in M with a metaphor: פֶּרֶה לִמֻּד מִדְבָּר, "a wild ass used to the wilderness." The orthography פרה is protected by a *masorah magna* (Weil, 3560) which specifies that the word is written five times with final *aleph* and once with *he*. M is directly supported by Sym (according to Syh) and V, and indirectly by S and T which only make a comparison out of the metaphor. On the other hand, G reads τὰς ὁδοὺς αὐτῆς ἐπλάτυνεν ἐφ᾽ ὕδατα ἐρήμου, "she has extended her ways over the waters of the desert." It is at least clear that the first three words are a rendering of the last word of the preceding verse: דְּרָכֶיהָ. It is hard to say where ἐπλάτυνεν comes from, whether it presupposes a *Vorlage* פָּרָה (Clericus) or פָּתָה (Cappel) or simply translates the next-to-the-last word of verse 23: מְשָׂרֶכֶת (McKane). One can say with certainty only that למד has been read לְמֵי, "over the waters," presumably by error. In the light of such evidence, a mixed C/B evaluation of M becomes understandable.

Evaluation of Problems

In view of the fact that πλατύνω is a rendering of פרץ in Gen 28.14, Köhler (1909, 35) proposed the emendation פֹּרְצָה לַמִּדְבָר, "she breaks away toward the desert" and such a reading has been adopted by BH3 and BHS, and, translationally, by NAB. On the other hand, Driver emends M to מִפְרָדָה לַמִּדְבָּר, "fleeing alone to the desert" and this emendation has been adopted by NEB, REB, and probably by GNB. These emendations as well as others which did not enter into modern versions, were inspired by the misplaced uneasiness about the presence of two animals. M should be maintained, not because it is entirely satisfactory, but because it is at least more satisfactory than anything else which has been proposed (McKane, 46).

Translation Proposals

A rendering such as given in NJB: "A wild she-donkey, at home in the desert" can be used as a satisfactory model of translation. In some cases, it may be useful to follow the translational practice of S and T by changing the metaphor into a comparison as done, for example, in GN: *Du bist wie eine Wildeselin, die alle Fährten in der Wüste kennt,* "you are like a wild she-donkey which knows all the tracks of the wilderness."

2.31

Textual Decisions

In M verse 31 is introduced by the sentence הַדּוֹר אַתֶּם רְאוּ דְבַר־יְהוָה, "and you, O generation, behold the word of the Lord." The presence of the sentence is attested by all witnesses, but not in the same way. The most literal rendering is given in V: *generatio vestra videte verbum domini.* In view of the extra information, καὶ οὐκ ἐφοβήθητε, "and you did not fear," at the end of the preceding verse, G probably divided the first two words in the wrong way, reading רְיתֶם. The rest of the sentence has been rendered with ἀκούσατε λόγον κυρίου, "hear the word of the Lord," selecting a more appropriate verb of hearing instead of seeing as has been done in S and T. One can even say that G glosses the sentence a second time by adding τάδε λέγει κύριος, "So says the Lord." If this is an apostrophe, it had developed already before the completion of the first redaction of Jeremiah, represented in the Old Greek. However, M which is a witness of the second redaction of the book, has preserved the apostrophe in its most original form and therefore it received a mixed A/B evaluation.

Evaluation of Problems

Duhm was the first who proposed deleting the sentence as the marginal note of a reader which had got into the text. This insight has been borrowed by many scholars (see Janzen, 133) and it has been introduced in the apparatuses of BH3 and BHS. For that reason the sentence has been omitted in NEB and REB. However, Rawlinson Jones (93) is no doubt correct when he observes: "The omission of this expression in NEB, uncorrected in REB, is irresponsible in a version."

The question therefore is not whether the sentence should be translated or not, but how it should be rendered. If it is taken to be the parenthesis of a preacher who wanted to actualize the message of the prophet for his contemporaries, it could be rendered accordingly. FC: *Que les lecteurs d'aujourd'hui soient attentifs à ce que dit le Seigneur!* "May the readers of today pay attention to what the Lord says," is a rather anachronistic attempt in this direction. However, Rawlinson Jones has drawn attention to the important fact that this sentence introduces a new section, in which case it cannot be considered a parenthesis of a preacher or a scribe. It should then, following a new section heading, preferably be presented as an utterance of the Lord, as has been done in GN.

Translation Proposals

This last translation could be taken as a good model: *Der Herr sagt: "Volk Israel, achte auf das, was ich dir sage!"* "The Lord says: 'People of Israel, pay attention to what I tell you.'" Especially in projects with Orthodox participation, such a rendering should be encouraged, since it also shows traces of the meaningful second gloss of G.

2.34

Textual Decisions

This verse ends with the difficult sentence כִּי עַל־כָּל־אֵלֶּה, "but upon/because of all these." V and T are apparently based on M, the main difference being that they explicitly provide different verbs: *memoravi*, "I have brought to remembrance," and עבדת, "you have done." G, on the other hand, renders this sentence with ἀλλ᾽ ἐπὶ πάσῃ δρυΐ, "but on every oak," vocalizing the last Hebrew word as אֵלָה or אַלָּה, and it is followed by S. The translation ἐπί clearly shows that the translator read עַל in his Hebrew text. By rendering the preposition with ܬܚܝܬ, "under," S presents a facilitating reading.

A minority of the committee gave a C vote to G, taking it to mean "next to every terebinth," that is, "everywhere." The majority of the committee voted the same way for M, judging that the difficulty is only interpretational and that an acceptable solution can be found.

Evaluation of Problems

McKane (54) is certainly correct by saying that it remains doubtful whether there is any solution to these "baffling, final words of v. 34." The vast majority of modern versions connect the sentence with the following verse, rendering it with some variation as "Yet in spite of all these things . . ." (RSV, NRSV, GNB, NIV, NJV, NJB, FC). With a few exceptions they do not even signal in a footnote the uncertainty of their own rendering.

Translators have the following possibilities: (1) connecting the last sentence of verse 34 with the next verse as proposed already by Radaq and as realized in NAB: "Yet withal (you say)." Such a rendering, however, does not take the *sof pasuq* into account, the location of which was already admitted during the translation of G; (2) taking the sentence as elliptical and providing a verb in translation as has been done in REB: "For all these things I shall punish you"; (3) rendering G as suggested by Châteillon, Condamin, and Soggin (434–35), and as done in NEB.

Translation Proposals

In projects with Orthodox participation, a rendering of G along the lines of NEB: "but by your sacrifices under every oak," can be recommended. In other cases, one of the interpretations of M as presented above, could be chosen. In all cases, a footnote should signal the uncertainty of all renderings.

2.36

Textual Decisions

The first sentence in M reads מַה־תֵּזְלִי מְאֹד, which, if the verbal form תֵּזְלִי is considered to be a contracted form of the verb אזל (Bauer-Leander, 371r), would, literally rendered, mean "how do you go much." G, by rendering this sentence with ὅ τι κατεφρόνησας σφόδρα, "for you have been so exceedingly contemptuous," seems to presuppose a *hiphil* vocalization תָּזֵלִי from the verb זלל. The same seems to apply to V: *quam vilis es facta*, "how base you have become," and to S which uses a *pael* conjugation of ܓ with the same meaning. T by rendering the sentence with מא את מסתכלא לחדא, "what a great fool you have made of yourself!" seems to have been inspired by the immediate context.

The committee judged that it is not necessary to admit that the versions vocalized the Hebrew form differently from M. It considered the problem to be an exegetical one, and therefore M received a B evaluation.

Evaluation of Problems

Since Giesebrecht, almost all commentators change the vocalization of M in the sense indicated above, whereas the apparatuses of BH3 and BHS even make such a change obligatory. No wonder therefore that such a change is reflected in almost all modern versions, according to one interpretation: "How you cheapen yourself" (NJV, and with variations GNB and NAB), or another: "Why do you so lightly change your course" (NEB, REB), "How frivolously you undertake a change of course" (NJB with textual footnote). As Rawlinson Jones (95) has rightly seen, RSV and NRSV combine the meanings of M and the versions in one translation: "How lightly you gad about, changing your ways!" a practice not to be encouraged. Only NIV among English versions seems to make an attempt at rendering M: "Why do you go about so much, changing your ways?"

In spite of all this translational evidence to the contrary, an interpretation of M seems to make sense. Against the objection of Michaelis, and later of Rudolph, that מְאֹד cannot qualify a verb of moving, the case of 1 Sam 20.19 can be quoted where מְאֹד intensifies the speed of a movement (compare CTAT I, 198–99).

Translation Proposals

In a literal type of translation, BR can be taken as a model: *Was rennst du so sehr, deine Brunstweg wieder zu wechseln?!* "What are you running so much to change again the way of your sensuality?!" In a functional equivalent type of translation, GN could be taken as an example: *Warum hast du es so eilig, den Bündnispartner zu wechseln?* "Why are you in such a hurry to change partners?"

3.1A

Textual Decisions

The first problem in this verse is caused by the introductory לֵאמֹר, "in order to say, saying." Its presence is attested by Aq, and through Aq by the Origen recension of G, as well as by T. It is indirectly supported by the paraphrase of V: *vulgo dicitur*, "it is generally said." On the other hand, it is absent from G and S. It should be added that it is also lacking in one Hebrew manuscript, Kennicott 491 of the fourteenth century, but this late witness is of no textual importance. The committee, without making any judgment about the origin or interpretation of the introductory element, assigned a B evaluation to its presence in M for the following two reasons: (1) its rather strong support, including its protection in one of the oldest (Ginsburg, Massorah IV, 101) *masorah magna* lists (Weil, 3072), mentioning nine instances of the verse-initial position of לֵאמֹר, including also Jer 25.5 and 42.14; (2) the simple fact that the omission in G and S can easily be explained by embarrassment.

Evaluation of Problems

The same embarrassment has led to the omission of the introductory expression in the vast majority of modern versions such as RSV, NRSV, NJB, NAB, NEB, REB, NIV, etc. A minority of translations rendering the expression follow the oldest interpretation provided by Jerome, Yefet ben Ely, Zwingli and Olivetan. So BR: *Mit dem Spruch*, "With the saying." The only problem with such an interpretation is that it is without parallel in Biblical Hebrew.

As to the other solutions, whether one considers לאמר to be an explicit introduction to the content of מָאַס in the preceding verse (so Radaq, Luther, Tremellius) or a direct continuation of 2.35b (Barthélemy), they all amount translationally to the same: the speaker is the Lord. Most translations will therefore need an explicit identification of the participant.

Translation Proposals

A long paraphrase as provided in NJV: "[The word of the Lord came to me]," although basically correct, can better be avoided, especially since the square brackets might be misunderstood and seem to suggest the presence of a conjectural reading as proposed by Clericus or Michaelis. A brief introduction as given in GNB: "The Lord says" is largely sufficient.

3.1B

Textual Decisions

The second textual problem is found in the rhetorical question of this verse. The reading of M הָאָרֶץ, "the land," "would not the land be greatly polluted?" is supported by the Origen recension of G, Jerome, S, and T. On the other hand, G has the reading ἡ γυνή, "the woman," οὐ μιαινομένη μιανθή-σεται ἡ γυνὴ ἐκείνη, "shall not that woman be utterly defiled?" a rendering which also has the support of V. The committee was led by the following considerations: (1) V cannot be used as a witness for an original reading of הָאִשָּׁה because Jerome states in his commentary: " '*mulier illa*', *pro quo in Hebraico 'terram' legimus*," " 'that woman', for which we read in Hebrew 'the land' "; (2) in Greek, ΓΗ could first have been corrupted into ΓΥΝΗ, and then have been restored by recension; or, ΓΥΝΗ could be a mistaken correction of ΓΗ, wrongly considered a corrupted form of this word; (3) G may also testify to the intervention of the translator, who was disturbed by the rapid transition from the picture of the "woman" to the portrayed land (Wichelhaus, 134); (4) the transition from γῆ to γυνή in G can easily be explained but not the change from האשה to הארץ. M therefore received a B evaluation, as the more difficult reading.

Evaluation of Problems

The emendation האשה, first proposed by Houbigant, was adopted by several commentators, most recently again by McKane (58–59). It also entered into NEB: "Is not that woman defiled, a forbidden thing?" and it stayed uncorrected in REB. The vast majority of modern versions render M, encouraged by the apparatus of BHS, which mentions the recurrence of the expression in the next verse. For McKane the recurrence is instead an argument in favor of the emendation because the pollution of the land is the consequence of that of the woman, and a reference to it ought not to appear until verse 2. However, proleptic thoughts are not forbidden, and the reference in verse 1 follows the thought of Deut 24.4: "her first husband, who sent her away, is not permitted to take her again to be his wife after she has been defiled; for that would be abhorrent to the Lord, and you shall not bring guilt on the land that the Lord your God is giving you as a possession" (NRSV).

Translation Proposals

The transition can sometimes be handled more easily by rendering the rhetorical question as a negative answer to a preceding question, as has been done in FC: *peut-il la reprendre comme épouse? Non! Le pays en serait souillé*, "could he take her back as his wife? No! The land would be defiled by it." A reference to Deut 24.4 would be helpful (see NJV).

3.8

Textual Decisions

In M this verse starts with a first-person singular verbal form: וָאֵרֶא, "and I saw," "and I saw that for all the adulteries of that faithless one, Israel, I had sent her away with a decree of divorce . . . ," a reading which has the direct support of G: καὶ εἶδον, "and I saw," and the indirect support of T: וגלי קדמי, "it was clear to me." On the other hand, one manuscript of Kennicott reads ותרא, "and she saw," a reading, presupposed by the Antiochian recension of G: (ε)ιδε(ν), by S and even by V, in spite of the fact that the verbal form has not been translated. In fact, a rendering of the verb becomes redundant in the context: ". . . and her false sister Judah saw it; she saw that. . . ."

The reading of the late-thirteenth-century manuscript Kennicott 187 has no authority at all. The fact that the more-difficult reading of the first-person singular is attested by both M and the Old Greek, made it receive a B evaluation.

Evaluation of Problems

The correction to the third-person singular feminine verbal form was first proposed by Vogel and it has been used by almost all exegetes since then, most recently by Holladay, who considers the first-person singular form to be an assimilation to the same form at the beginning of verse 7 (58–59). It was also borrowed by the apparatuses of all editions of BH, from where it found its way into a great number of modern versions (RSV, NRSV, NJB, NAB, GNB, NEB, REB, etc.). Most of these versions provide abundant textual evidence for their choice, though not always the correct one. Thus, NRSV signals that the third-person reading is found in a text from Qumran, probably confusing the Greek manuscript Q with Q(umran)!

However, the first-person reading, parallel with the same at the beginning of verse 7, makes excellent sense when not connected with the immediately following information, but with verse 8b, introduced by וְלֹא with the "*waw* of resumption" (Joüon-Muraoka, 176b): "And I saw that—while for all the adulteries of that faithless one, Israel, I had sent her away with a decree of divorce—her false sister Judah did not fear."

Translation Proposals

Since such a long and involved sentence can hardly be a good model for translators, some restructuring may have to be done. The verbal form can best be shifted toward the beginning of verse 8b. NIV can be used as a good example: "I gave faithless Israel her certificate of divorce and sent her away because of all her adulteries. Yet I saw that her unfaithful sister Judah had no fear."

3.23

Textual Decisions

A literal translation of the first line of verse 23: "Truly to the delusion from the hills tumult the mountains," clearly shows the problems of text and interpretation. The first textual problem is presented by the reading מִגְּבָעֹות, "from the hills," in M. G, V, and S, by rendering "the hills," probably only read גבעות without the prefixed preposition, unless (which seems more unlikely) they considered the *mem* to be part of the noun and provided it with the non-attested meaning "hills." Only T by its paraphrase: "Therefore in vain we have worshiped on the heights," seems to support M, attesting the presence of a preposition. The second textual problem can be found in the reading הָמֹון, "tumult," of M. The *qames* vocalization of M indicates the absolute state and makes the noun the predicate of a very short phrase: "it is tumult, the mountains." However, by rendering the Hebrew as a genitive construction, the versions must have vocalized with a *hatef patah*, the construct state: καὶ ἡ δύναμις τῶν ὀρέων, "and the power of the mountains" (G), *multitudo montium*, "the multitude of the mountains" (V), ܪ̈ܝܫܐ ܕܛܘܖ̈ܐ, "and the power of the mountains" (S). The retroversion πλῆθος ὀρέων from the Syro-Hexapla for Aq and Sym also supports such a vocalization, and it is directly attested by 36 manuscripts of de Rossi. It is again only T, with its paraphrase: "it is without profit that we have been excited on the mountains," that seems to support M. Nevertheless, the committee reasoned in both cases that G, V, and S provided a syntactical facilitation, and it assigned a C evaluation to the more difficult reading of M.

Evaluation of Problems

Since Michaelis (1793), a correction of M has been proposed according to what was considered to have been the Vorlage of G and V. Such a correction also entered into the apparatus of our Hebrew Bibles and into some versions such as NRSV: "Truly, the hills are a delusion, the orgies on the mountains," and NJB: "The hills are a delusion after all, so is the tumult of the mountains."

On the other hand, recent commentators such as Holladay (61), McKane (81), and Caroll (154) keep M.

The major problem of the translator is that no textual base as such is sufficient to produce a translation. There are many implications, such as pagan worship on the hilltops, and the enthusiasm of the pilgrims as well as the pejorative hubbub evoked by the word הָמוֹן, which have to be expressed with a certain degree of explicitness in a translation in order to be intelligible. For example, to clarify M, Kimchi provides the following paraphrase of the two words of M: "The safety for which we hoped from the hills is vain." When rendering M, one could, with Venema (1765), attribute an emphatic value to the preposition *lamed* in לַשֶּׁקֶר: "that which comes from the mountains is pure delusion."

Translation Proposals

Depending on the degree of paraphrase allowed by the principles of a translation project, at least two models can be proposed. For a minimal paraphrase, NIV is a good example: "Surely the idolatrous commotion on the hills and mountains is a deception"; and for a maximum paraphrase, REB: "There is no help in worship on the hilltops, no help from clamour on the heights."

4.2

Textual Decisions

In the second line, M reads third-person masculine suffixes twice: בוֹ . . . וּבוֹ, "(and nations shall be blessed / will bless themselves) by him and by him (they shall boast)." However, Grätz (1883, 60) proposed the second-person emendation בְּךָ . . . וּבְךָ, "in you . . . and in you," and he has been followed by many scholars. The committee, on the other hand, assigned an A evaluation to M for two main reasons: (1) M is unanimously attested by all the ancient versions, and (2) the proposed conjecture seems to be a facilitating reading, motivated by an exegesis which wanted to assimilate the Jeremiah text to Gen 22.18 and 26.4.

Evaluation of Problems

The problem is therefore a purely interpretational one, involving the question of the antecedent of the third-person masculine suffixes. For the Greek translator, the antecedent clearly was Israel, and this is confirmed by the explicit information he adds at the end of the verse: καὶ ἐν αὐτῷ αἰνέσουσι τῷ θεῷ ἐν Ιερουσαλημ, "and by him they shall praise God in Jerusalem." For the Targum, it is the same antecedent, as can be seen from the explicit word "Israel" in the beginning of 2b: "then shall the nations be blessed through Israel, and shall glorify themselves through him." Alternatively, for the Vulgate with its active and transitive rendering of the verb, the antecedent seems to be the Lord: *Et benedicent eum gentes, ipsum laudabunt,* "And people will bless him, and him they will praise." The division between the ancient versions can be traced back in the history of exegesis: Rashi, and, most recently, McKane (84–86) followed G and T; Kimchi, and again recently, Thomson (213) followed the interpretation of V. Among modern versions NEB, REB, and NJV side with G and T; the others, insofar as they are unambiguous, side with V.

It is difficult to make a choice between different exegetical options. If the first one is chosen, a change to second-person pronouns may be necessary, but only for translational reasons.

Translation Proposals

If the first option is preferred, NJV: "Nations shall bless themselves by you and praise themselves by you," or REB could be used as a model, but not their notes. If the second option is selected, GNB could act as a model: "Then all the nations will ask me to bless them, and they will praise me." It may be good to mention the option which is not adopted in the text in a footnote, either in the form of a variant translation or a brief description of the variant interpretation, as has been done in EÜ. Such a procedure can be particularly recommended in interconfessional projects with Orthodox participation.

4.16

Textual Decisions

According to verse 16b in M, נֹצְרִים, "watchers," are coming from a distant land. M seems to be confirmed by 4Q-c, by Sym (φύλακες, "guards"), and by V (*custodes*, "guards"). It is more difficult to know where συστροφαί, "crowds," in G stems from. In Hos 4.19 and 13.12, the same Greek word renders a derivation from the root צרר, and a correspondence with such a root could possibly be presupposed in this case. The reading of S, ܐܢܫܐ ܕܟܢܫܬܐ, "crowds of peoples," seems to have been inspired by G, whereas the reading of T, משרית עממין, "armies of peoples," seems to have been motivated by S. In fact, T has a doublet, its second translation being חטופין כקטופין, "robbers like grape-gatherers." In 49.9, Obad 5, and Lev 25.5, the rendering of the second word in T corresponds to the Hebrew root בצר, so that most likely בצרים forms the key to the understanding of the second translation of T. In view of the external evidence and of the "watchers of a field," mentioned in verse 17, the committee has granted a B evaluation to M.

Evaluation of Problems

Since Oort, the conjecture צָרִים, "enemies," has been proposed, a conjecture which has had relative success in the translation field, since it has been accepted by NJB, GNB, GN, and FC. Closely related to this is the conjectural vocalization נְצֹרִים, which, according to Brockington (199), forms the foundation for "hordes of invaders" in NEB and REB. This last conjecture is based on a proposal made by Driver, and it has at least the advantage of respecting the consonantal text of M. On the other hand, it has the "disadvantage of postulating a *niphal* of צור not otherwise attested" (McKane, 100). In light of the textual decisions, both conjectures will have to be rejected.

However, a rendering such as "Watchers are coming from a distant land" (so NJV and NAV) can hardly be understood correctly by receptors. Therefore, a rendering such as "besiegers" (RSV, NRSV, NAB, NIV, RL, TOB) may have to be chosen, even if the aim of the besiegers is not to assault a town but to isolate it completely, so that nobody can get out of it.

Translation Proposals

NIV: "A besieging army is coming from a distant land," can be taken as an acceptable model. An explanatory note may be helpful.

4.29A

Textual Decisions

In verse 29 of M the expression כָּל־הָעִיר, "the whole city," occurs twice, once at the end of the first line and once at the beginning of the third. In its first occurrence it is confirmed by V and S. It is also attested by T, for the reading כל יתבי קרתא, "all the inhabitants of the town," found in all manuscripts quoted in Sperber's edition, Urbinates I, the editions of Felix de Prato, and the Antwerp polyglot, seems to be original. The variant reading ארעא, "(all the inhabitants) of the land," found in the second rabbinic Bible and in the London polyglot, could be considered a secondary assimilation to the same expression in verses 27 and 28. On the other hand, G has the rendering πᾶσα χώρα, "all the land," which for most scholars would represent an original Hebrew Vorlage כָּל־הָאָרֶץ. It should, however, be noted that in Jeremiah G frequently uses a word for "land" where M presents a word for "town" (29 [36].7; 31 [38].24; 34 [41].22; 40 [47].5). It is true that in all these cases the Greek word γῆ has been used, not χώρα. However, χώρα may well have been chosen here because of its attractive assonance with the preceding verb ἀνεχώρησε, "has taken to flight." The committee, therefore, considered G to be due to translational procedures and it assigned a B evaluation to M.

Evaluation of Problems

From Michaelis to van Selms (93) and McKane (110–11), scholars were rather unanimous that G has preserved the dissymmetry of the original text and that the first occurrence of כָּל־הָעִיר in M is due to an assimilation to its second occurrence (Movers, 29). This argument was followed particularly by older translations such as Goodspeed, Moffatt, and LV, but much less so by modern translators. Among those in English, only NEB with its rendering "the whole country is in flight" testifies to it, REB having preferred to render M again: "every town is in flight." Among non-English versions, EÜ and GN (without textual note) are the exceptions. Internal logic is, in fact, a strong point in favor of rendering M. It can only be said in 29c that every town has been abandoned after the statement that every town has taken to flight. And the hiding places mentioned in 29b make clear that the flight is within the country and not abroad. In addition, if the structural divisions of BHS are accepted, the chiastic position of כָּל־הָעִיר in 29 αβ and cα strongly favors its repetition.

Translation Proposals

The identical phrase repetition: "every town is in flight. . . . Every town is deserted," as, for example, in REB provides a good translational model.

4.29B

Textual Decisions

The second line in M only makes two statements: בָּאוּ בֶּעָבִים, "they enter the thickets," and וּבַכֵּפִים עָלוּ, "and up the rocks they clamber," and these are confirmed by V, S, and T. However, in G three statements are made: εἰσέδυσαν εἰς τὰ σπήλαια καὶ εἰς τὰ ἄλση ἐκρύβησαν καὶ ἐπὶ τὰς πέτρας ἀνέβησαν, "they have gone into the caves, and they have hidden in thickets, and they climbed the rocks." The extra information in G would therefore be εἰς τὰ σπήλαια . . . ἐκρύβησαν which would correspond to a longer Hebrew text בַּמְּעָרוֹת נֶחְבָּאוּ (Volz). These two words would have followed the initial בָּאוּ in the Hebrew Vorlage of G. This Vorlage seems to have been more original, for the accidental omission of the two words in M is clearly due to homoioteleuton, the scribe confusing the initial באו with the identical last three consonants of נחבאו. The committee therefore gave a B evaluation to the restitution of the two reconstructed Hebrew words.

Evaluation of Problems

The back translation provided by Volz seems to be correct. The verb חבא appears one other time in Jeremiah, in 49.10 where G renders it with κρυβῆναι

(29.11). The noun מְעָרָה is also found one other time in Jeremiah, in 7.11 where it is translated by G with (μὴ) σπήλαιον. As to the initial בָּאוּ, εἰσέδυσαν seems to be its natural equivalent since the verb בוא has been rendered thirteen times with δύειν in the Septuagint. Although the decision made by the committee is still supported by a number of scholars (Bright, Holladay, van Selms), it does not meet with general approval. This may be one of the reasons that the vast majority of modern versions still render M. The only exceptions are NEB, EÜ, and GN. Translators are nevertheless encouraged to pursue the conclusions of the committee.

Translation Proposals

A good example of translation is NEB: "they creep into caves, they hide in thickets, they scramble up the crags." A brief textual note, as in NEB and GN, may be useful.

4.30

Textual Decisions

Following the initial וְאַתְּ, which is the older form of the 2nd-singular feminine pronoun, M has the masculine participle שָׁדוּד, "desolate one." Aquila and Theodotion, by reading ἡ ταλαίπωρος, "miserable one," and also V, S, and T, in spite of their feminine endings, are indirect witnesses of M. They did not read שדודה, but most likely they provided a facilitating translation by adapting to the feminine pronoun. The reading of Theodotion also entered into the recensions of Origin and Lucian. However, it is lacking in the Old Greek. The omission in G can easily be explained as an avoidance of the syntactical problem created by the masculine form of the participle. Therefore, M received a B evaluation.

Evaluation of Problems

Cornill judged that שָׁדוּד should nevertheless be deleted for metrical reasons, and he is followed by the vast majority of modern scholarship. No wonder therefore that at least some modern versions (NEB, REB, EÜ, FC) reflect this insight.

There are, however, several ways to explain the syntactical difficulty in M. Grammatically, Ewald (1863: 457f.) has drawn attention to the fact that in Arabic certain *qatul* forms preserve the masculine gender when combined with feminine nouns. On the other hand, semantically, the masculine participle could be a reference to the condition of the people mentioned in the preceding verse: "you, who are doomed to ruin." Such an understanding, shared by most recent translations, seems to be the best one.

Translation Proposals

NJV is a good example of how the syntactical difficulty of M can be solved: "And you, who are doomed to ruin, What do you accomplish by wearing crimson?"

5.2

Textual Decisions

In M verse 2 starts with וְאַם, "and even," "and although," and this reading is also attested by V, S, and T. The particle is, however, lacking in G which has instead the rendering λέγει κύριος, "says the Lord," apparently attached to the preceding verse to introduce its speaker. This translation is probably due to a reading נאם, "oracle," as a shorthand for נאם יהוה, "oracle of the Lord." In the first chapters of Jeremiah, there are four cases in which G has λέγει κύριος (the usual translation of נאם יהוה), but in three of these verses M has zero (1.17; 2.2; 17.19), in contrast to one place where נאם יהוה appears (3.10). Since the identification of participants can be considered to be a translational necessity, M received a B evaluation.

Evaluation of Problems

The vast majority of modern translations follow M. The only notable exceptions are NJB and EÜ which follow G, the first one according to its textual note. Most translators may feel the need to identify the speaker for translational, not for textual reasons. It should be pointed out, however, that the whole discourse of 5.1–6 will have to be analyzed on its participants' structure before solutions on the level of specific verses can be suggested. Two different analyses have been proposed in this respect. Rudolph has analyzed the discourse unit as a dialogue between the Lord and Jeremiah, the Lord being the speaker of verses 1 and 6; the prophet, of verses 2–5. McKane, on the other hand, makes a slight correction by considering verses 1, 2, and 6 as spoken by the Lord, and verses 3–5 as spoken by Jeremiah. In view of the arguments developed (p. 115), the last analysis seems to be preferable.

Translators can, of course, use several devices for the identification of speakers. They could either mention the speaker between parentheses preceding his text, as has been done, for example, in FC, or they could make the identification within the text of the translation at what seems to be the most appropriate place in the receptor language.

Translation Proposals

If the last solution is followed, the minimal approach of GN could be employed, which puts an introductory "The Lord says . . ." at the beginning of the two paragraphs consisting of, respectively, verses 1–2 and 6, and which leaves the paragraph consisting of verses 3–5, with the prophetic speech, unmarked.

5.7

Textual Decisions

In M the last word is יִתְגֹּדָדוּ, "they have cut themselves," "they have cut themselves (in a harlot's house)." The rendering of V: *luxuriabantur*, "they revel," seems to be an interpretation motivated by the context, and the same can be said of the rendering of S ܐܫܬܪܚܘ, "they behaved riotously." The rendering of T מסתיעין, "they have joined," must be based on a derivation from the noun גְּדוּד, "band," "troop." G, on the other hand, by its rendering κατέλυον, "they lodged," "they lodged (in harlots' houses)," should have had a Hebrew Vorlage יִתְגּוֹרָרוּ. Since such a Vorlage provides the only possible correct meaning in this context, the committee assigned a C evaluation to G and decided to correct the graphical error of M accordingly. The same correction seems to have taken place in manuscripts 518 and 576 of de Rossi, unless these two accurate Spanish manuscripts preserved the original reading.

Evaluation of Problems

The correction of M was first proposed by Michaelis (1792, 265) and it has been adopted by many others, most recently by Bright (36) and van Selms (108). Remarkably, many modern versions interpret M in the same way as T by rendering "To the harlot's house they throng" (NAB and with minor variations NIV) or "and trooped to the houses of prostitutes" (NRSV, and with minor variations NJV) or "they hurried to the brothel" (NJB, FC). These versions may have done so under the influence of misleading dictionary presentations (compare Brown-Driver-Briggs 151a). Such a meaning, however, is nowhere attested. Translators are therefore advised to adopt the corrected text which is followed in NEB, REB, GNB, EÜ, and GN.

Translation Proposals

REB: "and frequented brothels," or GNB: "and spent their time with prostitutes," offer acceptable models of translation. A textual note is obligatory.

5.13

Textual Decisions

In M this verse ends with the sentence כֹּה יַעֲשֶׂה לָהֶם, "so let it be done to them." The presence of this sentence is also attested by V, S, and T. However, as Clericus already noted, based on the Sixtine edition of the Septuagint, it is absent from some Greek manuscripts, among which is Codex Alexandrinus. On the other hand, the sentence is well attested by the three oldest Greek witnesses: Codex Vaticanus, Codex Sinaiticus, and papyrus Chester Beatty 966 (end of second century) in the form οὕτως ἔσται αὐτοῖς, "so it will be to them." It therefore certainly was part of the Old Greek, as is also shown by the fact that it figures in the Syro-Hexapla without asterisk. The omission in A and other manuscripts can easily be explained as due to homoioteleuton (similar ending), the copyist's eye having shifted from בָּהֶם at the end of the preceding sentence to לָהֶם at the end of the sentence under discussion. M therefore received an A evaluation.

Evaluation of Problems

The omission of the sentence was proposed by Cornill and it is still defended by McKane (121–22), although he agrees that the evidence of Codex Alexandrinus is slender in support of such a deletion. Nevertheless, NEB quotes G as the textual basis for its omission, whereas REB, although maintaining the deletion, no longer quotes textual evidence to support it. GNB omits the sentence without footnotes, whereas EÜ keeps it within square brackets. It will be clear that none of these approaches can be recommended to translators.

Among scholars who preserve the sentence, many propose transposing it after the first line of verse 14 where, according to them, it belonged. So Duhm and, recently, Bright. This proposal has had some influence on translation in view of the first two editions of La Bible de Jérusalem. It has, however, been completely abandoned in recent translations, and rightly so.

The problem presented by the sentence itself still has to be solved. It could have been the gloss of a reader who wished that the disasters of war and famine predicted by the false prophets of doom would fall on their own heads. Depending on one's interpretation of "prophets," it may also have been the utterance of those who showed contempt for the prophetic message of Jeremiah. Such a gloss is very old and it dates from before the achievement of the first redaction of the book. It may even stem from Jeremiah himself (Schuttermayr, 228ff.).

Translation Proposals

If verses 12–13 are taken to be the speech of Jeremiah, quoting the people of Judah, NAB can be taken as a model: "May their threats be carried out against themselves." For a more explicit paraphrase of such an interpretation, GN can be consulted.

5.16

Textual Decisions

The first word in M is אַשְׁפָּתוֹ, "its quiver," "its quiver is like an open tomb." This reading is confirmed by Th and Aq: ἡ φαρέτρα αὐτοῦ ὡς τάφος ἀνεῳγμένος, "its quiver is like an open tomb," by V: *faretra eius*, and T: בֵּית אֲזֵינֵיהּ, "receptacle of weapons." On the other hand, verse 16a is lacking in the Old Greek, whereas S renders with ܡܘܪܝܓܗ, "its throat." The committee considered the latter rendering to be an assimilation to the Syriac translation of Ps 5.10: קֶבֶר־פָּתוּחַ גְּרוֹנָם, "their throats are open graves," and the assimilation to be inspired by the unsatisfactory character of the figure in M. For the same reason, G omitted verse 16a. Half of the committee therefore gave an A evaluation to M and the other half a B evaluation, noting that in this case M represents the first redaction.

Evaluation of Problems

Because of the difficulty presented by the comparison, several corrections of the Hebrew text have been proposed. Michaelis already suggested the correction שְׂפָתוֹ, "its lips," Driver (1960, 123) the related correction אֲשֶׁר שְׂפָתָיו, "of which their lips," and lastly Volz אֲשֶׁר פִּיהוּ, "of which their mouth." According to Brockington, it is the first correction which seems to be the base of the rendering of NEB: "their jaws are a grave, wide open." This translation was adopted unaltered by REB, and the footnotes in both editions call attention to the Syriac. In fact, S can be considered a kind of anticipation of modern emendations (McKane, 124). However, apart from NEB, REB, and the older Dutch Canisius translation, no modern version can be cited which adopts any of these corrections. NJV only mentions the one by Volz in a footnote.

Whether the figure is considered "infelicitous" (McKane, 124) or "one of the finest of Jeremiah's figures" (Hopper in IntB), one will still have to render it. Probably the container is only compared with an open grave because its arrows will kill everyone they meet. If the figure is considered inappropriate, some translational adaptation may seem necessary.

Translation Proposals

For a literal type of translation, the majority rendering, "their quivers are like an open grave," can be adopted. However, for a functional equivalence type of translation, GN can serve as model: *Aus den Köchern seiner Krieger kommt Tod und Verderben*, "Death and destruction come out of the quivers of his soldiers."

5.26

Textual Decisions

There are textual problems with each of the three words which may have constituted the second sentence: יָשׁוּר כְּשַׁךְ יְקוּשִׁים frequently rendered "they lurk like fowlers lying in wait." The first item, יָשׁוּר, is lacking in G and S. On the other hand, Jerome (Field II, 585a) attributes the transliteration *iasir* to Aq and Sym, showing by his translation, *rectus* (*rectus quasi rete aucupis*), that he considers them to have read here an adjective derived from the root יָשַׁר, "to be straight." The translation of V: *insidiantes*, "lying in ambush," points by its plural reading to a syntactical facilitation of the form יָשֻׁר. T, by using the root אשׁד and rendering אֶשְׁדִּין דָּם, "they shed blood," seems to have been inspired by certain form and sound resemblances (Komlosh, 40).

The second item, כְּשַׁךְ, is also missing in G. In the asterisked insertion found in the Origen recension: ὡς δίκτυον ἰξευτοῦ, "like a net of a fowler," the second item apparently is represented by ὡς δίκτυον which seems to be based on a derivation from the root שׂכך (Schleusner II, 170). The same type of derivation seems to be presupposed by the reading ܐܝܟ ܣܝܓܐ, "like a fence," in S, but to presuppose such a derivation in the case of the rendering of T: כלבוש, "like a garment," seems to be rather daring. The reading of V: *quasi aucupes*, "like fowlers," may simply testify to an exegetical treatment of the form in M.

The last item יְקוּשִׁים, "fowlers" is the only one rendered in G. The translation (καὶ παγίδας ἔστησαν), "(and they have set) snares" shows, however, that יקושׁים has been given the meaning "snares" and that the noun has been taken as the object of the following verb in M: הִצִּיבוּ. The same happens in V and S. T confirms M, whereas the Origen recension, which stems from Theodotion, Aquila, and Symmachus, makes a translational adaptation to the singular.

The sentence in M received a C evaluation since the textual traditions do not appear to produce a text to be preferred over M.

Evaluation of Problems

It is no wonder that in the light of textual uncertainties many emendations have been proposed by scholars. I will mention only those which had some bearing on translations: Rudolph (282) proposed reading the sentence as follows: יִשְׂרְכוּ שְׂבָכָ(ה) כְּיוֹקְשִׁים, "they have interwoven the snare like fowlers," and this emendation may be the basis for the rendering of REB: "who, like fowlers, lay snares." Brockington conjectures יִשְׂרְכוּ שֶׁךְ יֹקְשִׁים as the textual basis for NEB "who lay snares like a fowler's net," but this seems to be doubtful. In spite of the superficial resemblance between REB and NAB, the latter seems, according to its textual note (418), to follow G precisely in its omission of the first two items (reason: corrupt dittography) and its syntactical combination with the following verb: "like fowlers they set traps." NRSV does not give any justification for its rendering "they take over the goods of others. Like fowlers (they set a trap)." It must, however, be based on a different consonantal division of the Hebrew text: . . . יָ֫שׁוּ רֶ֫כֶשׁ כִּיקוּשִׁים, as proposed by Holladay (193).

In view of the recommendations of the committee, the best approach seems to be, with the majority of the modern versions, to make sense out of M. One could in this connection consider the necessity of changing the singular of the verb into a plural (יָשׁוּר → יָשׁוּרוּ). This is the only change McKane takes as "inescapable" (133). However, in maintaining the singular, one could see here (with Radaq and Keil) an effort to give a particularizing meaning to the verb: this behavior is not that of the whole society but that of isolated individuals.

Translation Proposals

An acceptable translational model can be found in RSV: "they lurk like fowlers lying in wait" (compare also the renderings of FC and GN). Translators may want to state that the meaning of the Hebrew is rather uncertain.

6.2

Textual Decisions

With the exception of the last two words, בַּת־צִיּוֹן, "daughter of Zion," the whole verse is textually problematic. To be able to deal effectively with the problems, one should first discuss the initial word pair, הַנָּוָה וְהַמְעֻנָּגָה, frequently rendered "beautiful and delicate," and, after this the verb דָּמִיתִי, the interpretation of which will be the subject of "Evaluation of Problems."

Regarding the first word pair, M is directly attested by Th, Aq, and the Targum and indirectly by Sym, V, and S. G has the rather puzzling rendering . . . γίνεται, καὶ ἀφαιρεθήσεται τὸ ὕψος σου, ". . . is becoming. And your grandeur shall be taken away." As Cappel (1684, 521b) has suggested, the translator seems to have derived the first word from the root הָוָה, "to be," after which he has connected this word with the preceding sentence. He may then have derived the second word from the root מנע, a possibility which is reinforced by the fact that this root has been rendered with the same Greek verb in Job 38.15 and Prov 30.7.

With regard to the verb, Sym and V on the one hand, and S and T on the other, although differing in their interpretation of the meaning of the verb and the grammatical person concerned, nevertheless support the reading of M. With τὸ ὕψος σου the translator may have preferred to read a *resh* instead of a *daleth*. Tov (24–25) supposes that the translator avoided the rendering of the roots דמה and דמם and read רמיכי.

The committee considered the difficulties of the text to be mainly exegetical: if a Vorlage of G could be reconstructed, it would not be preferable to M, which therefore received three C and three B evaluations.

Evaluation of Problems

In view of the interpretational difficulties, a number of conjectures have been proposed, a few of which can still be found in recent translations. So, according to Brockington (200), NEB presupposes the emendation (ה)דָּמְתָ when it renders the verse as follows: "Zion, delightful and lovely: her end is near." Without textual justification, REB translates the same way. It should be noted, however, that GN, without textual change, basically provides the same rendering, a sign that other paraphrases of a classical interpretation of M come very close to some of the emendations. Houbigant's proposal to correct the first word to לְנָוֶה and to omit the conjunction preceding the second word is still followed most recently in GrN and RGrN: *Sion lijkt wel een malse wei*, "Zion looks like a luxurious meadow." On the other hand, the emendation הֲלְנָוֶה, understanding ה as an interrogative particle as proposed in BHS, only seems to have been adopted by older translations, such as the first editions of BdeJ and Moffatt: "Is it a meadow fair?" Probably NRSV, without changing the verb, follows Houbigant's correction of the first word pair when it reads: "I have likened daughter Zion to the loveliest pasture."

Preferably, translators should not follow such text corrections. However, M presents considerable problems of interpretation. The options are the following: (1) the verb can either be interpreted as a second-person feminine singular (Bauer-Leander, §42, k–1) or as a first-person singular; (2) the verb can either be derived from דמה I, in which case its meaning would be "to compare," or from דמה III, with the meaning "to destroy"; (3) the word pair should probably be considered to consist of close synonyms. The first problematic word could then be analyzed as a defective form of נָאוָה and given the meaning "beautiful." It has sometimes been given the meaning "stay-at-home." With regard to decision-making, the following can be said: (1) the majority of exegetes have, in agreement with the Masoretes, read a first-person singular of the verb, therefore making God the implicit verbal agent; (2) a derivation from דמה I is unlikely, since what is being compared should normally be introduced by a *lamed* and, moreover, definite articles preceding objects of comparison are unusual; (3) with the great majority of exegetes, a meaning "beautiful" for the first item in the word pair should be preferred. These three options are those of RSV, NIV, NJV, NJB, and GNB.

Translation Proposals

Depending on the way in which participants are handled in the context, NJV could be used as a model: "Fair Zion, the lovely and delicate, I will destroy." In view of the remaining uncertainties, variant translations and/or interpretations may be given in a footnote (compare FC). This is even a must in projects with Orthodox participation.

6.6

Textual Decisions

The textual problem is with the last word, הָפְקַד, "which is to be punished," of the first half of verse 6c: הִיא הָעִיר הָפְקַד, frequently rendered: "this is the city that must be punished." The reading of the word with a final *daleth* is confirmed by a *masorah parva* found in the Ben Chayyim edition as well as in the manuscripts of Cairo, Aleppo, and Leningrad. On the other hand, ms 596 of de Rossi reads a final *resh*, in which case the word should be connected with the postbiblical root פקר, "to lead a licentious life," and probably vocalized as הָפְקֵר with the meaning "licence." Of the ancient versions, M has the direct support of S and the indirect support of T since its paraphrase, "whose debts have been stored up against her" (דאתפקידו לה חובהא), seems to be based on M. In addition, the readings τῆς ἐπισκοπῆς, attributed in the Barberini manuscript to Sym, and *visitationis* of V are based on the form of M, in which the initial ה has been interpreted as the definite article. Only the rendering of G, ὦ πόλις ψευδής, "O, false city," presents problems. A presupposition that G would have read הַשֶּׁקֶר in its Vorlage (Cappel 1684, 522) is only based on a consideration of the fact that ψευδής in almost all instances in Jeremiah renders שֶׁקֶר. And Schleusner (5, 558) may be correct in considering G as a free, but semantically close, translation of M. The fact that M seems to be at the base of all textual traditions has led to a C evaluation.

Evaluation of Problems

It cannot be recommended therefore to conjecture הַשֶּׁקֶר, as has been done by Moffatt: "Ah, the false city," and in NV and W, or to follow a few Hebrew manuscripts and editions in adopting the reading הפקר, as done in NEB: "the city whose name is Licence."

However, M is difficult to translate because of problems of grammar and semantics. Grammatically there is no concord between the feminine noun הָעִיר, "the city," and the masculine form of the verb הָפְקַד, which makes the standard rendering ("the city that must be punished") forced, to say the least (Bright, 43). Therefore, Rudolph (42), following in the tracks of Rosenmüller and Nägelsbach, gave a different and impersonal meaning to the verb, considering the

half-verse as an introduction to the second one: "This is a city of which it is established: oppression is everywhere within her." This solution was adopted in
EÜ and FC: *La preuve en est faite: c'est la ville qui se distingue par la brutal-
ité qui y règne.* Other proposals with regard to the semantics of the verb have
been made (see Barthélemy, 505), but they are extremely unlikely because of
an extended ellipsis. In order to solve the grammatical problem, Venema, disregarding the accents of M, took the first word of the second half-verse, כֻּלָּהּ, as
subject of the verb: "This is the city, the totality of which will be punished."
Such a rendering is so close to the traditional one that the standard translation
could be maintained.

Translation Proposals

Renderings such as "this is the city to be punished" (NJB) or "a city ripe
for punishment" (REB) can serve as a model for translators.

6.9

Textual Decisions

The content of the discourse of the Lord of Hosts in M begins with עוֹלֵל
יְעוֹלְלוּ which could either mean "they will glean thoroughly" or "let them
glean thoroughly." Such a reading also is the textual base of Aq, Sym, V, S,
and T. On the other hand, the rendering of G consists of two plural imperatives: καλαμᾶσθε καλαμᾶσθε, "glean, glean." This rendering could be based
upon a Hebrew Vorlage עוֹלְלוּ עוֹלְלוּ, a reading in which the initial *yod* of the
second word in M was taken to be a final *waw* of the first (Cornill). The committee assigned a B evaluation to M, maintaining that M presents the classical
case of an infinitive absolute reinforcing a verb of the same conjugation. The
reading of G was explained as being due to a harmonization with the plural
imperative ἐπιστρέψατε, "turn back," in verse 9b.

Evaluation of Problems

Most commentators propose reading two singular imperatives עוֹלֵל עוֹלֵל
(Volz) or one infinitive absolute and one singular imperative which amounts to
the same reading (Bright, 44 and Rudolph, 42). This proposal has been adopted
by RSV, NRSV, NEB, and REB: "Glean (thoroughly) as a vine the remnant of
Israel." It is based on pure conjecture and on the presupposition that the Lord of
Hosts addresses himself to the prophet.

On the other hand, translating M is not without problems, as is shown by
the rendering of NJV (which is not basically different from NJB and NIV):
"Thus said the Lord of Hosts: Let them glean over and over, as a vine, the remnant of Israel. Pass your hand again, like a vintager, over its branches." In the

first part of this confusing translation, the enemies of Israel seem to be spoken about, while in the second half, the prophet is exhorted to glean.

Explaining the second command as one enemy ordering another enemy (Radaq) or reading הָשֵׁב, "pass," as an infinitive with the value of a gerund, "by passing the hand" (Luzzatto), seems to be forcing the evidence.

The following considerations may guide translators: (1) the whole discourse unit 9–15 is a dialogue between God and Jeremiah, and verse 9 is addressed to the prophet; (2) preferably, עוֹלֵל יְעוֹלְלוּ should be rendered as an impersonal statement; (3) certainly in functional equivalence translations the image and object of comparison need a more explicit formulation.

Translation Proposals

For a full translation of verse 9, GN presents a good model: *Der Herr der ganzen Welt sagte zu mir: "Wie man am Weinstock Nachlese hält, so soll auch an dem, was von Israel übriggeblieben ist, noch eine Nachlese gehalten werden. Wie die Hand des Winzers noch einmal alle Reben durchgeht, so wende auch du dich noch einmal diesem Volk zu."* "The Lord of the universe said to me: 'As one gleans a vine, so the remnant of Israel will have to be gleaned. As the vintager passes his hand one last time over the branches, so address yourself one last time to this people.'"

6.11

Textual Decisions

The second line of verse 11 in M begins with שְׁפֹךְ, which could either be interpreted as an imperative: "pour out, " or as an infinitive: "to pour out." M has the support of both V and S which opted for the first interpretation and of Sym and T which chose the second one. On the other hand, G has rendered a first-person singular: ἐκχεῶ, "I will pour out," and it is followed by Th: ἐξέχεα, "I poured out." Although manuscript Barberini attributes the last reading to Aquila, Ziegler suggests that it should probably be ascribed to Theodotion. According to the committee, G assimilated the verb to the two first-person singular verbs which preceded, and Th made the assimilation even stronger through the use of the aorist tense. M therefore received a B evaluation.

Evaluation of Problems

Since Ewald, it has frequently been proposed to vocalize the Hebrew form as an infinitive absolute שָׁפֹךְ which can then be interpreted as an equivalent of a finite form at the beginning of a sentence, in this case the first-person singular (Joüon-Muraoka, §123u). This is what, according to Brockington, has happened in NEB which renders "I must pour it out" (unchanged in REB) and, according to the textual notes (418), in NAB, with its translation "I will pour it out." These translations come close to Robert Estienne and the Geneva Bible, which interpreted the form in M as an infinitive and rendered it freely as a first-person singular.

With the majority of modern translations (RSV, NRSV, NJB, NIV, NJV, GNB, GN, FC, EÜ), it seems wiser, however, to interpret M as an imperative, since it is more likely that 11b begins the answer given by God to the prophet (Rudolph, 44). The explicit marking of the speaker at the end of verse 12 may have to be brought up here as an introductory device (GNB, GrN), or a double marking may be used, as in GN.

Translation Proposals

GNB provides a good example of a single marking: "Then the Lord said to me, 'Pour out my anger. . . .'"

6.15

Textual Decisions

This verse in M begins with the verbal form הֹבִישׁוּ, "they are put to shame." This form is presupposed by G, V, S, and even by T, which para-phrases with עֲלֵיהוֹן לְמִבְהַת, "they ought to be ashamed." In view of the uniform textual tradition, M received an A evaluation both here and in the parallel passage 8.12.

Evaluation of Problems

Following Grätz, Ehrlich (257–58), and Driver (1937–38, 102), NEB emends הֹבִישׁוּ to הֲבוֹשׁוּ, reading therefore the interrogative particle הֲ followed by the *qal* perfect of בּוֹשׁ, and translating, "Are they ashamed (when they practice their abominations)?" For such an emendation there clearly are no textual grounds. However, it should be noted that, without changing the form, already Jerome and many medieval Jewish exegetes attributed an interrogative value to M by considering the particle to be presupposed. It is therefore on interpretational grounds that the interrogative can be found in many recent translations, such as RSV, NIV, GNB, EÜ, and FC.

Another exegesis of M with historical interest is the one provided by T, adopted by Rashi and Ibn Nachmiash, and most recently defended by Rudolph (44) and McKane (147). It has been perpetuated in other modern versions such as NJB, REB, GN, and GrN. Since this interpretation provides the best contextual meaning, it should be preferred.

Translation Proposals

REB is a good model for the preferred interpretation: "They ought to be ashamed (because they practiced abominations; yet they have no sense of shame)." If the interrogative mood is preferred, GNB can serve as an example: "Were they ashamed (because they did these disgusting things? No, they were not at all ashamed)."

6.27

Textual Decisions

After having read בָּחוֹן נְתַתִּיךָ בְעַמִּי, "I have made you an assayer of my people," verse 27a ends with the word מִבְצָר which creates problems for understanding. G renders 27a in the following way: δοκιμαστὴν δέδωκά σε ἐν λαοῖς δεδοκιμασμένοις, "I have caused you to be tried among tried nations." One can only say that the translation of the last Hebrew word has been inspired by the rendering of the first one, but with regard to a Vorlage of the Greek translation no conclusions can be drawn. The Targum, by rendering ככרך תקיף, "like a strong, fortified city," confirms the reading of M as well as one of the two existing translations of Aquila, which, according to Jerome, would have rendered *munitum*, "fortified." According to the Barberini manuscript, Theodotion and the other translation of Aquila read ἐν λαοῖς ἰσχυροῖς, "among strong nations," and it is this free rendering of M which has inspired the translations of V and S. On the other hand, the Barberini manuscript attributes to Symmachus the rendering ἐν λαῷ μου πολιορκουμένῳ, "among my besieged people," which is not too different from the rendering *circumdato*, "encircled," attributed by Jerome to Symmachus. In fact, these renderings could be derived from a reading מצר, or at least from the root צור which is frequently rendered πολιορκέω in Sym. If this is the case, they could be due to a graphical error. The renderings συγκεκλεισμένοις and συγκεκλεισμένῳ in the Origin and Lucianic recensions, respectively, could be based on the same type of error, since the Greek verb συνκλείω frequently translates the Hebrew verb צור. The committee, judging that all these variants probably derived from M, assigned a C evaluation to it.

Evaluation of Problems

Driver (1955, 85) has proposed redistributing the consonants of the last word, מבצר, and the first word of the second half-verse, ותדע, in such a way that מִבְצָרוֹ תֵדַע, "its testing you know," can be read. According to Brockington this solution is reflected in the rendering of NEB: "I have appointed you an assayer of my people; you will know how to test them and will assay their conduct." This solution has rightly been abandoned by REB since, as McKane has pointed out (154), the circumstance that the same Hebrew word בְעַמִּי would have been resumed once by a singular suffix (at מבצרו) and once by a plural one (at דרכם) speaks sufficiently against it.

Three interpretational possibilities present themselves: (1) מִבְצָר has its normal meaning of "fortress" and is considered to be an explanation of the hapax בָּחוֹן, understood to mean "watch-tower." This is still the understanding of older translations such as StV and KJV: "I have set thee *for* a tower *and* a fortress among my people, that thou mayest know and try their way"; (2) מבצר is judged to be a gloss on בָּחוֹן, taken to mean "a tester (of metals)," in which case it should be repointed as a *piel* participle מְבַצֵּר, "examiner." This option is chosen by RSV, NRSV, NJV, REB, FC, and EÜ; (3) מִבְצָר is an intrusion from 1.18 and should be deleted (Giesebrecht; Rudolph, 48; Bright, 49). Semantically, the last option seems to be the most natural one. It has been adopted by NAB, NJB, GNB, GN, and GrN.

Translation Proposals

If the last possibility of interpretation is selected, NJB can be quoted as a model: "I have appointed you as a tester of my people, to learn and to test how they behave." One should follow NJB in adding a footnote: "Hebr. adds 'as a fortified city', same word as in 1:18." If the second interpretation is followed, REB can be cited as an example: "I have appointed you an assayer and tester of my people; you will know how to assay their conduct."

6.29

Textual Decisions

According to the *qere*, M reads two words, מֵאֵשׁ תַּם, "by fire is consumed," in verse 29: נָחַר מַפֻּחַ מֵאֵשׁ תַּם עֹפָרֶת, "the bellows blow fiercely, the lead is consumed by the fire." According to the *ketib*, one word is read, מֵאֶשְׁתַּם, "from their fire." Among the versions, S follows the *ketib* with its rendering ܡܢ ܢܘܪܗܘܢ, "without their fire," "the bellows are left without their fire and lead." The *qere* division into two words has the support of G: ἀπὸ πυρὸς ἐξέλιπε, "failed (to make) fire," "The bellows have failed (to make) fire, the lead has failed." It also is supported by V "*in igne consumptum est,*" "it is consumed in the fire," and even by the very long paraphrase of T which uses the first word, מֵאֵשׁ, "in the midst of the fire," and the second, תַּם, with the interpretation "is silent." The *ketib* figures in a Masoretic list of fifteen words which are written as one and read as two (Diaz Esteban, §82). Cappel (1775–86, 189) considered the *qere* to be a simple correction of a mistake. The committee signaled the fact that S testifies to the existence of two different interpretational traditions, although it preferred the *qere*, with a B evaluation.

Evaluation of Problems

NEB renders 29a: "The bellows puff and blow, the furnace glows" which according to Brockington should be based on a different consonantal division of the second and third words: מַפֵּחַ אֵשׁ. This conjecture was apparently adopted from Driver (1955, 85). On the other hand, REB by translating "The bellows blow, the fire is ready," follows an earlier proposal made by Driver (1937–38, 104) to render אֵשׁ תַּם with the highly improbable sense of "the fire is prepared."

However, the *qere* of M can be rendered as it is when translators are made aware of metallurgical techniques in antiquity. The impure silver combined with lead or the argentiferous lead to be refined was smelted in shallow vessels made of some porous substance, usually bone-ash, in a furnace heated until a temperature between 900 and 1000 degrees was reached. A blast of air was then blown across the molten lead, converting it to lead oxide, which was absorbed into the porous cupel, leaving the silver intact (Holladay, 231). In the comparison in Jer 6.29, the lead has been transformed and absorbed, but the pure silver has not been extracted. The wicked in Israel are symbolized by refuse silver because of their sins. It is essential that this comparison be correctly worked out and that the transition from image to object of comparison be smoothly made.

Translation Proposals

In a literal type of translation NRSV can be taken as a model: "The bellows blow fiercely, the lead is consumed by the fire." One may, however, want to use a footnote to describe briefly the technique involved. None of the existing functional equivalence translations can be quoted as a satisfactory example.

7.3

Textual Decisions

Verse 3 ends in M with the conditional promise וַאֲשַׁכְּנָה אֶתְכֶם, "I will let you live (in this place)." In the same way, verse 7 starts with the same promise, וְשִׁכַּנְתִּי אֶתְכֶם, "I will let you live (in this place)." Both the Aleppo and Leningrad Codex indicate in each verse by means of a *masorah parva* that the unique transitive *piel* form represents the authentic reading of M. In both verses, this reading is also supported by G, S, and T, and in verse 3 also by Sym who, according to Jerome, rendered *et confirmabo vos*, "and I will establish you." On the other hand, in both verses V provides the intransitive translation (*et*) *habitabo vobiscum*, "(and) I will dwell with you," a rendering which in the case of verse 3 has the additional support of Aq. Such a rendering can only be based on a *qal* vocalization וְאֶשְׁכְּנָה אֶתְכֶם (verse 3) and וְשָׁכַנְתִּי אֶתְכֶם

(verse 7). In verse 7 de Rossi has found the *qal* vocalization in five of his manuscripts and in the first hand of the three others. The committee theorized that the *qal* vocalization and its translation were probably inspired by a theology of the *Shekhinah*, and it gave a C evaluation to the *piel* vocalization of M.

Evaluation of Problems

The interpretation of contextual features has led Baumgartner (HALAT, 1388b), BHS, and many commentators (Ehrlich, 259–60; Rudolph, 50; Bright, 55) to prefer the reading with *qal* vocalization. The understanding of בַּמָּקוֹם הַזֶּה, "in this place," as either a reference to the temple (which would privilege the *qal* reading) or to Jerusalem and the country (which would favor the *piel* reading) has played an important part in the debate. Very few translations followed the intransitive reading. Only NAB with "so that I may remain with you in this place" in verse 3 and NRSV, RL, and TOB with "will I remain with you in this place" in verse 7 can be mentioned as exceptions.

In fact, the transitive reading of M should be preferred and not only on textual grounds. Although it is frequently said that God dwells "among" his people, it is never said that he dwells "with" them. In addition, in the 30 cases in which מָקוֹם, "place," is used in Jeremiah, only 4 could refer to the temple; all the others are referring either to Jerusalem or to the holy land as a whole (Barthélemy, 515). As McKane (160) correctly observes, the theme of the possession of the land cannot be excluded from the discourse unit 1–15. Translators, especially in projects with Orthodox participation, are therefore encouraged to follow the transitive reading of most modern versions.

Translation Proposals

The renderings of GNB, "and I will let you go on living here" (verse 3) and "I will let you go on living here in the land" (verse 7), can provide a model for translators. If they prefer, they could give the variant reading and interpretation in a footnote, as done in NJV and NEB. Care should be taken not to ascribe the reading of Aq to both verses, as has mistakenly been done in NJV and FC.

7.7; see 7.3

7.25

Textual Decisions

After having dealt with אֲבוֹתֵיכֶם, "your fathers," in 25a, 25b mentions אֲלֵיכֶם, "to you," "I sent you all my servants the prophets." The reading אֲלֵיכֶם

is supported by G, V, and T. On the other hand, one manuscript of the Masoretic tradition has the reading אליהם, "to them," which also has the support of the catenae text of G, of the Theodulph recension of V, and of S. The one manuscript in question is the first hand of Kennicott's manuscript 93, and the committee thought that a copyist's blunder cannot constitute a textual witness. It took the readings of the versions as a secondary assimilation to verse 25a in which G, V, and S translated "their fathers" instead of "your fathers." The result, therefore, was a B evaluation of M.

Evaluation of Problems

Following the footsteps of Oort and Bright, a number of modern versions (RSV, NRSV, NEB, REB, NJV) followed the variant reading. In the case of NEB and REB alone, the textual evidence of one Hebrew manuscript has been footnoted. The main reason for this kind of translation, however, seems to have been to solve the problem that the "you" addressed did not yet exist at the time of the exodus of the fathers. In M אֲלֵיכֶם, "to you," is used in an inclusive way, comprising all the generations of Israel. Independently from sentence divisions, most recent translations (NAB, NIV, NJB, GNB, RL, FC), by presenting a rather literal rendering of M, seem to presuppose that the inclusive understanding of M can be perceived by their receptors. If such is not the case, or if the device of a specific inclusive second-person plural pronoun fails in the language, a more explicit paraphrase may be given, as has been done in GN.

Translation Proposals

In the first case, GNB is a good model: "From the day that your ancestors came out of Egypt until this very day I have kept on sending to you my servants, the prophets." In the second one, GN can be compared: *So war es schon damals, als ich eure Vorfahren aus Ägypten führte, and so ist es geblieben bis auf den heutigen Tag. Immer von neuem schickte ich euch meine Diener, die Propheten*, "So it was already at the time that I led your ancestors out of Egypt, and so it remained until this very day. Again and again I sent you my servants, the prophets."

7.31

Textual Decisions

In M the object of the first verb is plural: בָּמוֹת, "high places," "They have built high places of Tophet in the valley of Ben-Hinnom." This plural reading has the support of 4Q-a, Aq, Sym, V, and S. On the other hand, G renders with a singular: τὸν βωμὸν (τοῦ Ταφεθ), "the altar (of Taphet)." T is normally quoted as another witness of the singular reading because of its rendering במת.

However, since the difference between singular and plural is only a difference of *patah* and *qameṣ* in the last syllable and since the vocalization of T is a matter of great uncertainty, it seems more correct to consider the reading of T as indeterminate. The strong textual support for the plural as well as the occurrence of the plural בָּמוֹת הַבַּעַל, "high places of Baal," in the parallel passages 19.5 and 32.35 produced a B evaluation of M.

Evaluation of Problems

The reluctant proposal of Giesebrecht to reestablish the singular reading has since then, without any hesitation, been adopted by most commentators, recently by McKane (179). For that reason, a number of modern versions (RSV, NRSV, NAB, NEB, GNB, FC) followed this decision. More than half of the recent translations (NIV, NJB, REB, NJV, GN, GrN, EÜ), however, maintained the plural of M, and rightly so. There seems to be no reason, whatsoever, why there could not have been a plurality of shrines in the valley of Ben-Hinnom.

Translators particularly face a problem with the meaning of the genitive construction "shrines of the Tophet." "Tophet" could be taken as a proper name which should be expressed in the translation (GN) or it could be considered a noun with the meaning "oven" (HALAT, 1638b–1639a).

Translation Proposals

In the first case, GN is a good model to follow: *die Opferstätte, die man Tofet nennt*, "the sacrificial sites called Tophet*. With regard to the second option, GrN offers an acceptable example: *offerhoogten met vuurovens*, "sacrificial high-places with ovens."

8.3

Textual Decisions

In the second part of the verse, M repeats the expression הַנִּשְׁאָרִים, "who survive," "which remain," and it is supported by the corrector of 4Q-c (although the scribe uses the feminine form), the Origen recension of G, and by V and T. The repetition is lacking in one Kennicott manuscript and erased in another. It is also missing in the first hand of 4Q-c and in G and S. The committee was rather divided in its judgment. Two members considered the repetition accidental and assigned a C evaluation to it. One member credited M with an A evaluation, considering the repetition a literary initiative. The other half of the committee voted C for M, judging that the multiple abbreviations of G do not necessarily imply that the word did not figure in the first redaction.

Evaluation of Problems

All commentators, with the notable exception of Ehrlich (262), opt for the deletion of the repetition. At least three modern translations do the same, quoting textual evidence: NEB and REB, by citing one manuscript of Kennicott; NJB, by quoting G and S.

If the rendering of M is preferred, translators are faced with a problem of interpretation. They could take הַנִּשְׁאָרִים as a qualifier of the preceding noun, בְּכָל־הַמְּקֹמוֹת, "in all places which are left over," that is, all the places which had been spared and which had not yet been destroyed by the enemies. This is the option of the Vulgate: *in universis locis quae derelicta sunt*, "in all the places which remain"; and of the (mainly medieval) translations of the Vulgate. It is the interpretation recommended by Ehrlich, but clearly abandoned by modern translators.

The other possibility would be to consider the second הַנִּשְׁאָרִים to have the same antecedent as the first one. TOB testifies to such a choice: *ceux qui survivront dans tous les lieux*, "those who will survive in all places." The only problem with such an interpretation is that it presupposes a text in which הַנִּשְׁאָרִים precedes בְּכָל־הַמְּקֹמוֹת. Moreover, if such an option is chosen, the repetition would be omitted in most receptor languages for stylistic reasons. This is what probably has happened in most recent versions.

Translation Proposals

Regarding the first interpretation, translators are encouraged to reintroduce the interpretation of the Vulgate.

For the second interpretation of M, a good example can be found in GNB: "And the people of this evil nation who survive, who live in the places where I have scattered them, will prefer to die rather than go on living." If the same interpretation of M is selected and the repetition left implicit for stylistic reasons, NJV can serve as a model: "And death shall be preferable to life for all that are left over of this wicked folk, in all the other places to which I shall banish them."

If translators decide to omit the repetition for textual reasons, the complete evidence as stated above could be printed in a footnote.

8.5

Textual Decisions

Following the grammatical subject הָעָם הַזֶּה, "this people," M reads יְרוּשָׁלֵַם, "Jerusalem." This reading is probably supported by 4Q-a: although after בה העם הזה[, the text has a lacuna, the length of this lacuna suggests the original presence of the word "Jerusalem." M is certainly confirmed by Aq,

Th, V, S, and T. The word is lacking, however, in the late Kennicott manuscript 126 and in G. The committee did not exclude the possibility that the word "Jerusalem" had been added in the pre-Masoretic tradition as explicit information and a justification for the feminine ending of the preceding verb. Such an addition would, however, constitute a literary initiative and not a textual accident. The evaluation of the committee members was quite diverse: one A and three B votes for M, one C vote for G, and one C vote for the conjectural omission, not of "Jerusalem," but of "this people."

Evaluation of Problems

From Hitzig to McKane (183), the omission of "Jerusalem" as an exegetical gloss was defended by commentators. No wonder, therefore, that many modern versions leave out the word, with textual note (NRSV, NAB, NEB, REB) or without (RSV, GNB).

With the majority of recent translations, translators are nevertheless encouraged to render it. This could be done in several ways: (1) "this people" and "Jerusalem" could be displayed in complete parallel sentences, as has already been done in T; (2) although the combination הָעָם הַזֶּה יְרוּשָׁלַם cannot be analyzed as a genitive construction grammatically (Gesenius-Kautzsch-Cowley, §128c), semantically nothing prevents such a translation; (3) if translators regard "Jerusalem" as a gloss, it could be rendered as an apposition set off with punctuation (such as commas, dashes, or parentheses).

Translation Proposals

In the first case, NJB could be taken as a model: "Why does this people persist in acts of infidelity, why does Jerusalem persist in continuous infidelity?" In the second one, FC could serve as an example: *Alors pourquoi ce peuple de Jerusalem, qui fait fausse route, persiste-t-il dans sa trahison?* "Why then does this people of Jerusalem, which goes astray, persist in its betrayal?" In the last case, NJV could be selected: "Why is this people—Jerusalem—rebellious with a persistent rebellion?"

8.8

Textual Decisions

At the end of the first half-line of verse 8b, M reads the verbal form עָשָׂה, "has made," "has done," and, in spite of their divergent syntactic interpretations, this reading has the support of Aq (ἐποίησεν, lit., "For iniquity the iniquity of the scribes has made the pen"), V (*operatus est*, "It is falsehood the lying pen of the scribes has worked"), and T (עבד, "In vain the scribe has made a lying pen"). G, however, renders with ἐγενήθη: εἰς μάτην ἐγενήθη σχοῖνος ψευδὴς γραμματεῦσιν, "In vain has a false pen come to be for the scribes," which, in more comprehensible language may mean: "In vain have the scribes used a false pen." The rendering of G may be based on a *pual* vocalization of the verbal form (Cornill) or it may be the result of a passive transformation of the *qal*, understood as an impersonal form. S could present the same transformation as G. The comittee considered therefore that all witnesses could have read a text like M, but that some doubt prevails as to G and S. By way of conclusion, a majority assigned an A evaluation to M and a minority a B evaluation to the same.

Evaluation of Problems

Most scholars either correct M by reading a *mappiq* in the *he* as indication of a feminine object, referring back to "law," or, without correction, understanding such an object to be implicit. Translationally, this was already the option of the Geneva Bible, adopted literally by KJ. Despite the differences in wording, it remained the option of the vast majority of translations. So, for example, NRSV: "when, in fact, the false pen of the scribes has made it into a lie." It should be seen, however, that such an option is inspired by certain syntactic and semantic considerations. Since Michaelis, it has been stated that the verb עשׂה followed by the preposition *lamed* would have the meaning "to transform something into something else," and such a semantic decision requires, of course, the presence of a grammatical object.

Translators should at least know that there is another option. In the tracks of G, Radaq, and Qimchi, we can take לַשֶּׁקֶר to mean "in vain," "to no purpose the pen of the scribes has labored," where עשׂה is given an intransitive meaning, as in 1 Kgs 20.40 and Ruth 2.19.

Translation Proposals

If the last option is chosen, NJV can be taken as a model: "Assuredly, for naught has the pen labored. For naught the scribes!" Such a rendering can particularly be recommended in projects with Orthodox participation.

8.13A

Textual Decisions

The first two words of this verse, אָסֹף אֲסִיפֵם, present many problems. אָסֹף, as vocalized in M, can only be the infinitive absolute of אסף, "to gather." V by rendering the two words with *congregans congregabo eos*, "I shall surely gather them," respects the particular meaning of the infinitive absolute and supports M. Although G translates καὶ συνάξουσιν, "and they shall gather," its rendering does not presuppose a different Vorlage. In G, verse 13 is the continuation of verse 10a, and for contextual reasons the translator has interpreted the infinitive absolute as a third-person plural, assimilating to κληρονόμοις, "inheritors." Aq, S, and T also seem to have interpreted an infinitive absolute, reinforcing the action expressed by the following conjugated verbal form.

As to the conjugated form אֲסִיפֵם, M seems to have the support of Aq, S, and T which all interpreted it as a first-person *hiphil* form plus third-person plural object suffix of the verb סוף with the meaning "to destroy." On the other hand, V with its translation *congregabo eos* seems to have vocalized the consonant text as אֹסְפֵם, relating it to the verb אסף. And G with its rendering τὰ γενήματα αὐτῶν, "their fruits," must have read the noun אָסִיף with third-person plural suffix: אֲסִיפָם.

The committee, which judged the last reading of G to be a graphical error, was divided between a B and a C vote for M.

Evaluation of Problems

Following G partly, Movers (14) was the first to propose the following vocalization: אֹסֵף (= אֶאֱסֹף) אֲסִיפָם, "I will gather their harvest." This proposal has received the approval of many commentators, and it was adopted, according to Brockington, by NEB: "I would gather their harvest . . . but." In spite of the absence of textual notes, such an interpretation may also be presupposed in many other translations, such as RSV, NEB, GNB, EÜ, GN, GrN, and so on. However, this "is not the sense which is desiderated" (McKane, 188).

Three interpretational possibilities remain: (1) the same verb, אסף, "to gather," is read twice (NAB, REB, NIV); (2) the same verb, סוף, "to destroy," is read twice (NJB, NJV, CEV); (3) the two verbs are associated stylistically and semantically, the verb אסף being read first and the verb סוף last (Barthélemy, 527; McKane, 189). Translational decisions will be conditioned by the way in which the images of the harvest are handled.

Translation Proposals

For the first option, REB could be a model: "I shall gather them all in." For the second one, CEV can be proposed: "I will wipe them out." And for the last one, the translation of McKane might be used: "I will gather them for final destruction."

8.13B

Textual Decisions

This verse ends with the rather obscure sentence וָאֶתֵּן לָהֶם יַעַבְרוּם, "I have given to them that which they have . . ." (". . ." standing for the meaning of the verb עבר). It is true that four de Rossi manuscripts and the first hand of four others in the same collection read יעבדום which could mean "I have handed (them) over to them (their enemies) (and) they will serve them." This seems to be a facilitating reading, however, or simply a graphical error. The absence of the *rafé* (usually occurring on the *begadkefat* letters) in the manuscripts of Cairo, Aleppo, and Leningrad is a clear indication that the Tiberian tradition read a *resh*. The ancient versions did the same. V with its rendering *et dedi eis quae praetergressa sunt*, "and I have given to them these things which passed by," confirms M. The same applies to T which makes certain information explicit: "because I gave them my law from Sinai, and they have transgressed it." Th, Aq, and S also support M, the only difference being the addition of a conjunction before the second verb in order to ease the syntax. The important exception is G which omits the whole sentence. The committee considered the reading of M too complex to be a later gloss. It judged it to be at the origin of all versions, and it explained the omission in G, following Michaelis and Wichelhaus (108), as due to a lack of understanding on the part of the translator. For these reasons, M received a B evaluation.

Evaluation of Problems

From Cornill to recently, McKane (188), several commentators proposed the deletion of the whole sentence. Some modern translations (NAB, NEB, REB) followed this advice, basing their decision on G in an explicit footnote. Although such a solution might be tempting, especially in projects with Orthodox participation, it should not be preferred. Rudolph (62) proposed an extensive emendation which is so highly improbable that it, correctly, did not have any following among translators.

The problem, therefore, mainly seems to be one of interpretation. Four different interpretations can be considered: (1) "and I have given to them the commandments which they have been transgressing." This is the interpretation of T, Rashi, and some recent translations, such as CEV; (2) "and what I have given them (that is, the land and the produce thereof) shall pass in ownership of them (that is, the enemies)." This is the interpretation of Kimchi and some modern versions, such as GNB; (3) "and I have given to them those (that is, the enemies) who shall overrun them (that is, Israel)." This has been the option of several commentators since Venema, and of NJB and TILC; (4) "And I have given to them (the land, goods, etc.) which will pass away." This is the interpretation of V and of the majority of modern translations (RSV, NRSV, NIV, NJV, RL).

Translation Proposals

For the first interpretation, CEV can be quoted as a model: "They have not done a thing that I told them"; for the second, GNB: "Therefore, I have allowed outsiders to take over the land"; for the third, NJB: "I have found them people to trample on them!"; and for the last one, NIV: "What I have given them will be taken away from them."

8.18

Textual Decisions

In M this verse starts with the rather obscure expression מַבְלִיגִיתִי. This expression seems to have been read by Aq, transmitted via the Syro-Hexapla only, which interpreted it as a noun. There is some doubt about the Greek retroversion from the Syriac. Both Field and Ziegler propose τέρψις μου, "my delight," or ἱλαρότης μου, "my cheerfulness." Barthélemy (531), however, makes a strong case for an improved retroversion, μειδίαμά μου, "my smile." V seems to have used Aq, for, although Jerome renders with *dolor meus*, "my affliction," he specifies that the Hebrew has the equivalent of μειδίαμα which can be interpreted as the expression of a face contorted with pain bearing the resemblance of a smile. Sym with his rendering χλευάζεις μέ, "you scoff at me," has interpreted the Hebrew expression as a verbal form, probably לעג. This certainly is the verbal form used in the paraphrase of T: "because they were scoffing at the prophets who prophesied to them." The translation of T also suggests an interpretation of the initial *mem* as the preposition מִן, "because." S, by using ܒܠܝܬ, "I am worn out," may have compared Aramaic בלי or Hebrew בלה.

In G, the first word of the verse has been translated ἀνίατα, "incurable." As Spohn has suggested, the translator did not read one, but two words: מבלי גיתי, deriving the last one from the root גהה, "to heal," "without cure"—reading, thus, something like מִבְּלִי גֵהוֹת. In fact, Th (if Ziegler is correct to attribute a reading to him which had been attributed to Aq in the Barberini manuscript) also read two words, but he derived the last one from the root גאה, "to be proud," to judge from his rendering διὰ τὸ μὴ εἶναι ὕβριν, "because of the absence of pride." It should also be noted that the same division into two words has been attested by a number of manuscripts of Kennicott–de Rossi, the oldest of which seems to be British Library Add 21, 161 from the twelfth century. These manuscripts did conserve a reading of two words, of which G and Th are the oldest witnesses, and which may have been superseded by a reading of one word, to which Aq is the oldest witness.

Since the committee considered the division into two words as an error, M received a C evaluation.

Evaluation of Problems

Modern translations can be divided into those which follow the word division (RSV, NRSV, GNB, NEB [?], REB, NJB, FC, GrN) and those which interpret the form in M (all others). Regarding the first, two things should be observed: (1) although these versions follow G in word division and interpretation, they do not, with the partial exception of EÜ, imitate its syntactical division. G connects ἀνίατα, "incurable," with the preceding verse: "and they shall bite you, mortally aggravating (lit.: with) the pain of your distressed heart." The sentence division in the editions of Rahlfs and Ziegler is wrong, whereas Swete's is correct. McKane (194) rightly remarks, however, that word division and sentence division do not need to be associated and that verse 18a can be understood to mean: "Incurable sorrow has overwhelmed me."

Translations which follow the undivided form of M can be grouped into those which follow V (CEV, GN) and those which interpret the root, with David ben Abraham, Buxtorf, and Grotius, as meaning "live in comfort" (NJV, NIV).

The rendering of the unbroken form, in spite of its difficulties, should be preferred, but the translation of the division into two words should certainly be considered in interconfessional projects with Orthodox participation.

Translation Proposals

For the interpretation of Jerome, CEV could be used as an example: "I am burdened with sorrow." If, however, translators want to go back (with Jerome's observation) to Aq, they could follow the translation proposal in the note of SEB: *Mein (verzerrtes) Lächeln verdeckt meinen Kummer*, "my distorted smile covers my sorrow." For the second interpretational option, NJV can be selected: "When in grief I would seek comfort." If, for well-defined purposes, the word division and word meaning of G without the syntactical implications of the Greek version are preferred, NJB could function as a model: "Incurable sorrow overtakes me." In the last case, a textual footnote seems to be indicated.

9.2 (3)

Textual Decisions

The main textual problem of this verse is a syntactical one. According to the punctuation of M, the expression שֶׁקֶר, "falsehood," has to be taken with the preceding information: וַיַּדְרְכוּ אֶת־לְשׁוֹנָם קַשְׁתָּם, "And they bend their tongue, their bow of falsehood." But M is followed only by T, ואליפו ית לישנהון פתגמי שקר דמן אנון כקשת נכילא, "And they have taught their tongue words of falsehood: they are to be compared to a deceitful bow." All other versions, however, take the term שֶׁקֶר, "falsehood," as the first word of the contrastive word pair שֶׁקֶר וְלֹא לֶאֱמוּנָה, "falsehood, but not (for) truth." They only differ in their respective syntactical divisions. G takes שֶׁקֶר as the grammatical subject of the verb in the second clause, read as a singular: ψεῦδος καὶ οὐ πίστις ἐνίσχυσεν ἐπὶ τῆς γῆς, "Falsehood and not faithfulness has prevailed on the earth." V considers both verbs to have the same grammatical subject and it takes "falsehood and truth" as characteristics of the bow: *et extenderunt linguam suam quasi arcum mendacii et non veritatis confortati sunt in terra*, "They have extended their tongue like a bow of falsehood and not truth; they are strong in the land." S does the same, but it makes "falsehood and truth" the symptoms of domination: "through falsehood and not through truth have they dominated the land." The last interpretation could also have been Sym's interpretation. According to the committee, the variations in the versions are to be considered syntactical harmonizations that aim to join "falsehood and not truth" more intimately. The syntactically more-difficult reading of M was therefore preferred and received a B evaluation.

Evaluation of Problems

The vast majority of scholars, with the sole recent exception of Holladay (296), endorsed the reading and/or interpretation of G. Some think it necessary to make some emendations, such as reading אֱמוּנָה instead of לֶאֱמוּנָה; others consider such an emendation superfluous because they take the *lamed* as emphatic (Nötscher, 380; Soggin, 221f.). It is no surprise, therefore, that many modern versions follow G. So, for example, RSV: "falsehood and not truth has grown strong in the land," REB: "Lying, not truth, holds sway in the land," and, with minor variations NEB, NJB, and GNB. Other translations stay closer to M, following the interpretational pattern of S. So, for example, NRSV: "they have grown strong in the land for falsehood, and not for truth," and NJV.

Although it may be tempting to adopt the interpretation of G, especially in projects with Orthodox participation, an effort should be made to render the syntactical division of M. In some types of translations, a certain degree of syntactical restructuring may be obligatory, depending on the way in which the metaphor is handled translationally (compare RGN and RGrN).

Translation Proposals

CEV is a good model for the type of translation which respects the syntax of M: "Lies come from the mouths of my people, like arrows from a bow. With each dishonest deed their power increases."

9.4–5 (5–6)

Textual Decisions

The first word of verse 5 (6) in M is שִׁבְתְּךָ, "your dwelling," "your dwelling is in the midst of deceit." Such a reading is confirmed by V: *habitatio tua*, "your habitation," S: ܡܥܡܪܟ, "your dwelling place," and by the paraphrase of

T: יתבין בבית כנישתהון, "They sit in their assembly-houses." It is also supported by an anonymous marginal reading of the Syro-Hexapla: ܒܟܬܐ ܕܝܠܟ, back-translated as καθέδρα σοῦ, "your seat," and attributed by Field and Ziegler to Symmachus.

On the other hand, G has the following two sentences: ἠδίκησαν καὶ οὐ διέλιπον τοῦ ἐπιστρέψαι. τόκος ἐπὶ τόκῳ, δόλος ἐπὶ δόλῳ, "They act unjustly; they do not desist in order to repent. Usury upon usury, deceit upon deceit." As Cappel (1786, 689) has already seen, G has read the Hebrew consonants as two words שב : תך, the first one ending verse 4 (5), and the second one beginning verse 5 (6). The rendering ἐπιστρέψαι implies a vocalization of שֻׁב for the first word, and the phonetic transcription τόκος presupposes a vocalization of תֹּך for the second. The committee considered the Hebrew Vorlage of G, בְּמִרְמָה תֹּך בְּתוֹךְ מִרְמָה, "oppresssion upon oppression, deceit upon deceit," as stylistically superior to M because of its double repetition. It also considered the construction of the infinitive שֻׁב with the preceding verb נִלְאוּ a natural one if that verb can be given the meaning "no longer be able." Three B votes and two C votes were therefore given to the Vorlage of G.

Evaluation of Problems

In fact, considering the Hebrew Vorlage of G to be superior to M is the position taken by the vast majority of modern versions. Only NJB, NIV, and NJV render M, the first apparently without any hesitation; the last stating at least that the meaning of the Hebrew remains uncertain.

Translators should therefore follow the Vorlage of G. In the translation of the two sentences, they should, however, be aware of the possible divergencies between the interpretation of such a Vorlage by G and the interpretation which should probably be given to the corrected Hebrew text. Thus, Schleusner has correctly seen that οὐ διέλιπον renders נִלְאוּ negatively, in its sense of *laborare*, "to take pains," so that the meaning of the last sentence of verse 4 (5) in G could be *non intermiserunt retrogradi*, "they do not cease going backward" (II, 99–100). In fact this is the interpretation of REB: "they weary themselves going astray" (compare also RGrN). The other interpretation of (N)RSV: "(they) are too weary to repent" may, however, be preferred.

Translation Proposals

For the last sentence of 4 (5), (N)RSV can be taken as a model, or NAB with its simple statement "and cannot repent." The staccato sentences of the next verse may have to be rendered more elaborately as in REB: "Wrong follows wrong, deceit follows deceit."

9.6 (7)

Textual Decisions

The textual problem concerns the expression בַּת־עַמִּי, "the daughter of my people," figuring at the end of a rhetorical question כִּי־אֵיךְ אֶעֱשֶׂה מִפְּנֵי בַּת־עַמִּי, "because what else can I do because of the daughter of my people?" M has here the support of V and S. But G has, preceding the translation of this expression, the extra information πονηρίας, reading ὅτι ποιήσω ἀπὸ προσώπου πονηρίας θυγατρὸς λαοῦ μου, "for I will do (this) because of the wickedness of the daughter of my people." The same applies to T: חובי כנשתא דעמי, "the sins of the assembly of my people," "For how shall I act because of the sins of the assembly of my people?" In fact, πονηρίας could be regarded as reflecting a Hebrew Vorlage רעת which would have been accidentally omitted in M for reasons of homoioteleuton, בת and the preceding רעת having the same ending. It has also been argued that the Hebraism ἀπὸ προσώπου πονηρίας could hardly have been invented by a translator (Houbigant). On the other hand, it should be noted that πονηρίας has an *obelos* in the Origen recension as a sign of awareness of the absence of this word in the proto-Masoretic tradition, and it should be noted that it is lacking in Codex Sinaiticus. Moreover, the very frequent stereotype ἀπὸ προσώπου hardly permits any conclusions with regard to the following word. The extra information in G and T could therefore simply be a gloss provoked by ignorance of the meaning of M.

This is one of the cases treated by Barthélemy (535–37) which had not been submitted to the committee.

Evaluation of Problems

The reading רעת, restored on the basis of G, has been followed in a number of modern versions such as NRSV, NIV, and GNB. The last two versions do not even deem it necessary to provide a textual note.

Volz, on the other hand, proposed the emendation רָעָתָם, "their wickedness," to be read instead of בַּת־עַמִּי, which was defended by Rudolph and Bright and suggested in BHS. It has had little impact on recent translations, NAB being one of the rare exceptions.

It seems preferable, however, to translate M and to render the rhetorical question either as referring back to the process of testing (Kimchi) or as an exclamation of perplexity and exasperation (McKane, 202). The majority of modern versions follow the interpretation of Kimchi in this respect. Some recent translations were tempted to interpret בַּת־עַמִּי as a formula of endearment. So NJV; variant reading in NRSV: "my poor people"; RGrN: *mijn dierbaar Sion*, "my dear Zion." Although contextually this makes some sense, a more neutral rendering of the standard metaphor may be preferred.

Translation Proposals

If rhetorical questions are maintained, REB is a good example: "How else should I deal with my people?" Receptor languages giving preference to statements could take CEV as a model: "I have no other choice."

9.9 (10)

Textual Decisions

In M the verb of the first sentence of 9 reads אֶשָּׂא, "I shall raise," "Over the mountains I shall raise weeping and wailing." This first-person singular reading of the verb has the support of 4Q-a, Aq, and Sym: ἀναλήψομαι, "I shall take up"; and (inspired by the last) of V: *adsumam*, "I shall take up." It is confirmed by T: אנא מרים, "I lift up." On the other hand, G reads a plural imperative: λάβετε, "take up," and is followed by S: ܐܠܐܢܙ.

The reading of G could be based on a different Hebrew Vorlage such as שְׂאוּ, but the committee considered a literary initiative on the part of the Greek translator more likely. The aim of the initiative would have been to avoid the risk of attributing the first-person reading to God. The Syriac translator could have done the same independently, or could have adopted the solution he found in G. The possibility that M could be a secondary assimilation to the first-person verbs of the context was not entirely excluded. M nevertheless received a majority B evaluation.

Evaluation of Problems

The judgment of the committee is also the majority judgment of modern scholarship, Rudolph being the notable exception. Maybe the imperative recommendation of BHS has persuaded a few modern versions such as (N)RSV to follow G. It is clear, however, that such a recommendation should not be followed. Verse 9 (10) is spoken by the prophet, and if there is any confusion with regard to participants, it is, as in many other passages of this book, due to the emotional identification of the prophet with the message of the Lord. The reaction of G and S against such a blurring is fully acceptable, but other ways to solve the problem exist. The unmarked first-person speech could always be presented as prophetic discourse, and the marked first-person speech as the divine one. This is, for example, done in GNB, in which the preceding verse ends: "I, the Lord, have spoken," and in which our verse begins: "I said," and the following verse again has: "The Lord says." Another solution is to mark the speaker of the verse by means of a heading, as in CEV and RGN.

Translation Proposals

For possible translations on a global level, see the discussion above.

9.16 (17)

Textual Decisions

After an introductory formula, this verse starts in M with two masculine-plural imperatives: הִתְבּוֹנְנוּ וְקִרְאוּ, "consider and call." It is supported by the Origen and Antiochian recensions of G: σύνετε καὶ καλέσατε, "understand and call," a reading which is attributed to Th and Aq, by Sym: ἐννοήθητε καὶ καλέσατε, "consider and call," by V: *contemplamini et vocate*, "contemplate and call," and by T: אסתכלו וקרו, "reflect and call." On the other hand G, by reading only καλέσατε, "call," did not render the first imperative and the conjunction preceding the second. In this it is followed by S. The committee considered it very likely that G omitted the first imperative for reasons of stylistic abbreviation, and it voted a B evaluation to M.

Evaluation of Problems

At least two recent versions (NEB and REB) base their work on G, according to their notes, in rendering only the second imperative: "Summon (the wailing women to come)." Others (CEV, RGrN) omit the first imperative without any textual justification. This is probably due to the impact of a strong commentary tradition from Cornill through McKane. Only Holladay strongly supports the originality of M. He stresses the association of the first imperative with שִׁלְחוּ, "send," which occurs further on in 9.16 and elsewhere in Jeremiah (2.10). Furthermore, he demonstrates that there are assonances between the first imperative and other elements of the sentence.

Although M has to be recommended to translators as the textual base, the rendering of the first imperative is not as evident. Some modern translations such as GNB and RGN judge it necessary to embark on a long paraphrase which seems to be rather illegitimate. On the other hand, a brief translation such as "Attention!" (NAB) or "Listen" (NJV) could be considered an undertranslation. It seems that "alertness" and "insightful behavior" are the major components of meaning of the verbal form in this context (HALAT I, 118a). People needed to become aware of the paradoxical situation that they were going to have to warn the professional mourning women before anybody had died.

Translation Proposals

NJB can be cited as a good model of translation: "Prepare to call for the mourning women!"

9.25 (26)

Textual Decisions

In the last sentence of this verse, M states that all the nations are עֲרֵלִים, "uncircumcised." This is also the reading of Aq according to the Syro-Hexapla and its Greek retroversion, ἀκροβυστίαν, "uncircumcised," and of V: *habent praeputium* "they have the foreskin." G, however, glosses M with σαρκί, "in flesh," and it is followed in this by S and T. This gloss has clearly been inspired by the desire to create symmetry with the "uncircumcised in heart" in the same sentence. According to the committee, however, such symmetry was not intended by the author, and therefore M received a B evaluation.

Evaluation of Problems

In fact, 25b (26b) seems to comment on the expression מוּל בְּעָרְלָה of verse 24b (25b). Although NJV may be correct by noting that the force of the Hebrew expression is uncertain, literally it probably means "circumcised as to the foreskin," therefore: "circumcised physically" (Bright, 78). If this is true, the statement of verse 24b (25b) about the nations that are circumcised contradicts the statement of verse 25b (26b) about the same nations, which are uncircumcised. For this reason Rudolph (1930, 282 and 1968, 70–71) proposed reading הָאֵלֶּה, "these," instead of עֲרֵלִים, "uncircumcised," a daring conjecture which has been adopted (according to their respective textual notes) by NAB and NJB: "For all those nations (and the whole house of Israel too) are uncircumcised at heart."

It has been suggested in CTAT (1986, 542) that NEB, without noting anything, does the same. However, NEB, and now also REB, could very well be based on an interpretation of M which takes לֵב, "heart," also as the implicit object of עֲרֵלִים, "uncircumcised." Translators may deal with the issues in several ways: (a) they may interpret along the lines of NEB and REB; (b) on the basis of the same interpretation, they may restructure all of verses 25–26 for clarity's sake, as has been done in CEV; (c) they could maintain the contradiction of the source text in translation, as has been done in NJV. It seems less advisable to manipulate the source text, as is the case in NIV verse 25: "all who are circumcised only in the flesh," and verse 26: "all these nations are really uncircumcised."

Translation Proposals

If solution (a) is preferred, NEB/REB could be taken as an example: "for all alike, the nations and Israel, are uncircumcised in heart."

10.9

Textual Decisions

Parallel to "beaten silver from Tarshish," M speaks of gold מֵאוּפָז, "from Uphaz," a reading which is only confirmed by V. On the other hand, Th has the rendering ἐκ σουφειρ, which is corrupt and has been restored to ܡܢ ܐܘܦܝܪ, "from Ophir," in a marginal note of the Syro-Hexapla. Such is also the reading and interpretation of S and T and of part of the manuscripts and editions of the Vulgate. As to G, it has provided a transcription of M in the form Μωφας. The committee considered G a possible assimilation to the reading זָהָב מוּפָז, "finest gold," in 1 Kgs 10.18 and the readings of the other versions a facilitating assimilation to the frequently occurring "Ophir." Therefore, M received a C evaluation.

Evaluation of Problems

Since the rare place-name Uphaz never has been identified, it is rather attractive to use the correction "Ophir," with Gesenius (Thesaurus, 137a), Simons (§185), McKane (223), and a number of modern versions such as NAB, NJV, NEB, and REB. The parallel with מְרֻקָּע, "beaten," used for silver, has led some commentators to propose interpreting מאופז as a participle from a hypothetical root פזז (Van Selms, 162; Thomson, 329–30). Such an interpretation, however, has had no impact on recent translations.The even more conspicuous parallel with Tarshish here and in Dan 10.5 further supports the likelihood of a place-name. The search of geographers for an identification of Uphaz should therefore preferably continue.

Translation Proposals

With most contemporary versions, we suggest that "Uphaz" should be maintained. A textual note could explain the reasons for different readings, and texts such as Dan 10.5 and 1 Kgs 10.18 could be mentioned.

10.13

Textual Decisions

The verse opens in M with the syntactically difficult construction לְקוֹל תִּתּוֹ הֲמוֹן, literally: "At the sound of his giving a multitude (of waters)." According to the Barberini manuscript, this reading is matched by Th and Aq: εἰς φωνὴν δόντος αὐτοῦ πλῆθος, a literal translation of the Hebrew of M. The translation of T is also literal. Sym has taken the liberty of introducing a conjugated form of the verb "to give": πρὸς τὴν φωνὴν ὅταν διδῷ πλῆθος, "at his voice when he gives a multitude," and so do both V and S. G, on the other hand, only has καὶ πλῆθος, "and abundance," and it therefore seems not to have rendered the first two Hebrew words.

To the committee it appeared that it was the syntactical difficulty of M which discouraged the Greek translator from rendering his Vorlage. And since none of the other versions suggested a variant, an A evaluation was given to M.

Evaluation of Problems

The problematic syntax of M has stimulated commentators to propose a number of conjectural readings (Duhm, Volz, Rudolph, Driver). These commentators had little effect on translation, and rightly so. Only the textual revision of Volz has been used by a modern translation: NEB. It reads for the first two words יִתְמְהוּן לְקוֹלוֹ, "At the thunder of his voice (the waters in heaven) are amazed." This proposal is too hypothetical, however, to be seriously considered.

The difficult syntax in M should not be so easily abandoned, however, because it is confirmed by an identical passage, 51.16, where it is even rendered by G. And it is not absolutely necessary to amend לְקוֹל תִּתּוֹ to קוֹל לְתִתּוֹ (with BHS and McKane, 225) in order to make sense. For Rashi both formulations amount to the same thing, and Böttcher illustrates this by comparing an expression such as מְכוֹן שִׁבְתּוֹ, "place of his dwelling," in Ps 33.14.

For the translator the problem of interpretation remains. He or she must decide whether the "raising of the voice" should be rendered in a generic or a specific way. In the last case the referent of the expression could be either "thunder" or "command."

Translation Proposals

For a generic rendering, NJV can be cited as an example: "When he makes His voice heard, there is a rumbling of water in the skies." If the reference is considered to be specifically to "thunder," REB can serve as a model: "When he speaks in the thunder the waters in the heaven are in tumult." And when an order is envisaged, CEV can be used as a sample: "The waters in the heavens roar at (your) command."

10.18

Textual Decisions

After having noted the saying of the Lord: "I am going to sling out the inhabitants of the land at this time, and I will bring distress on them," M ends verse 18 with the sentence לְמַעַן יִמְצָאוּ, "so that they may find." This reading of M is supported by the paraphrases provided by S and T. These paraphrases differ only in the verbal object they make explicit. S understands the first-person singular to be the implicit object: "so that they may seek and find me," whereas for T the notion of punishment is implicit: "so that they receive the punishment of their sins." On the other hand, G, Aq, and V all seem to have vocalized the Hebrew consonant form as a *niphal*: יִמָּצְאוּ, "that they may be found." So G: ὅπως εὑρεθῇ ἡ πληγή σου, "that your plague may be discovered" (by anticipation introducing the verbal subject from the next verse), Aq: ὅπως ἐλεγχθῶσιν, "that they may be convicted," and V: *ut inveniantur*, "that they may be discovered." Since M is at the origin of the paraphases of S and T and of the facilitating *niphal* vocalization, it received a B evaluation.

Evaluation of Problems

The majority of modern commentators (Bright, 70; Holladay, 338; McKane, 228–29), however, adopt the emendation יְמֻצּוּ, "they are squeezed dry," "I will press them until they are squeezed dry," proposed by Driver (1937–38, 107), reading therefore a *niphal* of the verb מצה. Such an emendation is not without impact upon translation. Driver's emendation was the basis for NEB which vocalizes according to Brockington יְמַצְאוּ, "and squeeze them dry." REB stays with Driver's emendation.

Older commentators after Houbigant were inspired by S, and they emended M to include the first-person singular verbal suffix. This, according to the textual note, has inspired NJB, which renders: "so that they may find me," thereby making the return to God a result of the suffering. In this it is most likely followed by GrN, which gives no textual note. It certainly is the same intention which is behind the rendering of BR: *auf daß sie zu finden beginnen*, "so that they may start to find."

Most modern translators, however, with or without justification, seem to follow the *niphal* vocalization of G, Aq, and V with different paraphrases or alterations. So NIV: "so that they may be captured," FC: *qu'ils n'échapperont pas*, "that they will not escape." Similarly TOB and GN.

M is followed by NJV, RSV, and NRSV with minor variations: "so that they shall feel it." Barthélemy (547) reintroduces Michaelis's interpretation, rediscovered by Böttcher (1833, 130), that מצא *qal* can have the meaning "to reach an aim" in the context of shooting, and the preceding verb of the sentence צרר would in the *hiphil* mean "insert a projectile into a sling" (see also Ehrlich, 271–72).

Translation Proposals

The last interpretation would lead to the following translation: "I will sling out the inhabitants of the land at this time. I will put stones into the sling that they may reach their aim." If translators do not feel free to follow such a unique proposal, they can follow the traditional translation of M, as done by

2

JEREMIAH 11–20

11.2

Textual Decisions

This verse starts in M with a plural imperative, שִׁמְעוּ, "Hear," followed at the beginning of the second sentence by a masculine second-person singular verbal form with added object suffix וְדִבַּרְתָּם, "and you shall speak them" (namely: the words). M is here exclusively represented by the Leningrad Codex, all other Hebrew manuscripts and editions reading וְדִבַּרְתֶּם, "and you (plural) shall speak." Some doubt exists about the *qameṣ* vocalization of the Leningrad Codex since, due to the fact that the original writing had faded, the vowels have been rewritten. However, this vocalization seems to be confirmed by a *masorah parva* of the oriental manuscript New York JThS 232, dating to the ninth or tenth century. The Leningrad Codex is clearly supported by G, the original reading of which is, as correctly stated in Ziegler's edition, ἀκούσατε . . . καὶ λαλήσεις, "Hear (plural) . . . and you (singular) shall speak" (without object suffix). It also has the support of S, if a few manuscripts (among which is the authoritative Codex Ambrosianus) are considered to represent the original text. Finally, M, represented by the Leningrad Codex, has the backing of T if, against all the editions, the oldest Targum witness, Codex Reuchlin of the Prophets, with its reading ותמללינון, "and you (sg.) shall speak them," is taken as the base reading.

Only V: *audite . . . et loquimini,* "Hear (pl.) . . . and speak (pl.)!" by reading two plurals, apparently attests the majority reading, וְדִבַּרְתֶּם.

Since the divergent textual traditions of G, S and T can be explained as attempts at harmonization, the reading of the Leningrad Codex has a good chance of representing the original form of this text. Since this case was not submitted to the committee, no evaluation factor can be noted.

Evaluation of Problems

The history of Biblia Hebraica is extremely confusing for the translator because in former editions the majority reading of the Masoretic Text was given as the foundation text, but the translator was encouraged to follow the Leningrad Codex, whereas in recent editions the contrary is done: the reading of the Leningrad Codex is given as the base text, and translators are instructed to follow the majority reading.

However, if translators turn to the commentators for elucidation, they find the suggestion to delete the whole of verse 2 and the first two words of verse 3 for reasons of literary structure.

And if in despair they try to find a solution by consulting modern English translations, they find that these versions blur the problem by taking advantage of the fact that in English no distinction exists between singular and plural imperative.

If M is rendered in accordance with the Leningrad Codex, Hitzig's interpretation should be followed, according to which the attention of the general audience is seized first, and then the prophet is addressed. In this case it is not the source text that should be restructured, as suggested in some commentary discussions, but the translations.

Translation Proposals

GN can be quoted as an example of restructuring. The prophet is addressed before the general audience, which is now indirectly addressed by the Lord through the prophet. The object suffix of וְדִבַּרְתָּם is left implicit and the conjunction is not translated: *Das Wort des Herrn erging an Jeremia; er sagte zu ihm: Sprich zu den Leuten von Juda und den Bewohnern Jerusalems! Sag ihnen: "Erfüll die Verpflichtungen, die ich euch gegeben habe!"* "The word of the Lord was extended to Jeremiah; he said to him: Speak to the people of Judah and the inhabitants of Jerusalem! Tell them: 'Fulfil the obligations which I have transmitted to you.'"

The textual note of GN, being incorrect, should be omitted.

11.13

Textual Decisions

The last three words of this verse in M: מִזְבְּחוֹת לְקַטֵּר לַבָּעַל, "altars to make offerings to Baal," are preceded by the two words מִזְבְּחוֹת לַבֹּשֶׁת, "altars (you have set up) to Shame." Those two words are attested by the Origen and Lucianic recensions of G: τῇ αἰσχύνῃ θυσιαστήρια, "altars to Shame," as well as by Aq, Th, V, S and T. They are lacking in the Old Greek, however, and, according to Volz, in the Kennicott manuscripts 30 and 180. In the last manuscript they have been added in the margin by the person who did the vocalization. The majority of the committee judged that G had probably been a victim of either homoioarcton (same beginning) or homoioteleuton (same ending). G could also have deliberately abbreviated the text for stylistic reasons. A C evaluation was therefore attributed to M by the majority.

Evaluation of Problems

Since Movers (33), the two words under discussion have been considered a variant of the last three words of the verse, and from Giesebrecht to Janzen (12) and McKane (240), omitting them, as a gloss, has been proposed. Some translations such as NAB have taken this suggestion. In others, such as NEB and REB, the same omission can be noticed—based, however, on G.

The textual decisions do not favor such a practice. The absence of the two words could have been due to an accident, but not their presence. They are attributable to a literary initiative, maybe even that of the author. The text of 3.24, dealing with the actions of the "Shameful Thing," shows clearly that this expression can refer to Baal in the original of the book, as a contemptuous substitute. In translation the personification of "shame" may, however, lead to an incomprehensible sentence, so some type of change must be introduced.

Translation Proposals

An example of a change can be found in NIV: "and the altars you have set up to burn incense to that shameful god Baal are as many as the streets of Jerusalem." If a textual note is provided, it could contain a reference to Jer 3.24 (compare NJV).

11.14

Textual Decisions

This verse ends with the prepositional phrase בְּעַד רָעָתָם, "on account of their disaster," a reading which is attested by all the classical Tiberian manuscripts and by nearly all the editions. However, more than thirty Hebrew manuscripts, among which is the old and accurate Spanish manuscript Kennicott 23, read בְּעֵת רָעָתָם, "at the time of their disaster." This also is the reading of all the extant versions: G, V, S and T. A majority of the committee attributed a C vote to M for the following reasons: (a) בְּעַד can be considered the most authoritative reading of the Masoretic Text; (b) the reading בְּעֵת amounts to a burdensome and meaningless repetition; (c) the reading בְּעַד is a meaningful *lectio difficilior*. A minority of the committee attributed a C vote to the reading בְּעֵת in the light of the numerous repetitions starting with verse 11.

Evaluation of Problems

Many commentators adopted the reading בְּעֵת in the footsteps of Michaelis, who was the first to do so, even if with a bad conscience. The quasi majority of literal modern translations do the same by rendering either "in the time of their trouble" (RSV, NRSV) or "in the hour of their disaster" (NEB, REB). The paraphrase of so-called functional equivalence translations frequently is not distinctive enough to permit any judgment about the text being used as a base (compare GNB, FC and GN).

It should be noted that recent commentators such as Rudolph (76) and McKane (240) give preference to the reading בְּעֵד and that this also is the preferred reading of BHS. The question remains which particular semantic relationship is expressed by the proposition. A causal relationship may be intended or an apotropaic one: protection against threatening disaster (van Selms, 176).

Translation Proposals

NJV can be a model for literal rendering: "for I will not listen when they call to Me on account of their disaster." In languages in which causes cannot be expressed through prepositions, NJB may be a useful example: "for I will not listen when their distress forces them to call to me for help."

11.15A

Textual Decisions

The first word which has been creating major problems in this difficult verse is הָרַבִּים, "the many," which, according to the text divisions of the Masoretes comes at the end of the second Hebrew sentence. M is followed by Aq who according to Ziegler's retroversion from the Syriac τοὺς διαλογισμοὺς τοὺς πολλούς, "the many devices," attaches הָרַבִּים as a qualifier to the preceding noun. The same is done by V: *scelera multa*, "many crimes," S: ܪ̈ܚܡܐ ܣܓ̈ܝܐܐ, "much abomination," and by T: לִיחטא סגיאין, "(and they have made counsel) into many sins," if at least this translation of Walton is preferred to that of Hayward.

Whatever Hebrew was read by G instead of הָרַבִּים, it was not taken as the last word of the second sentence, but as the first word of the next one: μὴ εὐχαί, question particle + "prayers," "Will prayers and holy offerings take away your wickedness from you?" The question particle renders the initial ה, but since εὐχαί occurs only here in the Greek translation of Jeremiah, it is difficult to know what the source text equivalent could have been. Since the verb εὔχεσθαι elsewhere always corresponds with Hebrew נדר, a Vorlage הַנְּדָרִים, "vows," has been proposed. Second, on the basis of the reading *adipes*, "fat," in Irenaeus's *Adversus Haereses* IV, 17, which was considered to be the Old Latin version of this verse, a Vorlage הַחֲלָבִים or הַבְּרִיִּים has been advanced. Finally, a masculine-plural הָרֻנִּים of רִנָּה, "lamentation," has been suggested as another possible Vorlage of G, because of the presence of רִנָּה in the immediate context (verse 14) and the close relationship between this word and the notion of prayer. The first proposal of a Vorlage הַנְדָרִים for G has been rejected as improbable. Regarding the second proposal, the committee theorized that we only have a possible allusion to a Greek translation of this verse, because Irenaeus is not citing Jeremiah explicitly. In addition, it cannot be assumed that a secondary witness gives access to a more primitive text of G than attested by its own direct tradition. The last reconstruction was preferred and G was considered to be in error due to *beth/nun* confusion. As a result, a B evaluation was attributed to M.

Evaluation of Problems

Most recent translations follow G in their sentence division and at the same time take הַנְדָרִים, "vows," as the Hebrew Vorlage to be preferred. So, for example, RSV, NRSV, NJB, GNB combine "vows" and "consecrated meat." On the other hand, NEB and REB follow the recontruction הַבְּרִיִּים of BHS's second proposal, and therefore translate "fat offerings," "Can the flesh of fat offerings on the altar (ward off the disaster that threatens you?)." In a footnote reference is made to the Old Latin, which is, as signaled above, rather questionable.

If translators want to follow the text and text division of M, some syntactical decisions have to be made. In order to facilitate the syntax as in all versions except G, הָרַבִּים has to be taken as a qualifier of the preceding word הַמְזִמָּתָה, "abomination," "so many abominations." This conception, current in the sixteenth cetury, is still the one of NJV. Another option is to consider הָרַבִּים as "the many gods" and therefore as a more precise definition of the abomination: "she has committed abomination with the many gods" (Radaq); or to see in הָרַבִּים a multitude joining her in her evil designs as in KJV: "she has brought lewdness with many" and in NIV: "as she works out her evil schemes with many(?)" Such an interpretation, however, can hardly be correct.

A third possible solution is to take הָרַבִּים as the grammatical subject of the infinitive עֲשׂוֹתָה which has here the value of a participle, and to consider the third-person feminine singular suffix as anticipating the following noun: "they are many who commit it, the abomination." This option of the Talmud, Rashi, and Rosenmüller is followed by BR.

Translation Proposals

If the first syntactical option is preferred, NJV can be quoted as an example: "(Why should My beloved be in My house,) who executes so many vile designs?" If the last one is chosen, BR presents the following model: "(Was hat mein Freund noch in meinem Haus,) wo die Vielen es bereiten: das Ränkewerk" "(Why should my friend still be in my house,) where so many prepare intrigues."

11.15B

Textual Decisions

The third sentence of this verse in M ends with מֵעָלָיִךְ, "from you," and the fourth sentence starts with כִּי, "for." The last word has been rendered by Aq as ὅτι, by S as ܡܛܠ, and by T as מִן קדם. G, by rendering ἀπὸ σοῦ τὰς κακίας σου, "from you your wickedness," apparently did not read כִּי and it connected the last word of the third sentence מֵעָלָיִךְ syntactically with the second word of the fourth: רָעָתֵכִי, "your wickedness," with its rare, Aramaizing second-person feminine singular suffix. It seems quite certain therefore that G, instead of two words, only had מעליכי in its Vorlage. V seems to have been guided by G in view of its similar reading *a te malitias tuas*, "from you your malice."

The committee judged that the first word of the fourth sentence, כִּי, was matched by the first word of the fifth sentence: אָז, "when . . . then," which would plead for the originality of M. It discerned, on the other hand, that a dittography of כִּי in M could not be excluded, which is why M only received a C evaluation.

Evaluation of Problems

If translators are convinced that M contains a dittography, they can simply follow the text division and interpretation of G, as has been done in many modern versions such as RSV, NRSV, NJB, etc. They are then left with the interpretation and rendering of the last sentence as אָז תַּעֲלֹזִי, which most likely expresses a bitter irony, such as "Surely you would then rejoice!" or "Then you would have reason for self-congratulation!" (McKane).

If the originality of M is accepted, translators will not have many problems with the rendering of the last two sentences. If רעה is given the meaning of "wickedness," they can follow the interpretation and rendering of NJV or NIV. But if "disaster" is considered to be its meaning, the rendering of the sentences could be: "When disaster reaches you, then you will surely rejoice!"

The real problem of interpretation and translation is with the third sentence. Since the verb is plural, a translation such as NJV, "The sacral flesh will pass away from you," is impossible. The verbal subject can only be an impersonal one or a double duty הָרַבִּים (see the preceding case). The sentence would then refer to the religious chiefs: "Let them remove far from you even the sacrificial meat!"

Translation Proposals

For a rendering according to G, NRSV can be chosen as an example: "Can vows and sacrificial flesh avert your doom?" If M is preferred, the last two sentences can be rendered as in NIV, "When you engage in your wickedness, then you rejoice," if the first interpretation of רעה is followed. For the second meaning, see above. The third sentence can only be translated as indicated at the end of the preceding section. No existing translation can be quoted as an example.

11.16A

Textual Decisions

In this verse the people is compared with an olive tree which in M is qualified three ways: רַעֲנָן, "full of leaves," יְפֵה, "beautiful," and פְּרִי־תֹאַר, literally: "fruit of appearance." All of these qualifications in M have been rendered by Aq and V, and also by S which for reasons of explicitness repeats a translation of יָפֶה between פְּרִי and תֹאַר. G, on the other hand, does not seem to have read פְּרִי, "fruit," but instead introduces εὔσκιον, "shadowy," as one of the characteristics of the olive tree. The same features of absence of fruit and presence of shadow can be found in the paraphrase of T: "Behold, like the olive tree which is handsome in its appearance and beautiful in its looks, and among the trees its boughs are providing shade," deriving מטלן from טלל and translating it: "are providing shade," and not from נטל, as is done by Hayward, who translates "are exalted."

The committee judged that G's wording could be due to a simplification of the florid style of a Vorlage like M. It also concluded that the omission of fruits and the introduction of shade in G and T could have been influenced by the description of the lofty cedar to which Pharaoh is compared in Ezek 31.3–9. In view of the otherwise strong support of M, it received a B evaluation.

Evaluation of Problems

Since 1793 (Michaelis), most commentators have proposed deleting פְּרִי on the basis of G. Relatively few modern translations follow the emendation of, for example, NAB: "A spreading olive tree, goodly to behold," and NEB and REB: "an olive tree, leafy and fair."

Translators are, however, encouraged to follow M, which can be understood as presenting an ellipsis of ויפה, "and beautiful (of)," before the last word תֹאַר, "appearance," an ellipsis, "corrected" by S, and in its tracks by Abulwalid (1886, 259, 12f) and Radaq. It is even possible, without the assumption of ellipsis, to interpret פְּרִי־תֹאַר as "fruits of (beautiful) appearance" as has been done by Venema in his commentary.

Translation Proposals

An example of translation can be found in NJV: "Verdant olive tree, / Fair, with choice fruit."

11.16B

Textual Decisions

In the second part of the verse, after the statement that he (the Lord) has set the olive tree on fire, the verb used to describe what happened to its branches in M is וְרָעוּ, which frequently has been taken as derived from the verb רעע, meaning "(and) are broken." Such a meaning does not find any direct support in the versions. G renders with ἠχρεώθησαν, "they have become useless," Aq and Sym in Ziegler's retroversion from the Syriac render with ἠσθένησαν, "they have become weak," V with *combusta sunt*, "are burned," S with ܐܬܚܒܠܘ (according to the Paris and London polyglots), "are destroyed," and T with ויתברון, "they shall be joined," deriving the Hebrew consonantal form from the root רעה II.

It was deemed that all the versions probably presuppose M. Moreover, V was considered contextually inspired in view of Jerome's gloss: *ita ut comburerentur et redigerentur ad nihilum rami . . . eius*, "so that its branches . . . are burned and reduced to nothing." M therefore got a B vote.

Evaluation of Problems

The contextually inspired translation of V is also that of some modern versions such as GN and GrN. In view of the absence of a textual note, they do not seem to follow the textual emendation וּבְעֲרוּ which Grätz had proposed based on V and which was still adopted by former editions of BdJ.

Driver, on the other hand, explained the consonantal form of M as archaic, retaining the final *waw* of a *lamedh/waw* verb which, unrecognized by the Masoretes, would have been pointed as a plural. The form of M would therefore be equivalent to וְרָעָה, "and it (namely, the fire) consumes." This interpretation has been taken over by NEB: "(fire sets its leaves alight) and consumes its branches." REB, though not following Driver like NEB, still takes "to consume" to be the meaning of the Hebrew verb: "(he [namely, the Lord] has set it on fire) and its branches are consumed." RSV and NRSV ascribe the same sense to the Hebrew verb. It is very doubtful, however, whether this can be the meaning of רעה I since the root is never used of the devouring power of fire (McKane, 251).

A derivation from a root רעע remains the best solution. Translators could then either adopt a meaning "be broken" or "be desolate."

Translation Proposals

If the first meaning is chosen, NJB can be taken as a model: "its branches are broken," and if the second meaning is preferred, EÜ can serve as an example: *so daß seine Zweige häßlich werden*, "so that its branches become desolate."

11.19

Textual Decisions

In the plot against Jeremiah his opponents say: נַשְׁחִיתָה) עֵץ בְּלַחְמוֹ), literally, "(let us destroy) the tree with its food." The presence of the two words of M is attested in G: (ἐμβάλωμεν) ξύλον εἰς τὸν ἄρτον αὐτοῦ, "(Let us cast) wood into his bread," although it reads a different verb and understands "wood" to be a poison. It is also attested by Aq: ξύλον ἐν ἄρτῳ αὐτοῦ, "wood in his bread," by Sym according to Ziegler's retroversion: (διαφθείρωμεν) ἐν ξύλῳ τὸν ἄρτον αὐτοῦ, "(Let us destroy) in the tree its bread," by V: (*mittamus*) *lignum in panem eius*, "(Let us cast wood) into his bread" and by S: ܡܘܡܐ ܒܠܚܡܗ (ܢܪܡܐ), "(Let us destroy) the tree with its food." Finally, it is presupposed by the paraphrase of T: נרמי) סמא דמותא במיכלוהי), "(Let us cast) deadly poison into his food." Since all witnesses support M, it received an A evaluation.

Evaluation of Problems

Since Moshe ben Sheshet and Clericus, a different analysis of the consonantal form of M has been given. The *mem* in בלחמו has been considered part of the suffix, and the word has been analyzed as consisting of two parts: the noun לַח, "sap," and the suffix מוֹ. Repointed בְּלֵחָמוֹ, the meaning would be "with its sap." Dahood (1966, 409) comes to the same conclusion by regarding the *mem* as enclitic. This is the basis of NEB: "(Let us cast down) the tree while the sap is in it" and of other modern versions such as REB, GNB, FC, GN. Translations such as NJB: "(Let us destroy) the tree in its strength" and NAB, "in its vigor," show the same conception, but they are based upon the emendation בְּלֵחוֹ, first proposed by Hitzig.

If translators want to stay with the pointing of M, they have some interpretational problems. It is true that לֶחֶם is not found elsewhere with reference to the fruits of a tree. However, in Deut 20.19–20, in a rather identical context, the synonymous expression עֵץ מַעֲכָל, "fruit trees" occurs. And it should be noted that "food" is the standing metaphor for the "word of God" (compare 15.16). Translators can still hesitate about the meaning to be attributed to the preposition בְּ. A causative meaning has sometimes been ascribed to the preposition: "because of its (poisonous) fruit," that is, the unacceptable prophecies. The *beth* could also be interpreted with König (1936, 198b) as a *beth* of concomitance: "at the same time as." The last interpretation has to be preferred.

Translation Proposals

If the need is felt to make Jeremiah's comparison with a tree explicit, CEV is a useful example with its rendering: ". . . to chop me down like a tree—fruit and all."

12.4

Textual Decisions

This verse ends in M with the prophet Jeremiah's quotation of a statement made by his enemies: לֹא יִרְאֶה אֶת־אַחֲרִיתֵנוּ, "He will not see our end." In fact, there are two textual problems in this short sentence, the first relating to the verb, the second to the noun.

As to the verb, a first hand of 4Q-a seems to have written a *kaf* before the last letter, and after some space the tetragrammaton, reading therefore: "The Lord will not make you see." A later hand seems to have erased the *kaf* (Janzen, 176), reading therefore: "The Lord does not see." G, by reading οὐκ ὄψεται ὁ θεός, "God shall not see," supports the second hand of 4Q-a. On the other hand, V and S, and—if something can be deduced from its paraphrase—also T, confirm M. Although this case has not been submitted to the committee, M clearly presents the oldest form of the text. This is proved by the very fact that 4Q-a and G make two different divine names explicit.

With regard to the noun, M is, according to the Barberini manuscript, endorsed by Aq: τὰ ἔσχατα ἡμῶν, "our ends," and Sym: τὴν ἐσχάτην ἡμῶν, "our end"; by V: *novissima nostra*, "our latter end," by S: ـهته, and T: סופנא, both: "our latter end." The only exception is G, with its rendering ὁδοὺς ἡμῶν, "our ways." This translation is clearly based upon the metathesis אָרְחוֹתֵינוּ with *waw/yod* confusion. It is hard to say whether the metathesis was accidental or part of G's Hebrew Vorlage. The fact that the translator made God explicit as the grammatical subject of the verb may have motivated him to assign the classical blasphemy to Jeremiah's enemies, that God does not pay attention to human behavior (Ps 73.11 and 94.7 and other texts). Considering M to be both well supported and meaningful, the committee attributed a C evaluation to it.

Evaluation of Problems

A great number of modern versions simply adopt G in both cases. So NEB: "God will not see what we are doing," and with the same or similar wordings, REB, NAB, GNB, and FC. Others such as NJB follow G in the first instance and M in the second: "God does not see our fate." Others again, such as NRSV, follow M by leaving the verbal subject implicit, and follow G in the rendering of the noun: "He is blind to our ways."

Translators may not want to maintain the ambiguity of the verbal subject in M. They may therefore want to make a grammatical subject explicit, not for textual, but for translational reasons. Although a majority of commentators advocate the view that God is the implicit agent of M, a minority of exegetes since Joseph Qara have considered Jeremiah to be the implicit subject of the verb. For some of them this is even the only possible exegesis of M (van Selms, 183).

Translation Proposals

If the last interpretation is preferred, the variant translation of CEV can be chosen as a model: "Jeremiah won't live to see what happens to us." If the first interpretation is selected, NJB can be taken as example: "God does not see our fate," but no textual note should be provided. In projects with Orthodox participation, a case could be made for the adoption of G along the lines of GNB: "God doesn't see what we are doing," the textual note being only reserved for the noun. In view of the precariousness of interpretation, translators may want to propose a variant translation in a footnote.

12.9A

Textual Decisions

The first problem in this verse is connected with the second word in M צָבוּעַ which in association with the preceding noun of M עַיִט has been rendered by the versions in various ways. G translates the combination with σπήλαιον ὑαίνης, "a cave of a hyena," "Is not my inheritance to me a hyena's cave . . . ?" Josephus and the Hebrew, according to Chrysostom, have ὄρνεον ποικίλον, "speckled bird," "Is not my inheritance to me like a speckled bird . . . ?" V has *avis discolor*, "a parti-colored bird," and S, similarly, ܪܚܠ ܪܚܝܠܬܐ, "a speckled bird." In the paraphrase of T: כעופא דמתבדר, "like fowl that have been scattered," only עופא has a recognizable relationship with M.

The committee attributed an A evaluation to M, considering (a) with HALAT 936a, that צָבוּעַ does not need any form of correction in order to be understood as meaning "hyena," and that (b) the problem is not of a textual but of an exegetical nature.

Evaluation of Problems

The interpretational problem is complicated by the fact that צָבוּעַ is a hapax legomenon. Many modern versions have taken refuge in the majority interpretation of the ancient versions as, for example, NIV: "(Has not my inheritance become to me) like a speckled bird of prey (that other birds of prey surround and attack)?" and, with some variations, NJV, RSV, BR, etc.

Such a translation is conditioned by the interpretation of עַיִט in both occurrences in the verse as "bird of prey." If this is the meaning of the word, the second word of the connective construction צָבוּעַ cannot possibly mean "hyena," as had already been proposed by Bochart in his Microzoicon (I 830, 72 ff. and 838, 35–840, 6). NJV tries the impossible by rendering "Like a bird of prey [or] a hyena," but such a translation is unacceptable.

However, as has been well argued in HALAT (772b) and by Barr (235) and Emerton (182–88), עַיִט can have the meaning of "den" and צָבוּעַ the signification "hyena" so that the connective construction stands for "a hyena's den." In the classical exegesis עַיִט has been taken to mean the same thing in both its occurrences: "birds of prey." In the same way, G renders both occurrences similarly with σπήλαιον, "cave." Driver (1955, 139) and Barr (128), however, see here an intentional play on two homonyms by the writer, the first having the meaning "lair, den," the second, "bird of prey." Such an interpretation, although rarely represented in translation, is more likely.

Translation Proposals

The variant translation, found in the footnote of CEV, provides a model: "My land has become a hyena's den with vultures circling above." Or, if the rhetorical question of M is maintained, NEB and REB can be used as an example: "Is this land of mine a hyena's lair, with birds of prey hovering all around it?"

12.9B

Textual Decisions

In the second line of M, after the two imperatives לְכוּ אִסְפוּ, "go, assemble (all the wild animals)," a third imperative reads הֵתָיוּ, "bring." Among the versions, this reading has the unique support of S. However, four Hebrew manuscripts—Reuchlin of the Prophets, the MS of the Jesuits of Cologne, Urbinates 2, and London BL Add 14760—have the reading אָתָיוּ, "come." This is also the reading of G: καὶ ἐλθέτωσαν, "and let them come," of V: *properate*, "hasten" (plural imperative), and it is the reading presupposed by T: יתון עלה, "(the kings of the nations and their armies) will come against her."

Nonetheless, the committee decided to attribute a B evaluation to M for two main reasons: (a) the reading of M is protected by a *masorah parva* (Ginsburg, א, §1457), which specifies that this form occurs three times in the Bible; and (b) the other textual tradition can be explained as an assimilation to the parallel text of Isa 56.9: "all you wild animals in the forest, come to devour!" (NRSV).

Evaluation of Problems

Abulwalid (1886, 90.9f.) and also others such as Radaq maintained that the *he* is here equivalent to an *aleph*, and this permitted them to give a *qal* rendering of M. Such an analysis, however, has not been resumed in modern times. Since Houbigant, most commentators follow a correction of M according to the parallel tradition. No surprise, therefore, that this had an effect on recent translations such as NAB, NEB and REB.

It is, of course, very convenient for translators to picture the Lord as addressing himself directly to the wild beasts. If M is rendered, he must command a third party which is difficult to be identified. Are the vultures of the preceding line summoned? Do they have to invite the wild beasts? In view of these uncertainties, no participants can be made explicit, not even in the most extreme functional equivalence translation. On the other hand, the absence of any difference between singular and plural imperative forms in English may deceive translators to such an extent that they may consider Jeremiah as the addressee, which is certainly false. If, however, languages distinguish between the two forms, the use of the plural may imply a reference to the birds of prey, which is at least a possibility.

Translation Proposals

Taking into account the plural form of all imperatives, NJV can be quoted as an example: "Go, gather all the wild beasts, Bring them to devour!"

12.13

Textual Decisions

After having said in the first half line of the verse, "They have sown wheat and have reaped thorns," M continues the second half line with נֶחְלוּ, "they have tired themselves out." Among the versions M is only sustained by S: ܐܠܝܘ, "they have been wearied by labor." The others do not seem to have derived the Hebrew form from חלה, but from נחל, vocalized as נָחֲלוּ. Thus we have, most literally, Aq with his rendering: ἐκληρονόμησαν, "they have inherited," according to the Barberini manuscript, and V: *hereditatem acceperunt*, "they have received as an inheritance," and less literally, G: οἱ κλῆροι αὐτῶν, "their portions," Sym according to Ziegler's retroversion κληρονομήσετε, "you will inherit," and T: ומיעללתהון, "and from their harvest."

Although almost all versions did assimilate the Hebrew form with the root נחל, the committee considered the vocalization of M, protected by a *masorah parva*, connecting it with Amos 6.6, as meaningful, and it decided to attribute a B evaluation to M.

Evaluation of Problems

Since the sixteenth century (Vatable), the majority interpretation of the versions has correctly been abandoned. Only recently, Driver (1937–38, 112) has detected here and in Ps 82.8 the use of a homonymous root נחל, equivalent to Arabic *nahala*, having the meaning "to sift." Being apposite in the context of sowing and reaping, McKane is one of the rare commentators to have been seduced by this proposal. Translationally, it has been adopted by NEB: "they sift but get no grain," and this has been taken over by REB.

It is difficult, however, to explain how such a verb, if it existed in Hebrew with this meaning, could have entirely disappeared from later traditions. Moreover, the process of sifting is expressed in Hebrew by הֵנִיעַ בַּכְּבָרָה, "to shake with a sieve." In addition, the structure of the verse does not suggest a chronological follow-up of specific actions, but rather a kind of summary of agricultural labor. Translators are therefore encouraged to follow the vast majority of modern versions in their rendering of M.

Translation Proposals

Among others, NJB can be cited as an example: "They have worn themselves out, to no profit."

13.12

Textual Decisions

In verse 12a God tells the prophet what he has to say to the people. Verse 12b then presents the reaction of the people, introduced in M with וְאָמְרוּ, "and they will say (to you)." This reading has the support of Aq, V, S, and T. G, however, reads καὶ ἔσται ἐὰν εἴπωσι, "and it will come to pass, if they say (to you)." It has been suggested that this rendering could reflect a Hebrew original וְאִם אָמְרוּ, and that M could have been the result of haplography, the sequence אם having been written once instead of twice. The committee judged, however, that such a hypothesis does not take into account the Hebraism והיה כי, which is recognizable behind the Greek formula καὶ ἔσται ἐὰν, which points to a different Vorlage of G, resulting from an autonomous literary tradition. Since it cannot be totally excluded that M has been the victim of a textual accident, however, a B vote was given to M.

Evaluation of Problems

The haplography hypothesis, originally launched by Volz, has been adopted by Rudolph, and most recently by Holladay (401). A few modern translations, such as NJB, seem to accept this theory according to their textual notes, considering G to be original: "And if they answer you." NAB and FC give the same conditional rendering, but without textual note. NAB gives no justification in the accompanying volume (420). The same applies to other versions such as NIV, which, because of their readership, never provide textual information. It will be clear, however, that a translation of M will have to be preferred.

Translation Proposals

For the linear developement of M, CEV offers an example: "The Lord said: Jeremiah, tell the people. . . . They will answer. . . . Then say to them." If, for stylistic reasons, the use of a relative is endorsed, the last two introductions could be rendered as in NJV: "And when they say to you, . . . say to them."

13.18

Textual Decisions

After having received the order to tell the king and the queen mother to take a humble seat, Jeremiah must continue to provide the reason. מַרְאֲשׁוֹתֵיכֶם (יָרַד), "(it has come down), your headdress/tiaras." This reading of M has the unique support of T: יקרכון, "your dignity," "(for) your dignity (has gone into exile from you)." G renders with ἀπὸ κεφαλῆς ὑμῶν, "from your head," "for removed from your head is your crown of glory," and so do V: *de capite vestro* and S: ܡܢ ܪܝܫܟܘܢ. This common rendering could presuppose a Hebrew Vorlage מֵרָאשֵׁיכֶם, "from your head," or, if Dahood's thesis of the existence of a feminine plural of רֹאשׁ, "head," in Hebrew is accepted, analogous to Ugaritic (1961, 462), could presuppose a consonantal form, identical with M, but with a different vocalization: מֵרָאשׁוֹתֵיכֶם.

The committee, however, regarded the existence of the last form as highly improbable since all of the 150 occurrences of the plural of רֹאשׁ in the Bible have the masculine flexional ending. Considering the variant of the versions to be facilitating, the committee attributed a C evaluation to M.

Evaluation of Problems

Since the first edition of Pagnini's translation (1527), the rendering *de capitibus vestris*, "from your heads," has imposed itself. It has been adopted by all the Reformers, by Cappel, Clericus, and by the vast majority of modern commentators and translations. Of the last, some do quote the versions as their base text; others, in the absence of a textual note, may have deemed that their rendering reflected the consonantal text of M.

Translators, when they want to render M, may have some semantic problems. They will hardly be inspired by the information provided in the footnotes of NEB and REB that the Hebrew means "your pillows." M, however, can refer to "your head-pieces," that is, "your head-ornaments" (Holladay, 408) which would make excellent sense in light of the parallel "crown." And, with Kimchi (1862, 165b), מַרְאָשָׁה may in the same way as מַמְלָכָה, "royal dignity," be taken to mean "princely dignity," the plural expressing the totality of the insignia of royalty. The fact that the verb precedes the grammatical subject takes away the difficulty of its singular form.

Translation Proposals

If the first interpretation is chosen, NJV provides a good model: "For your diadems are abased, your glorious crowns." If the second is adopted, KJV can be taken as a base: "for your principalities shall come down, even the crown of your glory" (compare also CEV).

13.25

Textual Decisions

As an apposition to גּוֹרָלֵךְ, "your lot," M reads מְנָת־מִדַּיִךְ, "the portion of your measures." This reading is confirmed by V: *parsque mensurae tuae*, "and part of your measure," and it is presupposed in the interpretation of S: ܡܢܬܐ ܕܝܪܬܘܬܟܝ, "and the portion of your inheritance," and of T: וחולק אחסנתיך, which has the same meaning. G renders his Hebrew Vorlage as follows: καὶ μερὶς τοῦ ἀπειθεῖν ὑμᾶς ἐμοί, "and the share for your rebellion against me." Such a rendering presumes a Hebrew reading מְנָת־מֶרְיֵךְ a *dalet/resh* confusion. It is impossible to know which Hebrew Vorlage is reflected in Aq according to the Syro-Hexapla: ܡܢ ܟܘܠܝܢܐ ܕܝܠܟܝ, *prohibitionis tuae*, "of your prohibition" or "hindering," according to the Latin retroversion in Ziegler. Since *dalet/resh* and *resh/dalet* exchanges can easily take place, the committee attributed a C evaluation to M.

Evaluation of Problems

From Schleusner to Rudolph, the reading of G was frequently adopted, but rarely in translations. NEB and REB: "This is your lot, your portion as a rebel," are the only notable exceptions.

As has been pointed out by McKane (311), it is not at all obvious that the sense of G is superior to that of M. Besides, the root מרה, "to be rebellious," is always used with the accusative or with the prepositions בְּ or עַם, but never with the preposition מִן which figures in the context of this verse.

It is true that M presents some semantic problems. Although מַד means "garment" in general, a meaning "measure" is not excluded since the extended garment was used for measuring. Moreover, the use of the plural in M is an indication that the garment had to be "filled" several times in order to obtain the full measure. If such arguments are not accepted, it is always possible to analyze the form of M, with Kimchi, as a masculine plural of מִדָּה, "measure." The vast majority of modern versions should therefore be followed in their rendering of M.

Translation Proposals

Even more literal translations will need some kind of restructuring as is shown by NRSV which can be taken as a model: "This is your lot, the portion I have measured out to you."

13.27

Textual Decisions

After the statement that Jerusalem is unclean, in the last line of the verse, the verse is completed in M with the interrogative sentence עַד מָתַי אַחֲרֵי which could be understood to mean "after how much time yet?" The only variant which can be clearly distinguished in this difficult sentence pertains to the vocalization of the last syllable of the first word: אַחֲרַי. M is only supported by Sym: μετὰ ταῦτα (πότε ἔτι), "after this (when yet)?" G renders with . . . ὀπίσω μου (ἕως τίνος ἔτι), ". . . after me; (how long yet?)," thus vocalizing the Hebrew consonant form as אַחֲרַי. So does Aq according to Ziegler's retroversion from the Syro-Hexapla: ὀπίσω μου (πότε ἔτι), "after me; (when then?)," and V: *post me* (*usquequo adhuc*), "after me (up till now)." S renders the problematic sentence with ܗܓܪܬܐ ܐܬܬܘܝ ܥܕܡܐ. If the last word is not the result of an inner-Syriac corruption, this could mean: "Until when? Repent! (feminine imperative)." No translation of אחרי can be found in the Syriac or in T, with its paraphrase: כען ליך ארכא יומין סגיאין, "Now you have respite for many days."

The committee judged that the omission in S and T was due to a lack of insight into the difficult syntax of M. It considered the readings of G, Aq and V to be caused by a vocalization error and the result, "you are not pure after me," as not providing a better sense. M therefore received a C evaluation.

Evaluation of Problems

According to its textual note which judges the Hebrew to be *déconcertant*, "confounding," it is only TOB which seems to have followed G and V by its somewhat forced rendering: "Hélas! Jerusalem, tu ne veux pas te purifier en me suivant . . . combien de temps encore?" "Alas! Jerusalem, you do not want to purify yourself by following me . . . how long still?"

Volz proposed to read the verb אחר and he emended M to תְּאַחֲרִי, "you delay." This emendation was taken over by NEB and REB which, according to Brockington (204), rearranged the sentence in such a way that it reads: תְּאַחֲרִי עַד מָתַי, "how long will you delay?"

The elliptical state of M makes it difficult to know precisely whether the final sentence suggests a faint gleam of hope or a veiled threat of judgment. If the first interpretation is chosen, the omitted elements of the ellipsis may have to be spelled out in order to complete the sense: "How long will it be before you decide to purify yourself?" In the second interpretation, the meaning would be: "How much longer can this state of affairs continue?" (McKane, 314). The first possibility found slightly more supporters.

Translation Proposals

For the first interpretation see NJB: "How much longer until you are made clean?" and for the second, GN: *Wie lange noch soll das so weiter-gehen, Jerusalem?* "How long will this go on, Jerusalem?"

14.4

Textual Decisions

This verse starts with the following sentence in M: בַּעֲבוּר הָאֲדָמָה חַתָּה, "Because of the ground, it is cracked." The initial preposition בַּעֲבוּר has the support of Sym in Ziegler's retroversion from the Syriac: ἕνεκεν τῆς γῆς ἡττήθησαν: "because of the ground they became weaker," of V: *propter terrae vastitatem*, "because of the desolation of the land," of S: ܡܛܠ, "because of," and of T: בדיל, "because of." G, on the other side, renders his Vorlage with καὶ τὰ ἔργα τῆς γῆς ἐξέλιπεν, "and the produce of the land has failed." In other words, G has rendered the noun עֲבוּר. It is also followed in this by S, because S does not translate the verb in the sentence, but it provides both a translation of בַּעֲבוּר (or of the preposition בְּ) and of עֲבוּר: ܡܛܠ ܕܥܒܕܐ ܕܐܪܥܐ, "because of the products of the earth."

Given the rather weak possibility of an early corruption distinguishing M from the Hebrew Vorlage of G, the committee decided to assign a B evaluation to M.

Evaluation of Problems

Since Houbigant the variant reading of G has occasionally been adopted by commentators and therefore also by translators. So, for example, the Dutch Canisius translation, which according to its textual note: *De akkerbouw is gestaakt*, "farming has stopped," is an interpretation of the Greek and, more recently NEB: "the produce of the land has failed." The latter translation, however, has been corrected in REB.

Although one should opt for a rendering of M, its syntax can create some problems. So NJV, considering the meaning of M uncertain, tentatively translates: "Because of the ground there is dismay." RSV, giving the same meaning to the Hebrew verb, presupposes the presence of a relative clause which it renders explicitly: "Because of the ground which is dismayed." In fact, the Hebrew verb is part of a relative clause with ellipsis of the relative particle אשר

(for zero-marked relative clauses, see Waltke-O'Connor 19.6). The verb, however, should not be given the meaning "be dismayed," but with Kimchi and most modern versions, the meaning "cracked" (namely, with drought).

Translation Proposals

NJB can function as a model: "Because the soil is all cracked / since the country has had no rain."

14.8

Textual Decisions

This verse begins with מִקְוֵה יִשְׂרָאֵל, "O hope of Israel," in M. In this, M is supported by V, S, and T. Kennicott, however, cites nine Hebrew manuscripts which add the name of God: יהוה, and G can be added to them in view of its rendering ὑπομονὴ Ισραηλ κύριε, "O Lord, hope of Israel." Kennicott's lists, however, are not always precise. For example, manuscript 158 of the Jesuits of Cologne shows, on close examination, that the vocalizer of this manuscript has erased the name of God. And the vocalizers of manuscript 180 (Hamburg 27) and 150 (Berlin Orientalis, folio 2) did not provide the name with any vowels or accents.

The committee ascertained that both the Hebrew and Greek textual traditions had made an assimilation to the parallel text of 17.13, and, judging this assimilation to be definitely secondary, it attributed a B evaluation to M.

Evaluation of Problems

From Cornill to, most recently, Holladay (419), the addition of the name of God was regularly proposed without argument. It has been added in NAB and NJB in different slots, respectively: "O Hope of Israel, O Lord" and "Yahweh, hope of Israel," on textual grounds, according to their notes.

It should be noted that it is hardly necessary in this context to identify the addressee explicitly for translational reasons since the preceding verse was already a prayer addressed explicitly to the Lord. In languages in which the use of the vocative in connection with abstracts is awkward, a statement in the form of a complete sentence may have to be made.

Translation Proposals

As an example of the last solution, GNB can be cited: "You are Israel's only hope."

14.18

Textual Decisions

The last sentence in M reads (יָדָעוּ) וְלֹא, "and (they have no knowledge)."
The conjunction is only clearly supported by S. Although all the editions of T
as well as the Yemenite manuscripts cited in Sperber read ולא בקרו, "and they
have not made enquiry," the Tiberian witnesses to T (MS of Jew's College
London, Codex Reuchlinianus, and MS Urbinates 1) lack the conjunction ו. It
is therefore difficult to know the authentic reading of T. The reading without
the conjunction is found in 13 manuscripts of Kennicott and five manuscripts
of de Rossi as well as in the Soncino edition of the Hebrew Bible of 1488. It
is presupposed by the rendering as a relative clause in G: ἣν οὐκ ᾔδεισαν,
"(for priest and prophet have gone to a land) which they did not know." The
same applies to the identical rendering of V: *quam ignorabant*. The committee
considered the reading and rendering without the conjunction as an assimilation to the four cases in Jeremiah in which אֶרֶץ, "land," is followed by a relative clause containing the verb יָדַע, "to know": 15.14; 16.13; 17.4; and 22.28,
and it assigned a B evaluation to the reading of M with the conjunction.

Evaluation of Problems

Of modern translations only NAB and RL: *Sogar Propheten und Priester
müssen in ein Land ziehen, das sie nicht kennen*, "Even prophets and priests
must go to a land they do not know," follow the variant reading without the
conjunction, according to their textual notes. However, other translations,
such as KJV, BR, and NIV: "Both prophet and priest have gone to a land they
know not," have given a similar rendering, presumably without basing their
translations on the variant. In fact, since Yefet ben Ely, commentators have
frequently ascribed the meaning of the variant to M, interpreting M as an allusion to exile in a foreign land.

Entirely different renderings of the text are found in NEB and REB. The
first version attributes the Syriac meaning "to beg" to the verb of the preceding sentence, סָחַר and, in the steps of D. Winton Thomas (273–74), it derives
the verb יָדַע from Arabic *wada'a*, "to rest," with the following result: "prophet
and priest alike go begging round the land and are never at rest." REB returns
to the traditional rendering of the first verb, but stays with the Arabic meaning
of the second: "Prophet and priest alike wander without rest in the land."

It seems preferable, however, to render M, with many modern versions
and commentators, as two coordinate independent clauses and interpret it as a
description of the spiritual leaders who are at a loss, overwhelmed by the
catastrophe.

Translation Proposals

For a good idiomatic rendering of the last interpretation, see NJB: "even prophets and priests roam the country at their wit's end." Translators may want to provide a variant interpretation or translation, according to the interpretation first mentioned, in a footnote, as has been done in GNB: "Prophets and priests have been dragged away to a land they know nothing about."

15.8

Textual Decisions

In the second line of the verse, M states what God has done, עַל־אֵם בָּחוּר, "against the mothers of youths," the singular being used as a collective. This reading has the support of G: ἐπὶ μητέρα νεανίσκου, "against (the) mother of a young man," of V: *super matrem adulescentis*, "upon the mother of a young man," and of T which renders אֵם metaphorically: עַל סִיעַת עוּלֵימֵיהוֹן, "against the company of their young men." This reading is also presupposed by the Greek variant reading found, among others, in the Vatican Codex: ἐπὶ μητέρα νεανίσκους, "(I have brought) against the mother young men." Note that such an interpretation is also suggested by the Masoretes, since the words אֵם and בָּחוּר are separated by the disjunctive accent *tevir* in M. The only variant reading is found in S: ܠܥܠ ܐܡܐ ܘܠܥܠ ܓܕܘܕܐ, "against the mother and against the young man," which repeats the preposition before the second noun. This repetition was considered by the committee to be purely translational in character and M therefore received a B evaluation.

Evaluation of Problems

Rudolph (102) has proposed emending M in the following way: עֲלֵיהֶם לְאֹם מַחֲרִיב, "upon them a devastating people." Of this emendation only the conjecture לְאֹם, "people," was sometimes adopted. McKane (340) has proposed the following emendation, closer to M: עֲלֵיהֶם לְאֹם בָּחוּר. In fact, he seems to have taken over the conjecture which, according to Brockington (204), was the basis of the rendering of NEB: "I brought upon them a horde of raiders." It is noteworthy, however, that REB has entirely abandoned this conjecture, given its rendering: "I brought upon the mother of young warriors."

Houbigant had already proposed emending M according to S, while others, without emendation, suggested rendering M like S since M would present a typical case of asyndesis. Only one modern version, NJV, seems to have been inspired by this interpretation: "I will bring against them—young men and mothers together—" although the same interpretation can be presupposed by the paraphrase of GN, CEV and GNB: "I killed your young men in their prime and made their mothers suffer."

It should be observed, however, that M may imply that the widows are already bereaved of their sons, who can therefore no longer defend them. W and GrN adopted this point of view, focusing on the mothers and leaving "the youth" implicit in their translation: *Op de moeders stuur ik soldaten af,* "Against the mothers I send soldiers."

Translation Proposals

If translators want to follow the last interpretation, NJB can be quoted as an example: "On the mother of young warriors I bring the destroyer. . . ."

15.11A

Textual Decisions

This verse is introduced in M with אָמַר יְהוָה, "The Lord said." The reading אָמַר is supported by Aq, Sym, V, S and T. G, however, has the introduction γένοιτο δέσποτα, "Be it so, Lord." As correctly seen by Cappel (1684, 525b), the rendering of G presupposes a reading אָמֵן. The committee decided that the Greek translator could have been victim of a graphical ambiguity, resulting in a *resh* / final *nun* confusion. Guided by the concern to put the utterances of this verse into the mouth of Jeremiah, he could also have made an assimilation to the immediate context. M therefore received a B evaluation.

Evaluation of Problems

Since Michaelis, the rendering of G has frequently been adopted by commentators, most recently by Jones (221), whose apodictic statements classify translations as "right" or "wrong." It has entered in one form or another into many recent translations such as RSV, NAB, NJB, FC, GrN, etc. Even BR seems to be in favor of the variant interpretation.

It should be observed, however, that, in spite of the considerable efforts of Talmon, who wants to prove that "amen" can function as an introduction to an oath formula (1969), no evidence has turned up that "amen" ever belonged to the introductory oath formulas with אִם or with אִם־לֹא. As to the rather truncated אָמַר יְהוָה, "said the Lord," two other examples can be provided, one within the book (46.25), one outside: Ps 68.23. The rubric of the first text is more elaborate, but the rubric of the last closely resembles the one used here. Further arguments in favor of M can be found in Holladay (446) and McKane (344). With the vast majority of modern versions (NIV, NRSV, CEV, NJV, NEB, REB, GN), M should therefore be endorsed.

It will be clear that the decision about the speaker will have a bearing on readings and interpretations of the following statements in the verse. Conversely, any interpretation of the following statements may influence textual decisions of the case under discussion. In this treatment, the definition of the Lord as the speaker will be taken as the starting point for the readings and interpretation of readings in the succeeding case.

Translation Proposals

"The Lord said" (NRSV, NIV, NJV) or "The Lord answered" (NEB) are appropriate renderings.

15.11B

Textual Decisions

The main problem is the form in the first sentence which reads in M according to the *ketiv* שרותך and according to the *qere* שֵׁרִיתִיךְ. Aq with τὸ ὑπόλειμμά σου, "your remainder," Sym with ὑπελείφθης, "you are left over," V with *reliquiae tuae*, "your remainder," S with ܢܫܒܩܟ, "will leave you behind," and T with סוֹפָךְ, "your end," probably all have interpreted M as a defective writing for שְׁאָרִיתְךָ, analyzed by some as a form of the verb שׁאר and by others as a noun, שְׁאֵרִיתְךָ, "your remainder."

G, on the other hand, renders κατευθυνόντων αὐτῶν, which can be translated "while they were prosperous" or "while they directed." The Greek translator therefore seems to have considered it as being derived from either אשׁר or ישׁר.

The committee considered the rendering of G as due to literary activity of the Greek translator. It regarded the *ketiv* as a graphical error, and the votes were equally divided: three B and three C for the *qere*.

Evaluation of Problems

In view of the textual decisions made in 15.11A, interpretations and emendations based on the hypothesis of Jeremiah's being the speaker will not be taken into consideration for translational purposes. This concerns mainly the conjecture שֵׁרַתִּיךְ, "I have served you," which was simultaneously proposed by Condamin and Volz (173) in 1920 and which since then has been enthusiastically endorsed by many commentators. It has been entered into many recent versions such as NAB: "have I not served you for their good?" and NJB: "Have I not genuinely done my best to serve you, Yahweh?" Compare also BR and FC.

However, it is not entirely clear how the *qere* should be rendered. The majority interpretation of the versions, dominant in the 16th century and visible in, for example, KJV: "Verily it shall be well with thy remnant," has almost totally been abandoned. Only NJV among the recent versions still clings to it: "Surely, a mere remnant of you will I spare for a better fate!" In spite of the fact that this was also one of the mainstream interpretations in Judaism since Menaḥem ben Saruq and Radaq, its correctness is doubtful. In fact, the word under discussion does not figure in the list of words which have an unwritten *alef.* This list of 16 words can be found in the *Masorah* edited in the second part of Oklah of the manuscript of Halle (Ognibeni, §153). However, there is another interpretation, initiated by Yefet ben Eli, which analyzes the *qere* as a *piel* of the verb שׁרה with the meaning "deliver." This is also the meaning retained in the French adaptation of HALAT (Reymond, 398b), and it has been adopted in NIV, NRSV, GN, SR, NV, and Chouraqui.

Translation Proposals

NIV presents a possible model with its rendering: "Surely I will deliver you for a good purpose."

15.12

Textual Decisions

The added information וּנְחֹשֶׁת, "and bronze," "Can iron break iron from the north and bronze," at the end of this verse in M created problems. M is literally supported by Aq: καὶ χαλκός, Sym: καὶ χαλκόν, and by V: *et aes.* It is indirectly confirmed by all the other versions which modify the nominal clause in order to adapt it to the new receptor context. Thus, we find G with its rendering χαλκοῦν, "brazen," καὶ περιβόλαιον χαλκοῦν ἡ ἰσχύς σου, "and a brazen covering is your strength," and, according to Jerome, Th with his translation *et operimentum aeneum*, "and a brazen covering." T seems to point to a transposition of the last two words of the verse: מִצָּפוֹן וּנְחֹשֶׁת, "from the north and bronze," in view of its paraphrase וכנחשא ייתי מציפונא, "(A king who is as strong as iron shall come up to help a king who is as strong as iron) and brass: he shall come up from the north; (he has come up to shatter)." S has made another arrangement by moving מִצָּפוֹן, "from the north" back to verse 11 and by describing the enemy by whom Judah is threatened in verse 12 as ܒܪܐ ܐܝܟ ܦܪܙܠܐ ܘܐܝܟ ܢܚܫܐ, "as strong as iron and bronze."

Because of all these translational operations going off in different directions, the committee attributed a B evaluation to M.

Evaluation of Problems

In view of the decision described above, there seems to be little reason to adopt the "probable" reading of NEB and REB in which the last word of M has been omitted by conjecture: "Can iron break steel from the north?" There is no reason, however, to deny that the verse as a whole is problematic. Bright considered the whole of verses 12–14 as a "damaged variant" (109) of 17.1–4 and he suggested omitting them in translation. Some recent versions such as NAB followed this advice literally.

The main problem concerns the interpretation of the rhetorical question. Is "iron from the north" a reference to the quality of the iron? Greek and Roman sources have referred to the tribe of Chalybes on the Black Sea, famous for their steel production. If so, the verse can be understood as reassurance for Jeremiah by God in light of the statement from the vocation narrative, 1.18: "I have made you an iron pillar, and a bronze wall." Such is the opinion of, for example, Rashi and Grotius and probably of RSV: "Can one break iron, iron from the north, and bronze?" and NJB according to its note.

Or is "iron from the north" a reference to the Babylonian military power, as is suggested by the paraphrase of T, Jewish medieval exegetes, Calvin, and, most recently Reventlow (215)? This is the interpretation of NJV which brings "from the north" back to verse 11 as a direct qualification of the enemy (compare S), and of CEV according to its Targumic paraphrase.

In the light of prevailing uncertainties, it seems to be preferable to provide a translation which is open-ended and leaves room for multiple interpretations.

Translation Proposals

RSV, as quoted above, can be considered a model for such a translation. A footnote could explain that it is unclear whether this verse refers to the "enemy from the north" or to the solidity of the prophet.

15.13

Textual Decisions

After the statement that the Lord will hand over all the wealth of Judah as spoil, M continues with the words לֹא בִמְחִיר וּבְכָל, "without price, and for all (your sins)." Both the second and the last words are protected by a *Masorah magna*. The last one is particularly important as unique textual evidence for a reading with the conjunction *waw*, because it states that this is one of the five cases in which וּבְכָל is found twice in the same verse (Weil, §2543). All that is known of the texts of Aq and Sym are, respectively, the readings οὐκ ἐν ἀλλάγματι, "not in exchange," and ὑπὲρ οὐδενός, "for nothing," which support the first two words of M, the one in a literal way and the other in an idiomatic way. Except for the conjunction, both V and T support M—V: *gratis in omnibus* (*peccatis tuis*), "for nothing for all (your sins)," and T, which renders the first two words literally: לא בדמין, "not for a price," and continues with a paraphrase: "because of the sins of your worship of idols."

S omits the first two words and the conjunction *waw* and restructures the whole verse, which then reads: "your belongings and your wealth and all your borders I will hand over as spoil because of your sins."

G renders neither the first word nor the conjunction: ἀντάλλαγμα διὰ πάσας τὰς ἁμαρτίας σου, "as a recompense, because of all your sins."

The committee decided that (a) the oracle of 15.13–14 is a quotation of the original oracle in 17.3–4 and that (b) it is normal that the quoted form is not identical with the original one and that the autonomy of the two parallels has to be respected. Further it contended that G has no translation of 17.3–4 at all and that G therefore is a textual witness of 15.13–14. It noted that M in 17.3 does not have the negation marker and that it reads the second word as במתיך. It therefore regarded the negation marker and the conjunction in M 15.13 as secondary elements, the one being the result of assimilation to texts such as Ps 44.13 or Isa 52.3, and the second having been introduced because of a wrong syntactical understanding. Two members of the committee judged M to be the result of an autonomous literary development and gave it a C vote. The other four members gave G a C rating. All agreed that M resulted from the Vorlage of G.

Evaluation of Problems

Both NAB and NEB—not REB—omit verses 13 and 14, although NEB provides a translation in a footnote. An omission, however, can hardly be recommended.

Although the rendering of the conjunction is not realized for translational reasons, most modern versions seem to render the negation marker of M in one way or another: "without price" (NRSV), "without charge" (NIV), "without repayment" (NJB). Recent commentators came totally (Rudolph, 104) or partly (McKane, 343) to the same conclusions as the majority of the committee and translators should pay particular attention to it, especially in projects with Orthodox participation.

Translation Proposals

If M is nevertheless followed, REB could be a model: "I shall hand over your health as spoil, and your treasure for no payment, because of all your sin throughout your borders." GrN renders the majority decision of the committee: *Jullie rijkdommen en voorraden laat ik plunderen; dat is de prijs die je moet betalen voor je zonden overal in het land*, "I will let your treasures and supplies be plundered; that is the price you have to pay for your sins everywhere in the country."

15.14

Textual Decisions

This verse starts in M with the verbal form וְהַעֲבַרְתִּי, "And I will make pass (your enemies" or "with your enemies)." This is also the reading of the other principal witnesses of the classical Tiberian text, such as the Aleppo and Cairo manuscripts and the Ben Ḥayyim edition. According to the Barberini manuscript, the verb has the backing of Aq: καὶ παραβιβάσω (σε), "I will pass (you) over" and of Sym: καὶ παράξω (σε), "I will bring (you)." M is further confirmed by V: *et adducam* (*inimicos tuos*), "and I will bring (your enemies)."

On the other side, de Rossi mentions thirteen manuscripts and the first hand of thirteen others, which do not read a *resh* but a *daleth*: והעבדתי, "And I will make serve." Only two manuscripts and the first hand of four others, however, have the additional suffix of the second-person singular masculine which is the reading of 17.4: וְהַעֲבַדְתִּיךָ, "And I will make you serve." Moreover, the reading with *daleth* is also attested by the Petrograd manuscript of the Prophets. The same reading is witnessed by S: ܘܐܫܥܒܕܟ, "And I will make you serve," as well as by T: ותשתעבדון, "And you will be enslaved (to your enemies)."

As has been demonstrated in the preceding case, serious attention should be given to the reading of G: καὶ καταδουλώσω σε, "I will make you the slave of (your enemies)," where a Vorlage, similar to the reading offered by M in 17.4, seems to have been read. With a C evaluation, this reading was preferred by four members of the committee; the other two committee members assigned a C vote to M, which they considered to be literarily autonomous. The majority therefore considered M to have a graphical error and possibly a euphemistic correction.

Evaluation of Problems

The majority decision of the committee is followed by most modern versions which can roughly be divided into those which provide a textual note, for example, NIV, NJB, CEV, and FC, and those which do not, for example, RSV, NRSV, REB, GNB, and BR.

From some of the textual notes, translators may get the impression that M is unintelligible. So, for example, CEV has the following rendering of M in a footnote: "I will make your enemies go through to a land you don't know about." Even some of the few modern versions that render M, as for example NJV, may give this impression: "And I will bring your enemies by way of a land you have not known."

However, depending upon the understanding of the implicit object of the verb, two self-evident interpretations present themselves: (a) "I will make *them*"—the treasures of the preceding verse—"to pass with your enemies into a land you don't know about," and (b) "I will make *you* to pass with your enemies . . ." (Friedman and Rosenberg, 109).

Translation Proposals

Preference should be given, especially in Orthodox projects, to translations expressing the majority decision, as for example, CEV: ". . . I will make you slaves of your enemies in a foreign land."

If M is taken as the source text, NAV is a good model: *Ek sal jou deur jou vyande laat wegvoer na 'n land toe wat jy nie ken nie*, "I will have you led by your enemies to a land you do not know."

16.18

Textual Decisions

The textual problem concerns the second word of the first sentence: רִאשׁוֹנָה, "first," "and first I will repay. . . ." The presence of the adverb of time is attested by V: *primum*, by S: ܠܘܩܕܡ, "first," and by T: כקדמאין, "(And I will repay to the second ones) as to the former ones," in a different grammatical class. As to the Greek witnesses, the word is also confirmed by Aq and Th in their reading πρῶτον, "first," and according to Origen (III, 231B) it was found in "the other editions." It is lacking in G, however.

The omission of the adverb in G or its Vorlage was considered deliberate because of the difficulty of interpretation it created in the context. According to the committee, even if the adverb was a later editorial addition, it was still part of the proto-Masoretic text type, which is why M received a B evaluation.

Evaluation of Problems

Van Selms sees in this verse a reference to the legislation on double restitution and considers רִאשׁוֹנָה to be a reference to the stolen animal or object and the following מִשְׁנֶה to refer to the second animal. The two expressions taken together would then mean "double" (224). If this were true, one could not state that רִאשׁוֹנָה has not been rendered in G, because the rendering διπλᾶς, "double," "(And I will recompense their mischiefs) doubly," would be the equivalent of the combination of the two words. In other words, there would be no textual problem at all. It is difficult to know whether such an understanding is shared by the many modern versions which do not render רִאשׁוֹנָה as an adverb of time (NJB, NIV, NJV, GNB, CEV, GN). They could also have been led by the suggestion of many commentators after Grätz to omit the word in question. Only RSV and NRSV clearly indicate in a footnote that they follow G in their omission.

More likely, however, רִאשׁוֹנָה is a gloss which was inserted after verses 14–15 were in place, simply to explain the sequence of events (Holladay, 479). Translators may feel justified in leaving the information implicit for translational reasons if the introduction of separate section headings for the units 14–15 and 16–18 prevents confusion. Otherwise, they may prefer to make the information explicit, as in NEB, REB, NAB, BR, GrN, and FC.

Translation Proposals

FC may have to be adopted: *Et pour commencer, je vais les payer doublement de leur crime . . .* , "And to start with, I will repay their iniquity doubly. . . ."

17.2

Textual Decisions

Verse 2 starts with the sentence כִּזְכֹּר בְּנֵיהֶם מִזְבְּחוֹתָם, usually translated "while their children remember their altars."

M is supported by V: *cum recordati fuerint filii eorum ararum suarum*, "because their children remembered their altars," and by T: כאדכרא בניהון איגוריהון, "while their sons remember their altars." The statement by Houbigant and Volz, still reproduced in BHK, that the sentence is lacking in S, only applies to the editions derived from the Paris Polyglot. One important manuscript, Ambrosianus, renders the sentence freely with ܟܕ ܕܟܪܝܢ ܒܠܒܗܘܢ, "as they remembered in their hearts." Since this sentence is preceded and followed in S by ܡܕܒܚܝܗܘܢ(ܢ), "their altars," it is clear that the sentence has been omitted in the source of the Paris Polyglot by homoioteleuton, and that Ambrosianus represents S as a free interpretation of M. The whole of verses 1–4 is lacking in G. However, in the asterisked addition of the Origen recension, the sentence of verse 2 is present: ἡνίκα ἂν μνήσθωσιν οἱ υἱοὶ αὐτῶν τὰ θυσιατήρια αὐτῶν, "when their sons remembered their altars." M received an A evaluation because of all this textual support.

Evaluation of Problems

Volz (184) has proposed emending the sentence in such a way that it reads לְזִכָּרוֹן בָּהֶם, "as a memorial against them," and he relates the emendation to the preceding information. This emendation may have influenced some recent versions such as NEB: "to bear witness against them," REB: "to witness against them." Compare also the variant translation in the footnote of NJV: "Surely the horns of their altars / Are as a memorial against them." Other modern translations such as GNB and GrN entirely omit the sentence, maybe following Duhm and Nötscher, who considered it to be a gloss that disrupts the flow of the text.

In this case a translation of M is clearly preferable. Apart from taking בְּנֵיהֶם as the subject of the remembering, as in the ancient versions, it is also possible, with Rashi and Kimchi, to consider it as its object. Then the meaning would be that they love their idolatry with the same affection that they have for their children (Freedman and Rosenberg, 117).

Translation Proposals

NIV is an example of the first interpretation: "Even their children remember their altars. . . ." And for the second, TOB can be mentioned: *Comme ils parlent de leurs enfants, ainsi parlent-ils de leurs autels*, "They speak about their altars the way they speak about their children."

17.3

Textual Decisions

The textual problem concerns the first word of this verse, הֲרָרִי, "my mountain (on the plain)." This reading of M is not confirmed by any of the ancient versions. Verses 1–4 are lacking in G, and the asterisked addition in which they appear has καὶ ὀρέων, "and of the mountains," at this point. Th has the same reading without the conjunction καὶ, whereas S has the rendering ܪܬ ܪܬܐܠܟܣܐ, "and on the mountains." All of them seem to have read a plural הֲרָרֵי, "mountains," in their Hebrew Vorlage. The same reading is the basis of the paraphrase in T: עַל טוריא, "on the mountains," "Because you worshiped on the mountains in the field." V takes the first two words of verse 3 with the end of verse 2: *in montibus excelsis sacrificantes in agro*, "who on high mountains made offerings in the field," where the reading הֲרָרֵי remains implicit because it was apparently judged to have been sufficiently expressed by the next to the last word in verse 2: גְּבָעוֹת, "mountains."

One member of the committee gave a C evaluation to the vocalization הֲרָרֵי, presupposed by the versions; all the others gave the same evaluation to M, taking הֲרָרִי to mean "mountain people."

Evaluation of Problems

From Houbigant and Schleusner to Bright and McKane, recently, the plural vocalization was adopted. It has also had a long translational tradition and it is therefore not amazing that it still is the choice of the majority of our modern versions: RSV, NRSV, NAB, NEB, REB, GNB, FC. Some of them take the following word, בַּשָּׂדֶה, as a reference to a plateau, such as NEB/REB: "the hills in the mountain country"; others, such as RSV/NRSV, speak about "the mountains in the open country."

It is possible, however, to render M according to two different interpretations. According to the first one הֲרָרִי is a first-person suffixed form: "my mountain." This could be considered accusative, as in NIV: "My mountain in the land (and your wealth and all your treasures I will give away as plunder)." More likely, however, the reference to Jerusalem is a vocative, as presented in BP, SR and NAV.

According to the second interpretation, הֲרָרִי should be compared with עֲרָבִי (Isa 13.20) and explained in the same way. Just as עֲרָבִי means "one who dwells in the Arabah," הֲרָרִי would mean "one who dwells on the mountains." This explanation, given by Rashi, among others, is behind the rendering of BR: *Bergler im Gefild*, "Mountaineers in the field." The insight of Yefet ben Eli should be mentioned: the relationship with the mountains is not one of origin or permanent residence, but one of pilgrimage.

Translation Proposals

Of the last interpretation GN can be the model: *Du Volk von Berg- und Hügelpilgern!* "You people of mountain and hill pilgrims."

17.4A

Textual Decisions

A problem is created by the second word in the first sentence: וְשָׁמַטְתָּה וּבְךָ מִנַּחֲלָתְךָ, "And you shall drop, and because of you, from your inheritance." For וּבְךָ M only seems to be represented by T if the rendering וּבְכוֹן, "and upon you," "And upon you I will execute just punishments," of Codex Reuchlinianus and of the London Polyglot is considered to be the authentic translation over against the rendering וּבְכֵין, "and so," of the Urbinates manuscript and the Antwerp Polyglot. The only difference between T and M is the use of the plural in the first, but this can simply be explained as a contextual assimilation. S has no clear equivalent of M and at the most it can be suggested that the second-person suffix of the verbal form ܘܐܫܒܝܟܝ, "And I will deport you," is a syntactic facilitation of M. As in the preceding cases, it should be noted that verses 1–4 are lacking in G. The original text of the asterisked addition of the Origen recension as reflected in the Syro-Hexapla and in Eusebius has translated the whole sentence as follows: καὶ ἀφεθήσῃ καὶ ταπεινωθήσῃ ἀπὸ τῆς κληρονομίας σου, "and you will be removed and brought down from your inheritance." As Doederlein (1777, 239) and Schleusner (V, 262) have suggested, ταπεινωθήσῃ may stem from either דך or מך. According to the Barberini manuscript, Aq has the first verb followed by μόνη σύ, "you alone," a rendering which seems to have inspired the translation *sola*, "alone," of V. This rendering has sometimes been related to the Hebrew לְבַד or לְבַדָּךְ, "(you) alone." The word μόνη has also been inserted into the Origen recension, probably because it was no longer understood that the second verb in Greek translated the second word of M. None of the variants was judged to merit more serious consideration, and M received a C evaluation.

Evaluation of Problems

Michaelis was the first to propose the emendation יָדְךָ, "your hand," "And you shall drop your hand from your inheritance." This has had a tremendous following among all commentators up to the present time. It also had an impact on most modern versions which either render literally: "You shall loosen your hand from your heritage" (RSV), or, more idiomatically, but according to Brockington still following the emendation: "You will lose possession of the patrimony" (NEB).

The acceptance of Michaelis's conjecture is somewhat amazing when one takes into account Ehrlich's remark (286) that the unique case of Deut 15.3, in which שָׁמַט is combined with יָד, would require a *hiphil* conjugation of the preceding verb; and Keil's observation that in Deut 15.3 יָדְךָ is the grammatical subject of the verb and not the object.

In spite of the appraisal which Michaelis's emendation has received, it seems therefore preferable to render M with NIV, NJV, NRSV, BR and GN.

Translation Proposals

NJV: "You will forfeit, by your own act, / The inheritance I have given you," can be chosen as a model.

17.4B

Textual Decisions

In the last sentence of this verse, the verb in M reads קְדַחְתֶּם, "you (pl.) have kindled," "you have kindled a fire in my anger." This reading has the support of V if the rendering *succendistis*, "you (pl.) have kindled," of the San Girolamo edition, based upon a few old manuscripts and Jerome, is preferred. Even the competing rendering, *succendisti*, "you (sg.) have kindled," of the Weber edition, can be considered to be a contextual assimilation of a reading, based upon M. S also confirms M: ܐܘܚܕܬܘܢ, "you (pl.) have kindled."

De Rossi, on the other hand, quotes three Hebrew manuscripts, the first hand of a fourth one, and the second hand of a fifth one, which have the reading קָדְחָה, "(a fire) is kindled," an assimilation to the same reading in the parallel of 15.14. The reversed assimilation seems to have taken place in manuscripts 30 and 82 collated by Kennicott, which have קָדְחְתֶּם in 15.14. קָדְחָה also is the basis of the reading ἐκκέκαυται, "is kindled," in the asterisked addition, ascribed to Th. The same applies to the paraphrase of T which is identical to the one of 15.14 : נפק מן קדמי, "has gone forth from before me," "an east wind as strong as fire has gone forth from before me." As noted before, G is lacking in verses 1–4.

In order to protect M against an assimilation to the parallel of 15.14, the committee decided in favor of M with a B evaluation.

Evaluation of Problems

The assimilation has nevertheless been proposed by most commentators and imposed by the apparatus of BHS. It has been taken over in various ways in a number of recent English translations (RSV, NRSV, NAB, NEB, GNB). Compare, for instance, NRSV: "for in my anger a fire is kindled" and NEB: "for my anger is a blazing fire."

One of the main reasons that the assimilation was advanced is the difficulty caused by the second-person plural in a second-person singular context. It should be noted, however, that the text of 17.4b also occurs in Deut 32.22a in a context which is in the third-person plural. It is very possible that the Deuteronomy text has been the source of the actualization in Jeremiah and that its plural context has been responsible for the introduction of the shift from second-person singular to second-person plural.

It is clearly preferable to render M, assimilating to the context, without bringing into focus such a shift, as has been done in a majority of modern versions (CEV, NIV, NJB, NJV, REB, BR, GN).

Translation Proposals

GN can serve as an example: *du hast meinen Zorn wie ein Feuer angefacht*, "you (sg.) kindled my anger like a fire."

17.16

Textual Decisions

The textual problem is mainly connected with the expression מֵרֹעֶה, "from a shepherd" or "from being a shepherd," "I have not run away from being a shepherd behind you." Although this expression of M does not have a literal equivalent in G, it is nevertheless possible to consider G's translation as a rendering of M: ἐγὼ δὲ οὐκ ἐκοπίασα κατακολουθῶν ὀπίσω σου, "I was not weary of following behind you." The same applies to V: *et ego non sum turbatus te pastorem sequens*, "I have not been unsteady in following you as shepherd," in which the rendering of G is combined with a literal equivalent of the expression under discussion. The paraphrase of T is such that, apart from the opening words, it cannot be correlated with M.

Aq, on the other hand, apparently vocalized his Hebrew Vorlage as מֵרָעָה, given his translation ἀπὸ κακίας, "from evil," and Sym did the same. S read in his Vorlage בְּרָעָה or מֵרָעָה, but in the latter case, he translated it as if it were בְּרָעָה, bringing it to the front position: ܘܐܢܐ ܒܒܝ̈ܫܬܐ ܠܐ ܫܒܩܬ ܕܐܙܠ, "And as for me, in evil times, I did not cease following you."

It should be noted that in 4Q-a the same consonants are found as in M, but, of course, nothing can be concluded regarding the vocalization.

Two members of the committee adopted the vocalization מֵרָעָה. The other four considered this vocalization to be due to an error. Two of these four members gave a B evaluation to M and two voted C.

Evaluation of Problems

In view of the rather open textual options and the various meanings which can be ascribed to the verb אוץ, three interpretational possibilities can be considered:

(1a) "I did not press after you because of disaster" (= מֵרָעָה). This is the option chosen by Michaelis, Giesebrecht, and more recently Hyatt as well as NEB and REB. Yet another interpretation of the same textual option is presented by BR: *aus Bössinn*, "out of malice."

(1b) A textual correction, namely, to read לְרָעָה, "to (send) evil," has been proposed by Volz, Rudolph and Bright, and this conjecture has been endorsed by many modern versions (RSV, NAB, NJB, GNB, FC).

(2) "I did not hastily abandon the office of shepherd (prophet) in your service." This is the exegesis of Yefet ben Eli and Ibn Nachmiash, adopted by NIV, NRSV, NJV, CEV, and GN.

(3) "I did not hesitate to follow you as shepherd." This interpretation has been chosen by McKane and it is represented in V and in all translations based upon V.

Of these three possibilities, (1b) can be disregarded since it is not based upon any textual evidence, and (2) could be favored in spite of the difficulty caused by the fact that this would be the only instance in which רֹעֶה would be used in connection with the prophetic office. Option (3), where the Lord is the shepherd, does not present this problem, but it is less in agreement with the syntax of M.

Translation Proposals

For option (1a) REB can be cited as a model: "It is not the prospect of disaster that makes me press after you," and for option (2) NRSV: "But I have not run away from being a shepherd in your service." A note about textual uncertainties and different possibilities of interpretation and translation seems almost indispensable.

17.19

Textual Decisions

The gate in this verse is, according to the *ketiv*, called "the gate" בְּנֵי־עָם, "of the children of people," and this rendering has the support of 4Q-a. Following the *qere*, the gate is called "the gate" בְּנֵי־הָעָם, "of the children of the people," a reading confirmed by Aq: υἱῶν τοῦ λαοῦ. Because the definite article does not exist in Latin, the textual basis of V cannot be ascertained. And, even though both S and T use an emphatic state of the second noun, this does not guarantee the presence of the definite article in their Vorlage. G does not provide the name of a specific gate, but gives a general description, making the second noun possessive: (ἐν πύλαις) υἱῶν λαοῦ σου, "(in the gates) of the children of your people." The *ketiv*, which has the essential support of 4Q-a, seems to be the origin of the later uses of definite article and possessive. It therefore received a B evaluation.

Evaluation of Problems

Linguistically, this problem is without any translational relevance for languages without definite articles as well as for languages which do possess them and in which their use in this context would be obligatory. It could therefore have been disregarded if Ewald, and in his tracks Grätz, Ehrlich, and Volz, had not proposed the conjecture בִּנְיָמִין, "the Benjamin (gate)" and if this conjecture had not been relatively well received in modern translations (RSV, NAB, NEB, REB).

Although the Benjamin Gate is mentioned in 37.13 and 38.7, and although the conjecture is attractive, it has no textual support at all and should therefore not be preferred. On the other side, however, the "People Gate" is unknown and it is impossible to decide whether it is a city gate (van Selms, 235) or a temple gate (Giesebrecht, 103), or whether the name is a reference to laity as opposed to priests. A rather literal translation with the use of majuscules to mark the proper name seems to be the only solution (NIV, NJB, NJV, NRSV, GNB, etc.).

Translation Proposals

The "Gate of the Sons of the People" (NJB) and, with less redundancy, "the People's Gate" (NJV, NRSV) therefore seem to be adequate translations.

18.4

Textual Decisions

In the relative clause, M reads בַּחֹמֶר, "of clay," "(the vessel he was making) of clay (was spoiled in the potter's hand)." This reading has the support of the asterisked addition in the Origen recension, ascribed to Th and Aq: ἐν τῷ πηλῷ, "in the clay," of V: *e luto*, "from clay," of S: ܒܛܝܢܐ, and T: דְטִינָא, "of clay." Although there is no explicit equivalent of this expression in G, Scharfenberg correctly considered G to be an adequate translation of M: καὶ διέπεσε τὸ ἀγγεῖον ὃ αὐτὸς ἐποίει ἐν ταῖς χερσὶν αὐτοῦ, "and it fell, the vessel, which he was making himself with his hands." In fact, G can be considered to be a stylistic abbreviation.

On the other hand, the prestigious rabbinic Bible of Venice, edited by Ben Chayyim in 1525, and many following editions, including the first two editions of the *Biblia Hebraica* of Kittel, read כַּחֹמֶר, "as clay," a shorthand for "as happens to clay."

The committee esteemed this reading to be due to a graphical error and it expressed its surprise that such an error, thanks to the prestige of Ben Chayyim, had dominated the Hebrew Bible editions up to the moment that it was decided to take the Leningrad Codex as the basis for the Hebrew Bible. In fact, 28 of the most important manuscripts which could be checked have the preposition *bet*. M therefore received a B evaluation.

Evaluation of Problems

The dominating view of Ben Chayyim is still detectable in the apparatus of BHS and in the recent commentaries of Bright (121), Rudolph (120), and Holladay (512). It can also be discerned in some recent translations, such as NJB: "as may happen with clay," NJV: "as happens with clay," and FC: "*ce qui arrive parfois avec l'argile*," "which happens sometimes with clay."

However, as demonstrated by McKane (421), the reading בַּחֹמֶר should be regarded as superior, and it should be followed by translators with the great majority of modern versions.

It is not true that such a reading would result in a tautology (Rudolph and Holladay). The precision makes clear that shaping, not baking, is concerned (van Selms, 239). Nor is it accurate to state that the preposition *bet* cannot indicate the material out of which something is made. Ehrlich (289) gives sufficient references to the contrary.

Translation Proposals

REB could be taken as an example of a translation without redundancies: "Now and then a vessel he was making from the clay would be spoilt in his hands."

18.14A

Textual Decisions

One of the greatest problems in the problematic first rhetorical question of this verse in M is caused by the reading שָׂדַי, "of the field," "Does the snow of Lebanon leave the crags of the field?" M seems to be confirmed only by V: *agri*, "of the field," and by T: חקלי, "fields," "Just as it is impossible that snow should cease coming down upon the fields of Lebanon."

On the other hand, G seems to have pointed שָׂדַי, considering its reading μαστοί, "breasts," μὴ ἐκλείψουσιν ἀπὸ πέτρας μαστοὶ ἢ χιὼν ἀπὸ τοῦ Λιβάνου, "Will breasts be missing from the rocks or snow from Lebanon?" Unlike the Hebrew, the Greek μαστοί can metaphorically be used for any breast-shaped object and it can therefore refer to the peaks of a mountain range. Sym reflects the same punctuation (according to Ziegler's retroversion from the Syro-Hexapla): μὴ ἐγκαταλειφθήσεται ἀπὸ πέτρας μαστῶν χιὼν τοῦ Λιβάνου, "Will snow ever be missing from the breasts of the rocks of Lebanon?" Finally, the same rendering is found in S: ܬܕ̈ܝܐ, "breasts."

According to the Syro-Hexapla, Aq renders the expression with ܕܣܦܩ, "of the Sufficient," in Greek retroverted ἱκανοῦ, which is his usual translation of the divine name שָׂדַי, "Shaddai."

The majority of the committee attributed a C evaluation to the reading of Aq. It regarded the punctuation of G, Sym, and S as an error and the reading of M as probably due to a *tiqqun sopherim*, a scribal correction, because of a possible association with pagan cults.

Evaluation of Problems

Translations made according to M are extremely rare, and either they make no sense at all (KJV, BR) or they make sense but cannot be accepted as a rendering of the source text (Chouraqui).

The many emendations which have been proposed have had a relative effect upon translation. Grätz (1883, 157) and, following him, Duhm, Cornill, and Rudolph, have suggested the emendation שִׂרְיוֹן, "Sirion," another name for Hermon. It has been taken over by both RSV and NRSV: "Does the snow of the Lebanon leave the crags of Sirion?"

The only other emendation which exerted limited influence upon translation was Albright's proposal (1950/51, 23f.) to change מִצּוּר, "from the rock" into צוּר, "flint," and to read: "Will flints forsake the fields or the snow Lebanon?" This emendation has been adopted, for example, by W.

Many recent versions (NEB, NIV, NJB, REB), however, give a rendering like: "Does the snow of Lebanon ever vanish from its rocky slopes?" (NIV), without stating clearly what is the basis of their rendering.

The committee's decision should nevertheless be taken seriously, in spite of the lack of modern commentary support (van Selms, 242, being the only exception). Already Abravanel, and in his tracks Luzzatto and Weiser, considered the "Rock of Shaddai" as the name of one of the peaks of the Lebanon chain, remarkable for its altitude and snow. Since the data for the use of this proper name are lacking in this respect, a general translation such as "mighty peaks" could be used. (NAB, GNB, GN, NAV, C, TILC)

Translation Proposals

C presents a model for translation: *Smelt ooit van de machtige spitsen / De Libanon-sneeuw*, "Does the snow of Lebanon ever melt from its mighty peaks?"

18.14B

Textual Decisions

In the following rhetorical question of verse 14b, the most problematic issue is the reading זָרִים, "strange," "strange waters" of M. Support for M is found in Aq and Sym according to the Syro-Hexapla, as well as in S, which all read ܢܘܟܪ̈ܝܐ, "strange." The rendering of verse 14b in G: μὴ ἐκκλινεῖ ὕδωρ βιαίως ἀνέμῳ φερόμενον, "does water which is driven violently by the wind deviate?" a rhetorical question to which the expected answer is "no," bears little resemblance to M, but it is at least clear that βιαίως, "violently," is the intended equivalent of the problematic word. It could correspond to a reading צָרִים since in Isa 59.19 נָהָר צָר has been rendered by G with ποταμὸς βίαιος, "a violent river" (Volz 1920, 158), or to a derivation from the root זָרַם, "pour forth in floods." (Schleusner I, 563). The case of the rendering of T מי מטר נחתין, "(so) the waters of rain (shall not cease) coming down," should, according to Sperber (IVB, 328), agree with a reading זֹרְמִים. The same correspondence has been established for the reading of V *erumpentes*, "bursting forth."

Considering the renderings of G, V, and T as due to either a graphical error or to exegesis, the committee preferred M with a C evaluation.

Evaluation of Problems

According to Brockington (206), the reading זֶרֶם, "heavy rain," forms the basis of the translation of NEB: "Will the cool rain streaming in torrents ever fail?" a rendering which, with a minor change of the first word, has been taken over by REB. McKane (430) has sufficiently pointed out both the grammatical and climatological difficulty of such a reading. It can therefore not be recommended to translators.

Remarkably, most modern versions adopt the old conjecture הָרִים, "of the mountains," defended in BH² and by Penna and Hyatt. So (N)RSV: "Do the mountain waters run dry, the cold flowing streams?" and, with minor variations, GNB, CEV, GrN, TILC. It goes without saying that no textual base for such a rendering exists at all.

If (with, for example, NIV, NJB and BR) M is chosen as the textual basis, it is possible to see here a reference to "rivers of foreign lands" such as Euphrates and Nile (so NJB, note e), or, closer to the geographical context, a reference to the distant sources of the Jordan River.

Translators might prefer the interpretation presented in the Preliminary and Interim Report (4, 235) to the one suggested in CTAT (624). Translations with textual notes should certainly mention the uncertainty of meaning for this sentence of M.

Translation Proposals

Keeping all these caveats in mind, NIV could present a satisfactory translational model: "Do its [that is, Lebanon's] cool waters from distant sources ever cease to flow?"

18.15

Textual Decisions

The second line of this verse in M begins with וַיַּכְשִׁלוּם, "and they made them stumble." The *hiphil* of this reading is only supported by T: ואטעיאונון, "and they have led them astray." G with its rendering καὶ ἀσθενήσουσιν, "and they will fail," Sym with ܘܢܬܬܩܠܘܢ, "and they will stumble" (according to the Syro-Hexapla), V with *et inpingentes*, "and dashing against," and S with ܘܢܬܬܩܠܘܢ, "and they stumble," did not read an object suffix, and they seem to have vocalized the Hebrew consonant form either as a *qal*: וַיִּכְשְׁלוּ or as a *niphal*: וַיִּכָּשְׁלוּ.

Since it is not easy to determine the grammatical subject of the causative verbal form of M, the last one clearly presents the more difficult reading. The committee theorized that, apart from an attempt at facilitating the syntax, G may have wanted to avoid a rendering in which the false gods of the preceding sentence would become the subject of an action directed against Israel. So M received a C evaluation.

Evaluation of Problems

Duhm and Ehrlich favored the *niphal* vocalization, taking the final *mem* with the following word; Giesebrecht and Bright the *qal* vocalization, the latter considering the *mem* (with Dahood 1962, 207–9) as enclitic. The rather weak attestation of M combined with these views of commentators had a considerable impact upon modern translators (RSV, NRSV, NAB, NEB, GNB, CEV, BR).

In spite of the difficulty in ascertaining the antecedent, an effort can nevertheless be made to render M. Two possibilities of translation seem to present themselves: (1) a passive transformation, as in NJV and NJB: "They have been made to stumble in their ways," and (2) a translation in which the idols of the preceding verse are unambiguously stated as the agent (REB, NIV, FC, and GN). The second possibility, being the clearest and the simplest one, may be preferred.

Translation Proposals

The introduction of a relative clause as in NIV may be the most appropriate solution: "(they burn incense to worthless idols) which made them stumble (in their ways)."

18.17

Textual Decisions

In the second sentence of the verse M stands alone in reading אֶרְאֵם, "I will see them," "back and not face I will see them." All the versions, G with δείξω αὐτοῖς, V with *ostendam eis*, S with ܐܚܘܐ ܐܢܘܢ, and T with אחזינון, show renderings which testify to a *hiphil* vocalization: "I will show them," "I will show them my back and not my face."

Since this case was not submitted to the committee, no textual decisions were made.

Evaluation of Problems

The uniformity of the versions is rather surprising in view of the monolithic character of the Masoretic textual tradition. Kennicott and de Rossi do not quote a single witness with a *patah* vocalization. The Bible editions of Halle and Minḥat Shay do not contain notes on this word. The information on which BHS and some commentaries base themselves, when they attribute the vocalization with *patah* to the "Oriental tradition," is unknown. According to Ginsburg the reading is found in manuscript London BL Or 1474, but this is a late witness from the end of the 16th century and without any special authority.

It is probably due to the great influence of V and Luther together that the reading of the versions has imposed itself upon the vast majority of commentators and translators.

If, in contrast with the translational tradition, translators want to follow M, a correct understanding of M is obligatory. In fact, the preceding words

עֹרֶף וְלֹא־פָנִים, "back and not face," should be analyzed as an accusative of limitation: "it is only a back-view and not a front-view that I shall have of them" (Joüon and Muraoka, §126g). This means that in the day of disaster, when the Lord scatters them before their enemies, he will look upon the back of these fugitives.

Translation Proposals

NJV can be cited as a model for an interpretation and rendering of M: "I will look upon their back, not their face, / In their day of disaster." As in NJV, the variant translation of the versions, based on a change in vocalization, should be mentioned in a footnote.

18.18

Textual Decisions

In the second exhortation of this verse, M reads בַלָּשׁוֹן, "with the tongue," "Come, let us strike him with the tongue." M is supported by 4Q-a, G, and V, and, indirectly, by the paraphrase of T: "Come, and let us bear false witness against him." The only variant reading is presented by S: ܒܠܫܢܗ, "with his tongue" (that is, Jeremiah's tongue), or "because of his tongue." This rendering has frequently been considered original, in which case M was the victim of either haplography (the word following our expression beginning with *waw*; Rudolph, 122) or a wrong interpretation of the initial preposition בּ (Ehrlich, 290–91).

However, the committee considered it very improbable that S would be the only witness of the original proto-Masoretic tradition, and it judged the pronominal suffix in Syriac to be explicit interpretive information provided by the translator. This consideration led to a B evaluation of M.

Evaluation of Problems

A very literal translation of M, such as has been supplied by BR, RSV, and NJV: "Let us smite (strike) him with the tongue," may have the advantage of maintaining the threat to Jeremiah's life that is possibly contained in the verb of M. It may have the disadvantage of not being very idiomatic in the receptor language. The same applies to partly modernized versions such as NIV: "let's attack him with our tongues."

On the other hand, linguistic paraphrases of the supposed meaning of the Hebrew idiom may take several forms, depending on which component of the meaning is put in focus. Emphasis could be given, as is done by T, to "slander" (so NJB) or to "bringing charges against" (so NRSV, GNB, NEB, and REB). If translators judge a lengthy paraphrase still to be acceptable, they could even add the component of threat to life, as has been done in TOB and FC.

From the textual decisions above, it is clear that S should not be followed, on textual grounds, as done by NAB. However, the interpretation of S according to which Jeremiah's own words are used against him is possible, although not likely. It has become the basis of some recent versions, such as GN.

Translation Proposals

FC is a good model of explicit translation: *Portons-lui un coup fatal par une campagne de dénigrement*, "let's demolish him by means of a campaign of defamation."

19.1A

Textual Decisions

The introduction to the divine speech in M reads כֹּה אָמַר יְהוָה, "Thus said the Lord." The first word, כֹּה, "thus," has the support of V, S and T. G, however, has the rendering τότε, "then," and it has been considered possible that this rendering would reflect a Hebrew Vorlage אָז (Ziegler 1958, 22). The committee judged, however, that G's rendering instead displays the intention of the translator to establish a connection with the preceding discourse unit and that the absence of such a conjunction in M witnesses its primitive character. M received a B evaluation.

Following יְהוָה, six manuscripts of Kennicott, the first hand of four others, as well as the Soncino editions of the Prophets (1486) and of the Bible (1488) have the reading אֵלַי, "to me." The same reading is reflected in the renderings of G and S and in some of the later Targum editions. V and T confirm M in the absence of such a reading. If the reading אֵלַי was present in the pre-Masoretic tradition, it is hard to understand why it was suppressed at a later stage. It is comprehensible, however, that translators felt the need to make the addressee of the message explicit. Here also, M received a majority B vote.

Evaluation of Problems

Since the new unit is speaking about Jeremiah in the third person, Volz (205) considers אלי to be an abbreviation of אֶל־יִרְמְיָהוּ, "to Jeremiah," and he is followed in this by Penna, Steinmann, and Weiser. Among the few translations that were influenced by this conjecture is NJB: "Then Yahweh said to Jeremiah," which also states in a footnote that it is following G with its rendering "Then."

For source-oriented translations of the literal and philological type it is preferable, however, to keep the minimal introduction of M, which clearly shows the "seams" of the text. This may even be preferred by receptor-oriented translations, at least when the context seems to make the addressee sufficiently clear. Otherwise, all information requested by the receptor language can be made explicit (GNB, FC, GN), if not on textual, at least on translational grounds.

Translation Proposals

For the first approach the minimal reading of CEV: "The Lord said:" can be quoted, and for the second one GN: *Der Herr befahl Jeremiah*, "The Lord told Jeremiah."

19.1B

Textual Decisions

Two nominal clauses: (וּמִזְּקְנֵי הַכֹּהֲנִים) וּמִזְּקְנֵי הָעָם, "and from the elders of the people (and from the elders of the priests)," form the second part of verse 1 in M. As to the initial *waw*, M is only supported by Jerome in the lemma of his commentary, *et de senioribus populi*, "and from the elders of the people," whereas in V the initial conjunction has been omitted: *a senioribus populi et a senioribus sacerdotum*, so that the two nominal clauses could be connected with the verb *accipe*, "take," used in the first part of the verse: "take a . . . flask from the elders. . . ."

It should be noted that the conjunction is also lacking in Kennicott manuscripts 112 and 150, in de Rossi manuscript 174, and in the first hand of two others (305, 440), as well as in the Soncino editions of the Prophets (1486) and of the Bible (1488).

With the exception of V, the versions supply the verbal information they judge necessary between the first conjunction and the first noun. So G: ἄξεις, "you shall bring," S: ܕܒ ܠܘܬܟ, "take with you," and T: תדבר עמך, "take with you."

In view of the presence of the conjunction *waw*, the committee did not consider it very likely that M had suffered the loss of a verb. Taking into account the absence of the conjunction in certain witnesses, however, it only assigned a B evaluation to M.

Evaluation of Problems

From Vogel, in his notes on Grotius, to McKane, a Hebrew Vorlage ולקחת (אתך) , "and take (with you)," was reconstructed and defended. A number of modern versions supply this information in footnotes, on textual grounds (so, for example, NRSV, NEB, NJB, and FC).

Even if one does not want to go as far as Rudolph by speaking about M as an "intolerable zeugma" (124), one must recognize that a literal rendering of M as presented in BR is deprived of any sense in the receptor language. The only way to render M, although not without difficulty, is to adopt the exegetical option of Rashi as is done by Chouraqui: *Avec des anciens du peuple, des anciens desservants, achète une gargoulette en grès, du potier,* "With the elders of the people, the elders of the priests, buy a jug of stoneware, from the potter."

If translators do not want to follow this interpretational option, their only option is to supply a verb of "taking," as do the versions, on translational grounds, and as has been done in the majority of translations (NJV, NIV, RSV, REB, CEV, NAB).

Translation Proposals

CEV with its rendering "then take along some of the city officials and leading priests" can be considered a solution in this respect.

3

JEREMIAH 21–30

21.7

Textual Decisions

After having referred to King Zedekiah with the accusative marker אֵת, M uses וְאֶת to connect to his officials and the people, and connects to a group which is described as "those of this city who have escaped the plague, the sword and the famine" with a third וְאֶת. This connecting in M is confirmed by Aq according to the Syro-Hexapla: . . . ܘ ܠܐܝܠܝܢ, "and those who . . ."; καὶ τοὺς according to Ziegler's Greek retroversion; by V: *et qui*, "and who"; and by the original text of T, found in the oldest and best manuscripts, such as Urbinates I and Reuchlinianus: וית, "and those who."

The accusative connection וְאֶת is lacking in nine Hebrew manuscripts. Two of these, 24 and 596, belong to the collection of de Rossi, who signals that the omission was corrected afterward. The same applies to the only one of the seven Kennicott manuscripts which could be checked (Paris BN hébr 2). The connection is also lacking in G and S and in two Yemenite manuscripts and Felix de Prato's edition of T, which therefore make the following information a qualification of "people."

The committee considered the omission to be a widely spread syntactical facilitation and it accorded a B evaluation to M.

Evaluation of Problems

Hitzig was the first to propose the deletion of וְאֶת and he has been followed by almost all modern scholars and translations. Only NJB provides a formal correspondence translation of M.

This in no way means that all modern translations follow the textual decision to omit וְאֶת. Most likely, the textual problem is of no interpretational and translational relevance at all. In fact, Noldius (293) has correctly classed this verse with nine others of the book in which the conjunction *waw* has the explicative meaning "namely." The only effect on translation that might be caused by the absence or presence of וְאֵת would be that, in the first case, the qualification which follows concerns only the people whereas, in the second case, the epexegetical remark could also refer back to the other groups mentioned—to the king and officials.

Recent translations are divided into those which only relate the qualification to the last group (NAB, NIV, GNB, GN, GrN, FC) and those which establish a relation with all categories (NEB, REB, CEV, NJV, NRSV).

Translation Proposals

The last interpretation could be expressed, as in NJV, by the use of two dashes: "—those in this city who survive the pestilence, the sword, and the famine—" or by an explicit mention of "all," as in REB: "all in this city who survive pestilence, sword and famine."

22.6

Textual Decisions

The last word of this verse reads נוֹשָׁבָה, "(towns not) inhabited" in the *qere*, and all the existing versions, G, V, S, and T, have a plural. The *ketiv*, on the other hand, vocalizes the consonant form as נוֹשָׁבָה, which has sometimes been considered as representing a singular.

In the footsteps of Bauer-Leander (315o and 384c), the committee judged the latter form to be a survival of the ancient third-person plural feminine, abandoned at a later time, when it could no longer be distinguished from the identical and more-recent form of the third-person singular feminine. In the absence of any semantic distinction between *ketiv* and *qere*, both forms received an A evaluation.

Evaluation of Problems

It is no doubt the misinterpretation of the *ketiv* which has led some recent versions, such as RSV and NRSV, to the "correction": "an uninhabited city." The same is done in NAB, which in its textual notes more precisely records the consequential change of the plural עָרִים, "towns," into the singular עִיר, "town." As indicated by the textual decisions, however, there is no need for any correction of a "slip of the pen" (Holladay, 583).

Moreover, a plural or singular distinction would only be of importance for a literal translation. A functional equivalent type of translation might prefer to make a stylistic adaptation to the singular in this context, for translational, not textual, reasons.

Translation Proposals

A literal translation, marking the comparison, could take NIV as a model: "I would surely make you like a desert, like towns not inhabited." A functional equivalent rendering could follow FC as an example: *je ferai de toi un désert, une cité morte*, "I will make you into a desert, a dead town." Compare also CEV: "as a ghost-town."

22.16

Textual Decisions

After the first sentence of the verse, which states that Jehoiakim's father defended the cause of the poor, M concludes with אָז טוֹב, "then it was well." The same words, at the same place and in the same form, are confirmed by 4Q-a. They are also attested in S: ܗܘܐ ܘܛܒ, "and it was well," and T: בכין הוה טב, "then it was well." On the other hand, Kennicott quotes five Hebrew manuscripts which add לוֹ, "with him," "then it was well with him." The same plus, in the form of αὐτῷ, is found in Th, Aq, and Sym, and in the form of *in bonum suum*, "to his benefit," in V. As to G, it has frequently been stated that these words are lacking in the Old Greek, but it should be noted that G offers a totally different redaction of verses 15b and 16a, as can be seen from the following English translation: "They do not eat and they do not drink. It would have been better for you to execute judgment and justice. They did not understand, they did not judge the cause of the afflicted nor the cause of the poor."

The committee considered the literary traditions of M and G distinct enough to avoid any kind of mutual contamination. The plus of the other Greek versions and V was judged to be an assimilation to the parallel expression at the end of verse 15: אָז טוֹב לוֹ, "then it was well with him." Therefore a B evaluation was attributed to M.

Evaluation of Problems

From Oort to the apparatus of BHS deleting the second sentence of verse 16 as an intrusion from verse 15 was proposed. This proposal has been followed by some translators, as is witnessed by LV, W, and, in English, by Moffatt and NEB. Among recent versions, NEB stands alone and it has been corrected by REB.

The probability, launched by van Selms (274), of a possible refrain in which, through an auditory error, לוֹ, "with him," fell out because of the following הֲלוֹא, "is that not," is better rejected, and no harmonization of the two formulas of 15b and 16a should be undertaken, neither in a literal way such as "it went well with him" (NAB 15b and 16a), nor with stylistic variation as in GNB: "and he prospered in everything he did" (15b) and "and all went well with him" (16a). The distinction between the practice of justice as profitable to a person (15b) and the same practice as assuring social peace and prosperity (16a) should be maintained in translation.

Translation Proposals

For a close-correspondence translation, NIV can be quoted: "so all went well with him" (15b) and "so all went well" (16a). For a more functional equivalent translation, still keeping formal correspondences, see FC: *et il s'en portait bien*, "and therefore he prospered," and *et on s'en trouvait bien*, "and they were all the better for it."

22.23

Textual Decisions

It is the first verb of the second line of this verse in M: נֵחַנְתְּ, usually translated "(how) you will groan," which has presented problems of interpretation and translation. G renders its Vorlage with καταστενάξεις, "you will sigh," V with *congemuisti*, "you groaned deeply," and S with ܐܬܬܢܚܬܝ, "you are groaning." All these versions presuppose a derivation from the Hebrew root אנח, "to groan"—more precisely, a reading נֶאֱנַחְתְּ, proceeding from נֶאֱנַחְתְּ (Bauer and Leander, 351), and therefore a metathesis, a permutation of consonants *ḥet* and *nun* with regard to the reading of M. On the other hand, the rendering of T: תעבדין(מה-), "(what) will you do," shows all the marks of a contextual improvisation, probably due to lexical ignorance.

Although the committee agreed on an interpretation "(how) you will groan," it was divided with regard to the metathesis. Half of the committee considered the metathesis phonologically justifiable; the other half judged the reading of M to be the result of a scribal error. Therefore, a C evaluation was given to both M and the Vorlage of the versions.

Evaluation of Problems

Although most modern versions follow the interpretational decision noted above, other solutions have nevertheless been proposed. One of these is to see in M a *niphal* conjugation of the Hebrew verb חנן, "be gracious," "have pity." This was the option chosen by Arius Montano already in his Latin version of the Antwerp Polyglot and by Yefet ben Eli. Such a derivation is found, for example, in NJV: "How much grace will you have," evidently with many ironical overtones, and most likely also in GNB: "but how pitiful you'll be," which seems to follow the translational gloss of BDB or the evidence of comparative Semitic philology (Jean and Hoftijzer, 92). However, the initial vowel *seré* in M is difficult to explain if the verbal form were to be derived from חנן; furthermore, no other *niphal* conjugation of this verb is attested in Hebrew. On the other hand, recent studies have revealed the existence of a Ugaritic root *nḥn* with the meaning "to groan" (Dahood 1962, 55–79). The probability of the interpretation proposed by the committee has therefore been reinforced.

Translation Proposals

A rendering as found in REB: "how you will groan when pains come on you," can therefore be a good model. Apodictic textual notes as given in NJB and NRSV are better avoided.

23.8

Textual Decisions

The problem in this verse is with the last verb of the relative clause, הֲדַחְתִּים, "I had driven them," "out of all the lands where I had driven them," particularly with the first-person singular in a context which speaks about the Lord in the third person. The first-person reading of M is confirmed by the insertion between verses 6 and 9 of ἐξῶσα αὐτούς, "I had driven them," in the Lucianic recension of G; *eieceram eos*, "I had driven them," in V; and דאגליתינון, "where I had exiled them," in T. On the other hand, G which renders verses 7–8 at the end of chapter 23, has the third-person singular ἐξῶσεν αὐτούς, "he had driven them," which was followed in this by manuscripts Cavensis and Toletanus of the Vulgate: *eiecerat eos*, "he had driven them." S stands alone with its rendering in the passive voice ܐܬܒܕܪܘ, "where they were dispersed."

The committee considered the reading of G to be a contextual assimilation and "he had driven them" to be an assimilation to the parallel Jer 16.15 M: הִדִּיחָם. S was judged to be a liberty taken by the translator, and M received a B evaluation, because it is the more difficult reading.

Evaluation of Problems

From Giesebrecht until, most recently, Holladay, many commentators adopted the assimilation of G, and, as witnessed by the footnotes, many modern versions as well (NEB, REB, NJB, RSV, NRSV). In fact, only NJV and NAB follow M, and in the NAB a dash in front of the last relative clause tries to compensate for the grammatical harshness of the translation.

It will be evident, however, that in most languages verse 8 in M cannot be rendered meaningfully without some kind of pronominal harmonization. No doubt the easiest way is to use a third-person pronoun for translational reasons, without making a textual reference in a footnote (so, for example, NIV, GN, FC).

However, since so much emphasis is placed on the nonassimilation of the present form, one could also consider, especially in functional equivalent translations, introducing the Lord as speaker of the whole verse (so GNB, CEV), for translational reasons.

Translation Proposals

In the first instance, verse 8 may be rendered as in NIV: "but they will say, 'As surely as the Lord lives, who brought the descendants of Israel up out of the land of the north and out of all the countries where he had banished them.' " In the second case, GNB is an appropriate example: "Instead, they swear by me as the living God who brought the people of Israel out of a northern land and out of all the other countries where I had scattered them."

23.10

Textual Decisions

M reads אָלָה, "curse," "because of a curse the land mourns," in the second line of this verse. This reading is confirmed by Aq, who renders M with ܪܕܠܚ, "(because) of malediction," according to the Syro-Hexapla. It is also attested by the Origen recension of G: ὅρκου, "oath," as well as by V: *maledictionis*, "of malediction." T, moreover, with its reading מומי דשקר, "oaths of falsehood," can only be considered a paraphrase of M. G, on the other hand, reads τούτων, "of these," "for because of these the land mourns," evidently vocalizing the Hebrew consonant form as אֵלֶּה, and it is followed in this by S: ܗܠܝܢ. The same vocalization is found in codex 295 of de Rossi and in the first hand of his codex 715.

The committee noted, however, as does I. Meyer (117f), that the different vocalization in G had taken place in a different literary context, for the first line of the verse is absent from G, having probably fallen out through *homoioarcton* (an identical beginning); and τούτων, "these," therefore refers back to the last two complements of verse 9: the Lord and the excellence of his glory. The reading of M was considered to be anchored in the proto-Masoretic tradition and received four B and two C evaluations.

Evaluation of Problems

Cappel already judged the vocalization behind G to be not less suitable than the one in M (1684, 527b). Since then, it has been adopted by many commentators, most recently by McKane (570). A number of recent translations do the same, either taking "these" to refer back to the "adulterers" in the preceding line, as in NEB and REB: "and because of them the earth lies parched" (so also NAB: "on their account the land mourns"), or taking "because of these (things)" as a logical connector, as in FC: *Voilà pourqoi la terre est en deuil*, "For that reason the land mourns." The first two translations do not provide a textual note as the last two do.

Most modern versions, however, are in agreement with the textual decisions outlined above. It seems to be sound exegesis to consider the curse a malediction from the Lord for the people's having transgressed the regulations of the covenant. Some translators may want to make such a link more explicit.

Translation Proposals

NJB can be taken as a model: "yes, because of a curse, the country is in mourning." Or, if more explicit information is wanted, GNB: "Because of the Lord's curse the land mourns." A textual note with the variant translation of G should certainly be supplied in projects with Orthodox participation.

23.17

Textual Decisions

After an introductory "They keep saying," M has the following two words, לִמְנַאֲצַי דִּבֶּר, the first of which indicates the addressees: "to those who despise me"; the second one, "says," being the verb of a new sentence: "(The Lord) says." The reading and division of M is followed in V: (*dicunt*) *his qui blasphemant me locutus est* (*Dominus*), "(They say) to those who blaspheme me: (the Lord) says," and also in the paraphrase of T: (אמרין בנבואת שקרהון) לדמרגזין קדמי מליל (יי), "(They say in their false prophesy) to those who provoke anger before me: (The Lord) has spoken." On the other hand, Babylonian manuscript Eb 22 vocalizes the first word as in M, but the second one as דְּבַר, "word," no doubt influenced by the frequency of the expression דְּבַר יהוה, "the word of the Lord." G does the same, and in addition vocalizes the first word as לִמְנַאֲצַי without a first-person singular object suffix: (λέγουσι) τοῖς ἀπωθουμένοις τὸν λόγον κυρίου, "(They say) to them who reject the word of the Lord." According to CTAT (643), S seems to vocalize as manuscript Eb 22 does, but this statement is hard to confirm. S has the following reading: ܐܡܪܝܢ ܠܐܝܠܝܢ ܕܡܪܓܙܝܢ ܒܡܠܬܗ ܕܡܪܝܐ, "(And they say) to them who provoke to anger with the word of the Lord." No period can be put after the participle since the verb is constructed here with the preposition ܒ. Therefore, S seems to follow G, as correctly indicated in the versional apparatus of the Jeremiah edition of HUB and as was seen already by Ehrlich (303).

The committee considered the vocalization of Eb 22 to be a first step toward the facilitating reading of G, and it judged the unusual reading דִּבֶּר יהוה, "says the Lord," to be an avoidance of placing an oracle: דְּבַר יהוה, "the word of the Lord," in the mouths of false prophets, by quoting verses 35 and 37 in the same chapter, where the same unusual reading is used. M received three B and three C evaluations.

Evaluation of Problems

Houbigant is not the only one of whom it can be said that he adopted the reading of G surreptitiously. Many important recent versions, such as (N)RSV, NEB, and REB do exactly the same, as shown by their renderings without any comment; for instance: "They say to those who spurn the word of God." This kind of procedure is only acceptable when the translation is defined as being based on the unvocalized Hebrew text exclusively. Some recent translations, such as NAB and FC, justify their adoption of G in a textual note.

A few translations, NJB, NJV, and NIV, clearly follow M; even in the restructured form of some recent functional equivalent translations, such as CEV, GN, and GrN, the textual base of M remains visible.

Although it may be attractive to follow G in projects with Orthodox participation, it is recommended to render M and explain the variant reading of G in a footnote.

Translation Proposals

NIV can be taken as one of the models: "They keep saying to those who despise me, 'The Lord says: you will have peace.'"

23.26

Textual Decisions

After a first interrogative: "How long?" M continues with a second interrogative sentence: הֲיֵשׁ בְּלֵב, "Is there in the heart (of the prophets) . . . ?" an anacoluthon. None of the versions has rendered the interrogative particle הֲ before יֵשׁ. They all render one interrogative sentence, G: (ἕως πότε) ἔσται ἐν καρδίᾳ (τῶν προφητῶν), "(How long) will there be in the hearts (of the prophets)?" V: (*usquequo*) *istud in corde est* . . . , "(How long) will that be in the heart . . . ?" and T: עד אמתי) אית בליבהון), "(How long) shall this be in their hearts?" S does the same, but reads in addition ܒܦܘܡܗܘܢ, "in their mouths," instead of "in the heart."

The committee considered the last reading a translational liberty, and it regarded the nontranslation of the interrogative particle in the versions as an apparent syntactical facilitation. M received a B evaluation.

Evaluation of Problems

Because the sentence(s) remains grammatically unsatisfactory, it is not surprising that several emendations have been proposed. The least radical one is the proposal made by Duhm and recently taken up again by Holladay (641) to redistribute the consonants of M so as to read הֲיָשֻׁב לֵב, "can the hearts (of the prophets) return . . . ?" According to Brockington (207), this was the reading on which NEB was based: "How long will it be till they change their tune, these prophets who . . . ?" REB has abandoned this base. Without any textual note, this emendation is still the preferred reading of NRSV: "How long? Will the hearts of the prophets ever turn back . . . ?"

Another, more drastic, emendation which reached translation is the proposal of Rudolph (154) to read הַשְׁמִי, "my name," instead of הֲיֵשׁ, "is there?" It has been taken over by NAB: "How long will this continue? Is my name in the hearts of the prophets who . . . ?"

For translators, it is clearly advisable to give the best possible interpretation of M. If the interrogative particle הֲ is considered to be superfluous and one interrogative sentence is rendered, several solutions present themselves. One is to provide a grammatical object of the verb "to be," as done in RSV: "How long shall there be lies in the heart of the prophets . . . ?" Another one would be to take בְּלֵב to mean "in the midst of" (van Selms, 289). This is apparently the solution adopted in NJB: "How long are there to be those among the prophets (who prophesy lies . . .)?"

The best solution, however, is to analyze verse 26 as consisting of two interrogative sentences and to take the initial הֲ of verse 27 as an interrogative particle like הֲ in verse 26. This is most consistently done in NJV: "How long will there be in the minds of the prophets (who prophesy falsehood—the prophets of their own deceitful minds—the plan to make My people forget My name, by means of the dreams they tell each other, just as their fathers forgot My name because of Baal?)." In most languages, however, the span of verses 26 and 27 will be too large for an acceptable flow of information.

Translation Proposals

FC can be taken as a clear model: *Jusqu'à quand en sera-t-il ainsi? Qu'y a-t-il dans l'esprit de ces prophètes, quand ils proclament ce qui est faux, ce qui n'est qu'invention trompeuse?* "How long will this continue to be? What do these prophets have in mind, when they proclaim what is false, what is only a deceitful invention?"

23.33

Textual Decisions

When the question is raised: "What is the message of the Lord?" Jeremiah is, according to M, supposed to answer אֶת־מַה־מַשָּׂא, "What message?" M has been paraphrased by V in the following way: *ut quid vobis onus,* "What does this burden matter to you?" It has been freely rendered in S: ܡܢܐܝܟܘܢ ܗܘ ܡܠܬܐ

ܢܒܘܬܐ (Codex Ambrosianus), "This is the word of the Lord," and in T: כדין נבואתא, "(you shall say to them) according to this prophesy." G, however, renders: ὑμεῖς ἐστε τὸ λῆμμα, "You are the burden," which presupposes a reading אַתֶּם הַמַּשָּׂא or אַתֶּמָה מַשָּׂא (Wernberg-Møller, 315–16), with a redistribution of consonants. Since the definite article is rather appropriate, the first reconstruction seems the most likely one. This is also the reading of the Old Latin, preserved by Jerome: *vos estis onus*, "you are the burden," which has entered the Clementine edition of the Vulgate.

The majority of the committee considered M to be the result of a theological correction to avoid the idea that anything could be a "burden" to the Lord. A majority C vote was therefore given to G. Two C votes went to M, since it was felt by two members that the fine irony of M could hardly have been introduced after the clear and straightforward reading אַתֶּם הַמַּשָּׂא.

Evaluation of Problems

From Houbigant to McKane (599), the Vorlage of G was generally adopted and, with it, the wordplay on the two homonyms spelled מַשָּׂא—one with the meaning "utterance," the other with the meaning "burden." As one might expect, the vast majority of translations up till recent times (even BR) follows such a Vorlage.

Only three versions (NJV, NIV, and Chouraqui) render M, understanding the "virtually inexplicable" (Holladay, 647) particle אֶת to mean "as to" (compare Waltke and O'Connor, 11.2.4), even if they do not translate it. Repeating the same question in an ironical way is certainly an acceptable stylistic device. Puns on homonyms can hardly be translated, however, and it should not be suggested that "burden" is a supplementary component of meaning of the homonym for "utterance" or "oracle." McKane's translation "burdensome word"—"burden" contradicts the sound warning he gives later (599). If no approximation can be made in translation, a footnote about the pun can be provided, as in GNB, GN, and GrNa. In projects with Orthodox participation, it seems preferable to render the Vorlage of G (which in Rashi is surprisingly identical with his interpretation of M!).

Translation Proposals

CEV has kept some assonance to hint at the pun: "Jeremiah, when a prophet or a priest or anyone else comes to you and asks, 'Does the Lord have *news* for us?' tell them, 'You people are a *nuisance* to the Lord, and he will get rid of you.'" If M is chosen as the textual base, NIV could be taken as a model: "When these people, or a prophet or a priest, ask you, 'What is the oracle of the Lord?' say to them, 'What oracle? I will forsake you, declares the Lord.'"

23.39

Textual Decisions

This verse begins in M with וְנָשִׁיתִי אֶתְכֶם נָשֹׁא, which could be taken to mean, "I will surely forget you" (Radaq). In the Leningrad and Aleppo Codexes the pointing as *shin* is protected by a *masorah parva* as a hapax. There is no further support for M. De Rossi signals the reading ונשׂיתי, "and I will lift up," with *śin*, as occurring in one manuscript (576) as well as in the first hand of four others (26, 304, 667, 815), and the punctuation נשֹׂא of the infinitive absolute in six manuscripts (174, 226, 411, 554, 596, 815) and in the first hand of eight others. It is this pointing as *śin* which is followed by G for the first verbal form: λαμβάνω, "I take up." G has not translated the infinitive absolute which is found in the asterisked addition ὑμᾶς λήμματι, "you as a burden" in the Origen and Lucianic recensions, attributed in the Marchalianus manuscript to Aq and Sym (for the dative case λήμματι as a rendering of the Hebrew infinitive absolute, see Thackeray, 48). It is this same pointing as *śin* which is presupposed by V: *tollam vos portans*, "I will lift you up, carrying you," and in S: ܐܢܐ ܡܛܥܢ ܐܛܥܢܟܘܢ, "I will lift you up." T with its rendering ואַרטוש יתכון מרטש, "I will surely drive you out," seems to have ignored the meaning of M and to have taken refuge in a contextually appropriate rendering.

For the majority of the committee, the pointing of the versions was preferred, with a C evaluation, and M was considered to be a theological correction, as described in the preceding textual problem.

Evaluation of Problems

In the absence of virtually any defense of M, the majority of modern Jewish and Christian versions follow the correction of *shin* to *śin* as proposed by the committee. They generally do so while also providing rather extensive textual footnotes in which a rendering of M is excluded. The only notable exception is REB which, apart from its translation "I myself shall carry you like a burden," gives the variant rendering in a footnote, "forget you" (with some manuscripts). No modern version seems to have embraced the hypothesis of Zolli (307–9) that a meaning "to seize" can be ascribed to M on the basis of Akkadian *nashu*.

The only two modern translations which render M with the sense of "to forget" are NJV and NIV. Both translations render the following verb of M, נָטַשׁ, with "cast out," "cast away." If "to forget" is selected as the meaning of נָשָׁה, however, it seems better to prefer the meaning "to abandon" for נָטַשׁ.

Translators can, therefore, be advised to render the correction of M, especially in projects with Orthodox participation and to provide a footnote on the text of M which they may present as a variant reading and translation.

Translation Proposals

CEV with its rendering: "I will pick you up and throw you far away" is an appropriate model for translation.

24.9

Textual Decisions

After quoting the Lord as saying: "I will make them a horror," M continues with לְרָעָה, "a disaster." According to the Syro-Hexapla, Aq and Sym support M with their reading εἰς κακά, "for evil," the same reading found in the Lucianic recension of G at the end of verse 9a. M also has the support of V: *adflictionemque*, "and (I will hand them over to) suffering," of S: ܠܒܝܫܬܐ, "and to evil," and of T: לביש, "for evil." The only differences are that S, immediately preceding the rendering of לרעה, has added even a third item: ܠܙܘܥܐ, "and for trembling." In G, however, the translation of לְרָעָה is lacking.

The committee noted that לְרָעָה, "for evil," matches לְטוֹבָה, "for good," in verses 5 and 6. It also considered לְרָעָה, even if it were a gloss, as an essential component of the proto-Masoretic tradition, and it therefore assigned a B evaluation to M.

Evaluation of Problems

Movers (32), taking into account that the expression is lacking in the parallel texts 15.4, 29.18, and 34.17, eliminated it in 24.9 as an interpolation. Others, such as Ewald and more recently Rudolph (156), considered the expression to be an erroneous dittography of the preceding word, לְזַוֲעָה, "to a fright," and they omitted it for this reason. Lastly, McKane (617) deleted it as disturbing the string of the preceding and following words.

With so much scholarly consensus, it is not surprising that many modern versions, such as RSV, NAB, NEB, and REB, omit the word in their renderings, basing their decision on G. In projects with Orthodox participation, translators may be tempted to do the same.

For good reasons, however, M can be preferred as textual base.

Translation Proposals

NJB could be a model for literal translation: "I shall make them an object of horror, a disaster," and CEV for functional equivalent translation: "I will punish them with a terrible disaster."

25.9

Textual Decisions

At the end of this verse the Lord states that he will make the land and its inhabitants an object of hissing, וּלְחָרְבוֹת, "and ruin (forever)." This reading of M is supported by Aq and Sym who, according to the Syro-Hexapla, have the rendering ܘܠܚܘܪܒܐ, "and a desolation," no doubt a translation of the Greek καὶ εἰς ἐρήμωσιν. The translation of S is identical. M is further attested by V: *et in solitudines*, "and desert places," and by T which reads, according to manuscript Urbinates 1: ולחורבת, "and (everlasting) destruction."

G, however, has the rendering καὶ εἰς ὀνειδισμόν, "and an (everlasting) disgrace," which would normally correspond to a Hebrew Vorlage that reads וּלְחֶרְפַּת.

The committee observed that in 25.18 M (= 32.4 G), where the same elements occur, לְחָרְבָּה has been correctly translated εἰς ἐρήμωσιν, "a desolation." It suggested that the different rendering of G in 25.9 was given in order to avoid the syntactical and semantical difficulty that "ruins" would have both the country and its inhabitants as antecedents. Three B and two C votes were given to M and one C vote to G.

Evaluation of Problems

Many commentators and translators agreed with G that inhabitants can hardly be transformed into ruins; thus the translators of RSV and NAB, with their common rendering "everlasting reproach," and the translators of NEB and NRSV, with their respective translations "a scandal forever" and "an everlasting disgrace."

It can very easily be shown that Hebrew syntax permits coordinating complements, some of which only refer back to some of the antecedents. This, however, is not a help for translators operating in a receptor language, the syntax of which does not allow for such a phenomenon. For them, two possibilities are left. They can either exploit verbs with metaphorical extensions, such as the verb "to ruin" in English (so NJB and REB), or—more likely—they will have to translate the sentence in such a way that the right complement goes with the correct antecedent.

Translation Proposals

For the first solution, REB presents a model: "I shall exterminate them and make them an object of horror and astonishment, ruined forever." For the second one, the antecedent of "ruins" could be specified: "I will exterminate them and make them a desolation, an object of hissing—their land ruins forever."

25.15

Textual Decisions

In this verse Jeremiah receives the order to take from the hand of the Lord the cup of the wine of הַחֵמָה, "of the wrath." This reading of M is supported by Aq with his rendering ܪܘܓܙܐ, "of anger," according to the Syro-Hexapla; by Th and Sym with their translation τοῦ θυμοῦ, "of anger," according to codex 86; by V: *furoris*, "of fury"; S: ܚܡܬܐ, "of rage"; and T: לוֹטָא, "of the curse." G (32.1), on the other hand, has the rendering τοῦ ἀκράτου, "of unmixed (wine)," which seems to presume a consonantal Vorlage הֶחָמֶר in Hebrew. This case is dealt with in CTAT (655), but it has been added there, and therefore it was not submitted to the judgment of the committee.

Evaluation of Problems

The consonant Vorlage of G has been adopted by some commentators, such as Oort and Condamin, and in some recent translations. NAB translates with "cup of foaming wine" and bases itself explicitly upon G in a textual note. NEB renders G without comment with "this cup of fiery wine," and GrN does the same by translating *deze beker met bittere wijn*, "this cup with bitter wine."

In the absence of any committee vote, translators could render G, especially in projects with Orthodox participation; however, they may want to consider the fact that G could only have been inspired by Ps 75.9: וְיַיִן חָמַר, "foaming wine," and its Greek translation οἴνου ἀκράτου, "of unmixed wine" (74.9).

Translators rendering M will have to take into consideration the fact that the presence of the definite article before the words "wine" and "wrath" indicates that the last word is in apposition to the first one (so also Gesenius-Kautzsch-Cowley, §131k and Rudolph, 164). The "cup of wine" being so frequently a symbol of the anger of God, they should disregard the attribution of different meanings to the word הַחֵמָה, as has been done by van Selms (II, 18–19): "poisoned cup," or by Chouraqui: *vin de fièvre*, "wine of fever."

Translation Proposals

NJV can be taken as an example: "Take from My hand this cup of wine—of wrath—and make all the nations to whom I send you drink of it."

25.24

Textual Decisions

After having mentioned כָּל־מַלְכֵי עֲרָב וְאֵת, "and all the kings of Arabia," M continues with וְאֵת כָּל־מַלְכֵי הָעֶרֶב, "and all the kings of הָעֶרֶב," the last word having been interpreted in different ways: "mixed peoples," "nomads," "rabble." Both sentences are attested by the Greek recensions of Origen and Lucian and by V, S and T, V interpreting the last word as *occidentis*, "of the West," S as ܕܡܥܪܒܐ, and T as עֲרָבָאֵי, both "of the Arabs."

The first sentence, on the other hand, has been omitted in Kennicott manuscript 145, and the second one in his manuscript 101.

More specific is the case of G (32.10) which has for both sentences only the following rendering: καὶ πάντας τοὺς συμμείκτους, "and all the mixed (people)," or, if συμμείκτους is taken to refer to irregular troops, "and all the soldiers of several nationalities."

The committee judged that G modeled the first sentence of verse 24 after the first one of verse 20 and that M added a doublet in which עֶרֶב was replaced by the הָעֶרֶב of verse 20. It also determined that no witness permits restoring an original reading. Therefore, with a majority C vote, the conflation of M was singled out as representing the proto-Masoretic text.

Evaluation of Problems

By the sole rendering "all the kings of Arabia," NEB and REB pretend, according to their textual note, to render G, which is, as can be seen above, certainly not the case. NAB, by putting "all the kings of Arabia" in square brackets, indicates that it considers the first sentence to be a gloss. It omits the second sentence which it characterizes in the textual notes as a dittography, thereby embracing the hypothesis first launched by Henderson in 1851 and repeated by many others up to Rudolph recently (164), that the second sentence is a dittography of the first one. Occasionally, earlier translators, such as LV, had already taken such a stand.

Translators are encouraged to take the advice of the committee seriously, however, and, with the vast majority of modern versions, render the conflated text of M, attributing one of the meanings given above to the last word. They may even signal the problem in a footnote and state that only the first sentence fits the context.

Translation Proposals

NIV is one of the models that can be used: "all the kings of Arabia and all the kings of the foreign people who live in the desert."

25.34A

Textual Decisions

After the announcement of the days of slaughter, M continues with the hapax וּתְפוֹצוֹתִיכֶם which is probably intended to mean "and I will shatter you." This is the reading of the classical Tiberian text as represented, among others, by the Leningrad and Aleppo Codexes and by the Reuchlin Codex of the Prophets. There are no direct witnesses to such a reading. It can only be noted that both S: ܘܢܬܒܕܪܘܢ, "and you will be shattered," and T: ותתבדרון, "and you will be scattered," have read a verbal form.

In a number of manuscripts, such as MS Petrograd of the Prophets, Erfurt 3, and Urbinates 1, the noun (Bauer and Leander, 599i) vocalization וּתְפוּצוֹתֵיכֶם, "and your dispersions," is found. This vocalization is presupposed by the asterisked rendering of the Origen recension, attributed to Aq, Sym, and Theod: καὶ οἱ σκορπισμοὶ ὑμῶν, "and your scatterings," as well as by *et dissipationes vestrae* of V, which has the same meaning.

In G (32.20), however, a translational equivalent of any Hebrew form is lacking.

The committee considered that G omitted the word because of its unintelligibility and that the vocalization of M was due to a syntactical facilitation. It therefore gave a C evaluation to the nominal form with *shureq* and *ṣerê*.

Evaluation of Problems

From Stade (1881, 68, note 2) to McKane (647, 652f.) and Holladay (677–78) the omission of M, with G, was promoted mainly for reasons of lack of (contextual) meaning. Many modern translations (NEB, REB, NAB, GNB, FC) therefore follow the omission in G as well as the variant reading of G in the last part of this verse (see next case).

The strange form of M is probably a mixed form, combining either a plural noun תפוצות with a verbal form והפיצותי (Kokovzov, 28) or two verbal forms: תָּפוּצוּ, "you shall be scattered," and הֲפִיצוֹתִיכֶם, "and I will scatter you" (Gesenius-Kautzsch-Cowley, §91 l). All Jewish versions (NJV, Chouraqui, BR) follow the first-person singular verb analysis of Saadya (Kutub al-Lughah, 209) as witnessed by NJV: "I will break you in pieces." Christian versions are divided between the noun interpretation, "dispersion(s)" (RSV, NRSV), and the verbal (NJB, NIV, CEV, GN, GrN) interpretation, the latter being mostly in passive voice.

For functional equivalent translation, the distinction between noun and verb analysis is without interest, since a verbal transformation may be required anyway in some receptor languages.

Translation Proposals

Depending upon the way participants are organized in the total discourse, NJV: "I will break you in pieces," or NIV: "(you will fall) and be shattered," can be taken as an example.

25.34B

Textual Decisions

The last sentence of M states that people will fall: כִּכְלִי חֶמְדָּה, "like a precious vase." M has the direct support of Aq and Sym: ὡς σκεῦος ἐπιθυμητόν, "like a precious vessel," and the indirect support of V: (*et cadetis*) *quasi vasa praetiosa*, "and you will fall like precious vases," S: ܘܬܦܠܘܢ ܐܝܟ ܡܐܢܐ ܕܪܓܬܐ, "(and you will fall) like vessels of desire," and T: ותיפלון) דהויתון רגיגין כמני חמדתא, "(and you will fall), you who were coveted like precious vessels." Apart from the paraphrase in T, the only difference between M and V, S, and T is the plural form of the noun in the versions, which should be considered a translational adaptation to the flectional ending of the preceding verb.

G, on the other hand, renders the last sentence with: (καὶ πεσεῖσθε) ὥσπερ οἱ κριοὶ οἱ ἐκλεκτοί, "(and you will fall) like the choice rams" (32.20), which means that οἱ κριοί, "the rams," presupposes a Hebrew reading כְּאֵילִי, "like rams."

The committee considered it unlikely, however, that such a reading could have figured in the Vorlage of G since חֶמְדָּה, "precious," can hardly modify an animal, whereas the expression כלי חמדה is a frequently occurring one (Hos 13.15; Nah 2.10; Dan 11.8; 2 Chr 32.27, 36.10). It therefore considered the rendering of G to be an assimilation to the text of 51.40 (28.40 G). M received a B evaluation.

Evaluation of Problems

From J. D. Michaelis to Holladay and McKane, many commentators adopted the presumed Vorlage of G, כאילי. McKane (651–53) does so after much hesitation, finally preferring the single image of G to the unsatisfactory sequence of "shatter" and "fall" in M. All modern translations which followed the omission of G in the preceding case also endorse G in this one (NEB, REB, NAB, GNB, FC). RSV which accepted M in the foregoing case, adopts G here.

G not being a reliable translational base, translators are encouraged to render M.

Translation Proposals

NIV can serve as a model: "you will fall and be shattered like fine pottery."

25.38

Textual Decisions

After the description of the country as a wasteland, M indicates as the first reason for this as being חֲרוֹן הַיּוֹנָה, "(the) fury of the devastating (one)."

The real textual problem is presented by the first word, but since the second word gives interpretational difficulties, both are treated together for translational purposes. Regarding the first word, M is attested by the rendering ὀργῆς, "of anger," ascribed in the Barberini manuscript to Aq, Sym, and Theod; by V: *irae*, "of anger"; and by S: ܪܘܓܙܗ, "his anger." On the other hand, 21 manuscripts of Kennicott and de Rossi read חֶרֶב, "the sword." This is also the reading of T and G (32.24): μαχαίρας, "of the sword."

Regarding the second word, the form of M is confirmed by the rendering τῆς περιστερᾶς, "of the dove," attributed to Aq, Theod, and Josephus in the Barberini manuscript, as well as by V: *columbae*, "of the dove." In these versions the form יוֹנָה has been interpreted as a noun with the meaning "dove."

The same manuscript offers still another reading for Aq: τεθολωμένης, "muddy," which etymologically seems to presuppose a reading יָוֵן (HUB), and a second reading for Sym: τῆς οἰνωμένης, "of the intoxicated," which assumes an etymological relationship with יַיִן, "wine." The reference to inebriation is also found in the paraphrase of T: "the sword of the enemy, which was like wine that intoxicated."

G, however, renders the second word with τῆς μεγάλης, "of the great," and S with ܕܡܪܝܐ, "of the Lord," probably resuming the translation of the end of verse 37.

The committee voted on the first word only. One member considered חֲרוֹן to be an assimilation to the second חֲרוֹן in the same verse and therefore gave a C evaluation to the reading חֶרֶב, "sword." The other members voted in the same way for M, taking the reading חֶרֶב as an assimilation to the parallels in 46.16 and 50.16.

Evaluation of Problems

The majority of modern versions render חֶרֶב, "sword," and the rendering חֲרוֹן is only found in NJV and NJB. The textual basis of most functional equivalence translations cannot be detected. Only "the horrors of war" in GNB points in the direction of "sword." The second word has been glossed in several ways: "oppressive (wrath)" in NJV; "devastating (fury)" in NJB; "(the sword of) the oppressor" in NIV and REB, where the last word seems to presuppose a vocalization of הַיּוֹנָה; "(the) cruel (sword)" in NEB and NRSV; "(the) sweeping (sword)" in NAB. RSV is the only translation to select the Syriac for the second word: "the sword of the Lord." In fact, it may be that no real problem exists, since חרון היונה may be considered shorthand for חרון חרב היונה, "the fierceness of the oppressive sword," as shown by Isaiah da Trani (Freedman and Rosenberg, 173).

Translation Proposals

GN is one of the possible models of translation: *Alles Land ist zur Wüste geworden durch das furchtbare Schwert*, "The whole country has become a wasteland through the devastating sword."

26.1

Textual Decisions

After an explicit indication of the time of the prophesy, M continues in the following way: הָיָה הַדָּבָר הַזֶּה מֵאֵת יְהוָה, "this word came from the Lord." M has the support of G, V, and T. After the third word, S adds: ܠܐ ܐܪܡܝܐ, "to Jeremiah." It is true that according to the edition of Sabatier the addition *ad Jeremiam*, "to Jeremiah," is also found in Vet Lat. However, Sabatier refers to a quotation of this verse by Jerome in his commentary on the beginning of chapter 27. In Jeremiah's lemma of 26.1, the addition does not figure. In fact, Reiter's critical edition of Jerome clearly shows that no manuscript of Jerome attests this supplementary reading (CSEL, 332,8). It is therefore only confirmed by a very secondary part of the late Latin tradition. For this reason M received a B evaluation, S being considered an assimilation to 27.1.

Evaluation of Problems

Over against the view point of Rudolph (168) that Jeremiah can hardly be missed as the addressee, Ehrlich (310) had already noted that S should not necessarily go back to a Hebrew Vorlage. It is certainly erroneous for NJB to base its addition "to Jeremiah" on Vet Lat, but even the citation of S as a witness in both NJB and NEB can hardly stand in light of what has been said above.

In fact, partisans of literal or philological translation should simply reproduce M, with NJV, RSV, NRSV, NIV, NAB, and REB, especially if they think that the receptor language makes sufficiently clear who the implicit addressee of the prophetic message is. Adherents of functional equivalence translation often make the addressee explicit, as has been done in GNB, CEV, FC, GN, and GrN for example, but without quoting textual evidence for such a procedure.

Translation Proposals

For a literal translation, NRSV could be followed: "this word came from the Lord." A functional equivalence translation could follow GNB: "the Lord said to me," or CEV: "The Lord said: Jeremiah."

27.1

Textual Decisions

The introductory verse to this chapter in M places the following events in the beginning of the reign of יְהוֹיָקִם, "Jehoiakim." This reading is supported by Aq, an asterisked addition of the Origen recension, the Lucianic recension, and by V and T. On the other hand, the second manuscript of Königsberg (Lilienthal, 227ff.), the first hand of the Reuchlin manuscript of the Prophets and the margin of Kennicott manuscript 590 have the reading צִדְקִיָּהוּ, "Zedekiah," also witnessed by S. It is true that the same reading is found in an Arabic manuscript in Oxford, but this translation by Pethion Ibn Ayyub has been made from the Syriac (Frank, 138–39). The whole verse is omitted in G.

The committee considered the replacement of the name Jehoiakim by the name Zedekiah to be a secondary correction influenced by verses 3 and 12. Although it agreed that verse 1 is not original, it regarded such a statement as being dependent on literary, not textual criticism. M, as reflecting the second redaction of the book, therefore received a B evaluation.

Evaluation of Problems

The contradictory statements made above are not very helpful to the translator, and even less to the uninitiated audience. One of the following three solutions can be adopted:

(1) M can be reproduced, as in all Jewish versions (BR, NJV, Chouraqui). This can hardly be done without an explanatory note, either in the form of a neutral textual statement (NJV), or a critical remark, as done in Chouraqui: scribal error for Zedekiah, with reference to 26.1. The note could also take a positive form if Rashi's explanation is given that the prophecy concerns Zedekiah but was communicated to Jeremiah at the beginning of the reign of Jehoiakim (cf. also Schenker, 510f.).

(2) Zedekiah can be substituted for Jehoiakim, with a textual note (RSV, NRSV, NJB, NIV, NEB, CEV, GN, FC).

(3) With Giesebrecht (147), Rudolph (174) and McKane (684–85), the whole of verse 1 according to M can be put in square brackets, and textual and discourse reasons for the secondary character of the whole verse can be given in a footnote (so NAB, which wrongly excludes the last sentence of the verse).

As becomes evident from modern versions, procedure (2) is most widely used, but procedure (3) should be taken into account in projects with Orthodox participation because of the absence of verse 1 in G.

Translation Proposals

If procedure 2 is selected, the note in NIV could serve as model for a textual note: "A few Hebrew manuscripts and Syriac (see also Jer 27:3, 12 and

28:1); most Hebrew manuscripts *Jehoiakim* (most Septuagint manuscripts do not have this verse)." If procedure 3 is adopted, the footnote could state: "This verse is lacking in the Septuagint. Jer 27.1 in Hebrew is most likely a secondary addition which picks up the introduction to the preceding section (26.1). Verses 3 and 12 of chapter 27 clearly indicate that the reported events took place during the reign of King Zedekiah." The two notes could be combined and, with slight adaptations, be provided for any of the solutions used.

27.3

Textual Decisions

This verse begins in M with וְשִׁלַּחְתָּם, "and send them," a word in which the pronominal suffix refers to the thongs and yokes mentioned in verse 2. M is attested by 4Q-c, G (34.2), V, S, and T. The Lucianic recension of G, however, has καὶ ἀποστελεῖς, "and you shall send," omitting αὐτούς, "them." Jerome has done the same, in fact, disregarding the *eas*, "them," of the Vulgate: *et mittes ad regem . . .* , "and send to the king," in his lemma.

The committee considered the omission of the translation of the suffix in the Lucianic recension to be an internal stylistic abbreviation comparable to G's translation of וּנְתַתָּם, "and put them," with καὶ περίθου (περὶ τὸν τράχηλόν σου), "and put (around your neck)," in verse 2. So M received an A evaluation.

Evaluation of Problems

According to their textual notes, a minority of modern versions (NAB, NEB, and REB) follow the Lucianic recension, presupposing a Hebrew Vorlage וְשִׁלַּחְתָּ, "and send." Even McKane, who is in favor of this reading, doubts very much that it could have been based on a Hebrew Vorlage (686).

A majority of English versions follow the same reading without textual justification, taking the verb as having "word" or "message" as its implicit grammatical object or even presupposing (with Hitzig) a Hebrew Vorlage וְשִׁלַּחְתָּ דָבָר, "and send word" (so RSV, NRSV, NIV, GNB, CEV).

The refusal to render M in many modern versions is not so much related to textual matters as it is to interpretation. It has generally been judged improbable that the envoys would have been willing to play such a symbolic role. According to Volz (259), however, such a transmission should be considered *durchaus möglich*, "perfectly possible." Moreover, with Ehrlich (312), one could ascribe a partitive value to the plural suffix: Jeremiah will put some of the thongs and yokes around his neck, and he will divide all the others among the kings. M could hardly imply, as suggested by NJB, that Jeremiah had put all the yokes around his own neck first.

Translation Proposals

BR could be a model for translation: *gib welche auf deinen Hals, sende welche an* . . . , "put some around your neck; send some to. . . ." Compare also TOB: *Tu en mettras sur ton cou, tu en enverras au roi* . . . , "Put some of them around your neck; send others to the king of. . . ."

27.9

Textual Decisions

The third term in a list of five terms for professional diviners is, according to M, חֲלֹמֹתֵיכֶם, "your dreams." This reading of M is only attested by the Greek recensions of Origen and Lucian: ἐνυπνίων ὑμῶν, "your dreams." All other versions have an agent here. G (34.7): τῶν ἐνυπνιαζομένων ὑμῖν, "those who interpret dreams for you"; V: *et somniatores*, "those who have faith in dreams"; S: ܘܚܠܡܝܟܘܢ, "and your dreamers"; and T with its paraphrase: ומן חלמי חלמיכון, "and from the dreams of your dreamers."

In view of the surrounding vocabulary, the committee considered it most likely that this term also concerned an agent. With Ehrlich (312–13), Volz (259), and Holladay (2, 113) it vocalized the Hebrew consonantal form as חַלֹמֹתֵיכֶם, analyzing it as the verbal adjective חָלוֹם, standing for a profession, followed by the Mishnaic plural ending וֹת-, as in Mishnaic דְּרוֹכוֹת, "grape-treaders," לָקוֹחוֹת, "buyers," and so on (Segal, 154ff.; HUB, apparatus 1, note 2). A B evaluation was given to this revocalized form with the meaning "your dreamers."

Evaluation of Problems

No modern version, not even any of the Jewish translations, follows M. NEB has the rendering "your wise women," which is not based upon an emendation such as חֲכָמֹתֵיכֶם (Carroll, 528), but which, according to its note: "*lit.* women who have dreams," takes the feminine plural suffix at its face value. The same is done by REB with its translation "your women dreamers." These translations seem both, in view of Brockington's note on NEB, to be based on a different vocalization, חֹלְמֹתֵיכֶם, the feminine plural participle of the *qal* of חָלַם, "to dream."

The revocalization חַלֹמֹתֵיכֶם is preferable, however, taking the feminine plural suffix as a profession marker, maybe a subdivision of the existing Hebrew abstract marker (Gesenius-Kautzsch-Cowley, §122r). Since "dreamers" is rather vague, a translation may have to focus particularly on the professional activity of dream interpretation.

Translation Proposals

NIV provides a useful example: "So do not listen to your prophets, your diviners, your interpreters of dreams. . . ."

28.1

Textual Decisions

בַּשָּׁנָה הַהִיא בְּרֵאשִׁית מַמְלֶכֶת צִדְקִיָּה מֶלֶךְ־יְהוּדָה בַּשָּׁנָת הָרְבִעִית בַּחֹדֶשׁ הַחֲמִישִׁי,
"In that year, at the beginning of the reign of King Zedekiah of Judah, in the fourth year, in the fifth month"; these are the time indications given in M. It is supported by the Origen and Lucianic recensions of G (35.1) and by V, S, and T. The Old Greek briefly notes: ἐν τῷ τετάρτῳ ἔτει Σεδεκία βασιλέως Ιουδα ἐν μηνὶ τῷ πέμπτῳ, "in the fourth year of Zedekiah, king of Judah, in the fifth month," which could reflect a Hebrew Vorlage: בשנת הרבעית לצדקיה מלך יהודה בחדש החמישי.

The committee considered the data of M as characteristic of the second redaction of the book (Schenker, 512). Although it judged the dating variant of G to be primitive, it related the variant to the literary and not to the textual level. For that reason M received an A evaluation.

Evaluation of Problems

If translators agree with the sophisticated motivation underlying the decision above, they can follow most recent English versions, without (RSV, NRSV, NJV, NJB) or with (NIV) receptor-oriented modifications.

They are certainly not encouraged to adopt the arbitrary translational decisions of NEB and REB, which change the "fourth year" into "the first year," since these are based on the hypothesis of an abbreviated Hebrew text put forward by Driver (1963, 84–87) which is, according to the correct judgment of Janzen (195, note 24) highly improbable.

On the other hand, translators cannot neglect the fact that the content of G is correct, whether it is based on a different Hebrew Vorlage or not. They may want to employ G as a textual base for their translation, especially for reasons of discourse cohesion. This has been done with textual justification in GNB, CEV, and FC; and without a textual note in NAB, GN, and GrNa, a procedure which may be preferred in projects with Orthodox participation.

Translation Proposals

Translators wanting to translate M could use NIV as an example: "In the fifth month of that same year, the fourth year, early in the reign of Zedekiah king of Judah. . . ."

For the second approach, GN could serve as a model: *Im fünften Monat desselben Jahres—es war das vierte Regierungsjahr von Zedekia—*, "In the fifth month of the same year—it was the fourth year of the reign of Zedekiah—."

28.8

Textual Decisions

This verse ends in M with a description of the content of former prophecies. After the mention of "war," the verse concludes with וּלְרָעָה וּלְדָבֶר, "disaster and pestilence." The reading of both terms is attested by the asterisked addition of the recension of Origen and Lucian, ascribed to Aq and Th by Codex Marchalianus: καὶ εἰς κακὰ καὶ εἰς θάνατον, "and concerning evil and death." It is supported by S: ܪܘܚܒܢܐ ܘܕܡܘܬܐ, "and of evil and of pestilence," and T: ולבישא ולמותא, "and of evil and of pestilence."

In G, on the other hand, both words are omitted. V omits only the last word.

As to the first item, de Rossi notes approximately 30 Hebrew manuscripts which have a reading לרעב, preceded or not by the conjunction *waw*, "(and) famine." V presents a conflated rendering *et de adflictione et de fame*, "about affliction and famine," underlined by Jerome's paraphrase: *et adversa et rerum omnium penuriam*, "and disasters and scarcity of everything." V therefore provides a translation of both וּלְרָעָה and וּלְרָעָב.

The committee considered וּלְרָעָה, "and disaster," to be the most stable element in the oldest layers of the textual forms. In view of the frequent occurrence of the triad sword-famine-pestilence, it judged that וּלְרָעָב, "and famine," could only be primary if preceded by חֶרֶב, "sword." Regarding the first expression, M therefore received a B evaluation. A C evaluation was given to M for the last word. Although the absence of both words in G was believed to be primitive, it was also held that the textual support of M for a nonprimitive reading excluded any correction of M.

Evaluation of Problems

From 1551 (Châteillon) until recently, many commentators defended the correction of "disaster" with "famine." They have been followed by a number of translations: RSV, NRSV, GNB, NEB, REB, and BR—usually without textual justification. The arguments developed above, reinforced by those of Rudolph (178) and Holladay (2, 125), do not favor such a procedure.

With the vast majority of all other versions, M should be preferred, and in contrast with the current translational practice, the textual issue should be footnoted. In projects with Orthodox participation, the omission of G could be adopted, in which case a rather exhaustive textual note may be needed to summarize the discussion.

Translation Proposals

If M is adopted, NJV can be taken as a model: "The prophets who lived before you and me from ancient times prophesied war, disaster, and pestilence against many lands and great kingdoms."

28.13

Textual Decisions

In contrast to the information "You broke bars of wood," M has וְעָשִׂיתָ, "but you shall make (bars of iron instead)." The second-person masculine singular is also attested by V: *et facies*, "and you shall make," S: ܬܥܒܕ, and T: ותעביד, both "(and) you shall make."

G (35.13), however, reads the first-person singular: καὶ ποιήσω, "and I will make," making the Lord the agent.

The committee considered the rendering of G as due to wrongly anticipating the content of the next verse, with its first-person verbal form, and it assigned a B evaluation to M.

Evaluation of Problems

Although recent commentators unequivocally defend M, a few modern translations still seem to prefer G. Whereas NEB relegates the reading of G to a textual note as a possibility, RSV, GNB, and CEV overtly adopt the versional evidence; in CEV, the adoption even becomes the basis of a translational restructuring of verses 13–14.

This practice can hardly be advised, and M should be correctly interpreted and rendered (McKane, 713). In fact, the second statement is a kind of automatic implication of the first. Rebellion against Babylon is counterproductive and increases tyranny.

Translation Proposals

NRSV can be quoted as a model: "You have broken wooden bars only to forge iron bars in place of them."

29.1

Textual Decisions

This verse deals with a letter which Jeremiah addresses first of all אֶל־יֶתֶר, "to the rest," of the elders of the exile community. The reading יֶתֶר of M is attested by V: *reliquias*, "remainder," S: ܫܪܟܐ, "remnant," and T: שאר, "rest." It is, however, lacking in the entire Greek text tradition.

The omission in G was considered by the committee as facilitating and motivated by the interpretational difficulties presented by the word יֶתֶר. M received therefore a B evaluation.

Evaluation of Problems

RSV honestly notes that it follows G with the omission of יֶתֶר, "rest." A number of translations, however, adopt G without any footnoting (GNB, FC, TOB, GrNa).

If יֶתֶר is considered original, the problem of its meaning has to be resolved. Already Houbigant, foliowed more recently by Wambacq and (with some hesitation) by Rudolph, suggested that the word might have the meaning "foremost," "leading" or "elite." BHS refers in its apparatus to Gen 49.3, where יֶתֶר seems to have the same sense. This meaning has occasionally been adopted in translation (W). This would imply, however, that only a select group of prominent elders received the letter, which would obviously be in conflict with the wide distribution described in this verse (McKane, 728).

According to van Selms (II, 52) M can only be interpreted as the elders who survived deportation (so NIV, C). The reason for the perishing of many elders remains obscure. Perhaps the exhausting travel to Babylon and the adaptation to exilic conditions made many victims among the aged exiles.

Translation Proposals

Either NEB: "the remaining elders among the exiles," or NIV: "the surviving elders among the exiles," could be taken as a suitable example.

29.19

Textual Decisions

In a context in which third-person plural pronominal suffixes dominate, M ends this verse surprisingly with a verb in second-person plural: שְׁמַעְתֶּם, "you (did not) listen." This reading of M is confirmed by Th: καὶ οὐκ ἠκούσατε, "and you did not listen," V: *et non audistis*, "and you have not heard," and T: ולא קבילתון, "and you did not listen," literally: "receive."

However, most of the Greek witnesses of the recensions of Origen and Lucian which have verses 16–20 (lacking in the Old Greek) render a third-person plural: καὶ οὐκ ἤκουσαν, "and they did not listen." S: ܘܠܐ ܫܡܥܘ ܐܢܘܢ, "and they did not listen," has the same rendering.

Considering the last rendering to be a syntactical facilitation, the committee assigned a C evaluation to M.

Evaluation of Problems

Quite a number of recent versions render a third-person plural, indicating in a footnote that they follow Greek and Syriac evidence (FC, GN), Syriac alone (NRSV), or that they make a conjecture (NJB) or simply do not follow M (NJV).

However, as has been correctly seen by Rudolph (186) and McKane (730), the existence of a different Hebrew Vorlage is extremely doubtful, and a justification based on textual evidence is hardly defensible. Modern translators may therefore be obliged linguistically to make the same contextual harmonization as their remote ancestors. They may particularly be inclined to do so if they consider the sentence "but you did not listen" to be the mechanical repetition of a frequently occurring phrase in Jeremiah—therefore almost a "slip of the pen of Baruch" (van Selms, II, 57).

They cannot do so, however, when they take the pronominal distinctions of M as reflecting different audiences, either "your forefathers and you" (Abarbanel) or the Jerusalem and exilic community (so NEB, REB, NIV). It is far from certain that such a history of apostasy is implied in this verse.

Translation Proposals

It seems preferable to take a translation such as NAB as example: "For they did not listen to my words, says the Lord, though I kept sending them my servants the prophets, only to have them go unheeded."

If the exegesis of the two audiences is adopted, NIV can be used as a possible model: " 'For they have not listened to my words,' declares the Lord, 'words that I sent to them again and again by my servants the prophets. And you exiles have not listened either,' declares the Lord."

29.25

Textual Decisions

According to M the letter of Shemaiah was sent: אֶל־כָּל־הָעָם אֲשֶׁר בִּירוּשָׁלַם, "to all the people in Jerusalem," וְאֶל־צְפַנְיָה בֶן־מַעֲשֵׂיָה הַכֹּהֵן, "and to Zephaniah, son of Maaseiah, the priest," and וְאֶל כָּל הַכֹּהֲנִים, "and to all the priests" —three addressees.

The three groups of M are also attested by V, S, and T. The first and the last addressee have been added in the Greek recensions of Origen and Lucian: πρὸς πάντα τὸν λαὸν τὸν ἐν Ιερουσαλημ, "to all the people in Jerusalem," and καὶ πρὸς πάντας τοὺς ἱερεῖς, "and to all the priests." The Old Greek, however, mentions only the second person: καὶ πρὸς Σοφονίαν υἱὸν Μαασαίου τὸν ἱερέα, "and to Sophonia, son of Maaseiah, the priest" (36.25).

The committee considered the omission of the first and the last group in G as probably deliberate since the following narrative only concerns Zephaniah. Even if M expounded on the text, the initiative would have to be considered literary. So M received an A evaluation.

Evaluation of Problems

Some recent commentators (Bright 206 and Holladay 2, 145) as well as the critcal apparatus of BHS advise translators to omit the first and the last group, with the Old Greek. This advice is followed in NEB and REB which base their translations on G according to their respective footnotes. NJB takes a unique position by mentioning the three groups in the text and placing the last one between parentheses "(and to all the priests)," thereby defining it as a gloss.

It is not advisable to use the Greek evidence in this way, however, especially since in the narration of G no letters are sent at all, but a person! Moreover, it is not unlikely that Shemaiah, in his inquisitorial zeal, sent several letters to several addressees and that only the one to Zephaniah is quoted because Zephaniah communicated its content to Jeremiah.

Translation Proposals

NIV is a useful model for translators: "You sent letters in your own name to all the people in Jerusalem, to Zephaniah son of Maaseiah the priest, and to all the other priests."

29.26

Textual Decisions

"The Lord has made you priest," לִהְיוֹת פְּקִדִים בֵּית יְהוָה, "to be officers (in) the house of the Lord." This is what Shemaiah says to Zephaniah according to M and what (not without difficulty) could be taken to mean "so that there may be officers in the house of the Lord." The plural פְּקִדִים, "officers," is only attested by M. All the versions render a singular noun, G (36.26): ἐπιστάτην, "superintendent," Sym: ἐπίσκοπον, "overseer," V: *dux*, "chief," S: ܪܒܝܬܐ, "officer," and T: סגן כהניא, "prefect of the priests."

In spite of the overwhelming evidence for the singular form, the committee assigned a C evaluation to the more difficult reading of M, considering it very likely that the versions adapted the reading of M to the context.

Evaluation of Problems

Since Luzzatto, the vast majority of modern commentators correct the plural of M to be singular. This explains the fact that very few recent translations clearly render M. The notable exceptions are BR, NAB, and NRSV.

On the other hand, not many translations produce textual justification for the singular noun in a footnote, except NEB, REB, and GNB. Moreover, the textual basis of these footnotes (only "G" in the first two and "some ancient translations" in the last) is unnecessarily presented as small.

Most modern translations offer evasive paraphrases with regard to the textual problem, moving the function of the officer to the foreground (RSV, NIV, NJV, NJB, CEV). This seems to be a correct translational solution since both the chief officer and other officers are involved (van Selms II, 58).

Translation Proposals

The paraphrases of NJV: "The Lord appointed you priest . . . to exercise authority in the House of the Lord . . ." or of CEV: "the Lord chose you to be priest in charge of the temple security force" offer useful examples of such an approach.

30.5

Textual Decisions

After the introductory formula "Thus says the Lord," M continues with a verb in first-person plural: שָׁמָעְנוּ, "(a cry of panic) we have heard." The first-person plural of M is also attested by Aq, V, S, and T.

G, on the other hand, renders with a second-person plural: ἀκούσεσθε, "you will hear." To the evidence provided in CTAT, 679–80, should now be added the fact that, according to a new collation made for HUB, the first hand of Kennicott manuscript 150 (end of the 13th century) has the reading שמעתי, "I have heard." This information was not available to the committee.

The reading of G was considered to be an assimilation to the plural imperatives with which the next verse starts, and a majority B vote was given to the more difficult reading of M.

Evaluation of Problems

Linguistically and translationally some adaptation of M seems necessary, in spite of RSV, NRSV, NAB, NJB, REB, and NJV, because a literal translation would suggest the presence of the plural of majesty, which must be excluded (Joüon, §114*e* N). Notwithstanding the difficulty in identifying the speakers, four possible adaptations present themselves:

1. to follow G as has been done in NEB: "You shall hear"
2. to adopt a first-person singular reading, as in Kennicott MS 150 and as proposed by Volz (285) and Rudolph (188). This is realized in GNB, CEV, and GrN

3. to produce an evasive passive rendering of the verb, as done in NIV: "Cries of fear are heard"
4. to identify the speakers of M as the exilic community and to introduce their utterance with a phrase such as "you say."

Solution 1, though restricted to NEB, could be taken into account in projects with Orthodox participation.

Even though solution 2 now has some textual support, it is not sufficient to serve as textual base.

Solution 3, in its evasiveness, is clearly an undertranslation.

Solution 4 probably presents the best interpretation, already proposed by Schnurrer in the 18th century, taken over by Rosenmüller a century later, and recently introduced again by Freedman and Rosenberg (197–98). An introductory phrase such as "you say" would merely be a matter of explicit information.

Translation Proposals

In the absence of any existing translation adopting the last solution, the following proposal can be made: "Thus said the Lord: 'You say: We have heard cries of panic.' "

30.7

Textual Decisions

This verse starts in M with the exclamation: הוֹי, "Alas!" a reading confirmed by the Origen recension: οὐαί, "woe!" V: *vae*, "ah," and S: ܘܝ, "woe!"

G (37.6) has ἐγενήθη, "have become," at the end of verse 6, a rendering presumably based upon a reading הָיוּ instead of the untranslated הוֹי, "alas!" in the beginning of verse 7 in M.

More difficult to judge is the rendering of T. HUB's first apparatus, signaling that T almost equals G, is vague. G seems to be based upon a *yod/waw* metathesis and different vocalization of the word under discussion; some manuscripts of T do not render the word at all. Sperber's edition omits וי, "woe," on the presumed authority of two Yemenite manuscripts in the British Library and Codex Reuchlinianus. The latter codex, however, *has* the reading וי and it is also found in manuscript Urbinates 1 which was not used by Sperber. Therefore T almost surely supports M.

Four members of the committee considered G as due to a graphical error and they gave a C evaluation to M, whereas two members assigned the same evaluation to G.

Evaluation of Problems

Rothstein in BH2 was the first to propose correcting הוֹי to הָיָה, and he has been followed in this in all editions, as can easily be seen from the editorial layout of the text. Among commentators, Volz, Rudolph, and Holladay defended the same correction which, according to their textual notes, has been taken over by NAB and NEB. It is doubtful, however, that the reconstructed Hebrew Vorlage of G is grammatically correct.

Most modern versions (RSV, NRSV, NJV, NJB, FC) follow M, as can easily be seen because of their literal character. The unnaturalness of "woe" exclamations in modern language causes linguistic changes in translation which make the choosing of a base text rather difficult.

Translation Proposals

For a literal but natural approach, compare FC: *Quel malheur! C'est un jour terrible, un jour sans pareil*, "What a disaster! This is a terrible day, no other like it." For a functional equivalent translation, REB can be taken as an example: "How awful is that day: when has there been its like?"

30.8

Textual Decisions

In a context in which third-person pronominal forms prevail, M presents two nouns with second-person possessive suffixes: צַוָּארֶךָ, "your neck," "(I will break his yoke from off) your neck," and וּמוֹסְרוֹתֶיךָ, "and your bonds (I will burst)." The suffixes of M are also attested by 4Q-c, Th, Aq and Sym (according to the Barberini manuscript), S and T, and for the first noun only, by the Lucianic recension of G and V.

G, however, has third-person plural possessives in both cases: αὐτῶν. The committee considered the second-person possessive suffixes as part of a quotation of Isa 10.27 and the brief transition to the second person in M as an affectionate echo of the announcement of the realization of the oracle in Isaiah. The third-person references in G were judged to be harmonizations and the more difficult reading of M was preferred, with a B vote.

Evaluation of Problems

Apart from NJV, BR, and NAB, none of our modern versions renders M. In fact, M can only be translated in an interlinear type of translation. Retaining M in translation and acknowledging in a footnote that M is unsuitable (McKane, 761) is not an acceptable translational procedure. It may be true that the change of person is of rhetorical nature and that it has to do with emotive meaning, but very few languages will express this in the Hebrew way.

On the other hand, the textual decisions above prevent the translator from following G, on textual grounds, even though doing so has frequently been advised by scholars from Houbigant to Bright and realized in translations such as RSV, NRSV, NEB, and REB. The translational procedure of G can be followed, however.

Actually, contextual harmonization in this domain is a must, and two different possibilities present themselves: a harmonization with regard to second-person forms (NJB, CEV) or third-person forms, as in G (NIV, GNB, GN, GrN, FC). The last possibility might be preferred, especially in projects with Orthodox participation.

Translation Proposals

For the latter harmonization, NIV can serve as a model: "I will break the yoke off your necks and will tear off their bonds; no longer will foreigners enslave them"; and for the first, NJB: "I shall break the yoke now on your neck, and snap your chains; and foreigners will enslave you no more."

4

JEREMIAH 31–40

31.3

Textual Decisions

The first sentence of this verse in M states that "from far away" or "long ago" the Lord appeared לִי, "to me." The first-person singular suffix of M is confirmed by Sym, V, and S. Nothing certain can be concluded with regard to T's Vorlage from its paraphrase: "Jerusalem said, from of old the Lord was revealed to our fathers. O prophet, say to them. . . ." However, "our fathers" could be based on a first-person plural transformation of M.

The Greek tradition (38.3), on the other hand, has the unanimous rendering αὐτῷ, "to him": κύριος πόρρωθεν ὤφθη αὐτῷ, "The Lord from afar appeared to him," a rendering certainly derived from a reading לוֹ, "to him."

The committee, considering the converging testimony of Sym, V, and S, concluded that M was rooted in the proto-Masoretic textual tradition and decided to assign a B evaluation to it.

Evaluation of Problems

From Châteillon to, most recently, McKane, many commentators proposed correcting M according to G and in conformity with the context. This proposal has been taken over on textual grounds by a majority of modern versions (NAB, RSV, NRSV, GNB, NEB, REB). Here again, the textual decisions above do not encourage translators to take G as textual base. But the contextual assimilation of G can serve as a translational model (see GN), especially in interconfessional projects with Orthodox participation.

One glance at literal translations such as NJV and NJB clearly shows that M cannot be literally rendered without producing confusion. At least some paraphrase with indication of speakers and/or addressees is necessary. Such a paraphrase could best be founded on Kimchi's interpretation, according to which verse 3 consists of a statement and a counterstatement—the first spoken

127

by Israel and the second by the Lord. The first interpretation is already present in T: "Jerusalem said," and the second in the paraphrase of S: "and he said to me." Translators could therefore opt for this kind of rendering, provided that they do not think (van Selms, 70) that the dialogues are too implicit, too rapid, and too fragmentary to be true.

Translation Proposals

If the last solution is preferred, the minimal paraphrase of FC could present an acceptable model for translation. Speaking of Israel: "*Il disait: 'De loin le Seigneur est venu se montrer à moi.' Et je lui ai dit à mon tour: 'Je t'aime depuis toujours,'*" "He said: 'From far away the Lord has appeared to me.' And I for my part said to him: 'I have dearly loved you from of old.'"

31.7

Textual Decisions

According to M the proclamation in this verse has the form of a prayer: הוֹשַׁע יְהוָה אֶת־עַמְּךָ, "Save, O Lord, your people." M is completely confirmed in this by both V: *salva Domine populum tuum*, and S: ܦܪܘܩ ܡܪܝܐ ܠܥܡܟ.

4Q-c has vocalized the initial verb as הוֹשִׁיעַ, "he has saved," but the last word is the same as in M, which results in the confused reading "The Lord has saved your people." The same textual picture is provided by Babylonian manuscript Eb10 (Yeivin III, 110) with a supralinear vocalization of the verb and עמך.

In G, on the other hand, the proclamation takes the form of a statement: ἔσωσε κύριος τὸν λαὸν αὐτοῦ, "the Lord has saved his people" (38.7), presupposing therefore the vocalization of 4Q-c and a reading עמו, "his people." The same reading is attested by T: פרק יי ית עמיה, "the Lord has saved his people."

The uncertainty with regard to a different Vorlage for the last noun caused a majority vote in favor of M, three members giving it a B and two a C evaluation. One C vote was given to G.

Evaluation of Problems

Since the eighteenth century, the majority of commentators have adopted the reading of G and T, which is partly the reading of 4Q-c, and most translations have done the same, with textual justification (NAB, NEB, REB, NJB, GNB, GN), some without (BR, RSV, GrN). The arguments against such a rendering in CTAT (684–85) are not very convincing, since the interrelation between the two textual problems of verb and noun-suffix has not sufficiently been discussed. Translators may therefore want to join the majority.

If, however, the combination of proclamation and supplication is not considered to be unnatural, translators could follow M with an important minority of modern versions (NRSV, NIV, NJV, CEV, FC).

Probably no translator will be tempted to follow Chouraqui in producing the mixed text of 4Q-c and Eb10.

Translation Proposals

For the first solution, REB is a model: "Sing out your praises and say: 'The Lord has saved his people' "; and for the last, NIV: "Make your praises heard, and say, 'O Lord, save your people.' "

31.9

Textual Decisions

In the second sentence of this verse, the Lord says that he will bring back his people בְּתַחֲנוּנִים, "with supplications." This reading of M is confirmed by V: *in precibus*, "in prayers," and by S: ܘܒܚܢܢܘܬܐ, "and in fervent prayer."

G (38.9) renders here ἐν παρακλήσει, which could either mean "in invocation" or "in consolation." Aq translates ἐν οἰκτειρμοῖς, and Sym μετ' οἰκτειρμῶν, respectively: "in mercies" and "with mercies." This is also the translation of Jerome: *in misericordia*, "with mercy," and of T: ברחמין סגיאין, "with great mercies."

The committee considered the different renderings of the versions, G included (Schleusner IV, 201), to be of an exegetical and not of a textual nature. The committee, being equally divided, gave A and B ratings to M.

Evaluation of Problems

Ever since Houbigant, commentators consider G to be based on a different Hebrew Vorlage, וּבְתַנְחוּמִים, "and with consolations." Many modern translations therefore follow G on textual grounds (RSV, NRSV, NAB, NEB, REB). G, however, could be followed as an acceptable interpretation of M, and any accompanying note could be of an exegetical kind. This has been done, for example, in NJV which references Zech 12.10 for the meaning "compassion" in M.

For G and T, "weeping" and "consolations" are contrasted, the first being related to deportation, the second to the return from exile. It is also possible, however, to relate "weeping" and "prayer"/"consolation" to the difficulties and dangers of the journey back.

Translation Proposals

Depending upon the exegetical option chosen, either NJV: "They shall come with weeping, And with compassion will I guide them," or CEV: "They weep and pray as I bring them home," can be taken as an example.

31.13

Textual Decisions

According to the first line of M and its syntactical division, there are two separate groups, one consisting of young women dancing and a second consisting of young and old men יַחְדָּו, "together." This reading is also attested in Aq according to the Syro-Hexapla: ܟܚܕܐ, "unanimously," V: *simul*, "together," and T: כחדא, "together."

G (38.13), on the other hand, reads χαρήσονται, "they will rejoice," which could be based on a different vocalization of the same Hebrew consonants: יַחְדּוּ or יֶחְדּוּ, conjugated forms of the verb חדה, "rejoice."

S, with its rendering ܢܚܕܘܢ ܟܚܕܐ, "together they will rejoice," takes a unique position. This translation could be the result of a conflation of two textual traditions, but it could also simply be a rendering of M with a repetition of the verb used earlier in the phrase, for translational reasons.

Another distinctive mark of G is that it probably had a Hebrew Vorlage in which the conjunction *waw* before בַּחֻרִים, "young men," was missing, as in 17 Kennicott manuscripts. The result is that the two groups are differently composed in G: young women and young men amuse themselves together and the old men do so separately.

The committee considered G's rendering to be as due to ignorance of a feature of Hebrew culture in which only the girls dance, and the men, young and old, have their own festivities. M therefore received a B evaluation.

Evaluation of Problems

From Venema to Holladay and McKane recently, the reading of G was adopted for textual reasons by many commentators. Only Ehrlich (321) has correctly observed that the use of the verb חדה is problematic in all its occurrences in the Hebrew Bible.

However, the textual problem is without any relevance for translation, since a second parallel verb for the second group of persons will have to be provided in many languages anyway and since the notion of "being together" can be expressed in several ways, even without the explicit use of "together." Therefore, a textual note is correctly lacking in all modern translations. Only Brockington states that NEB is based on G, but in NEB itself no indication is given.

The correct group distinctions are translationally important, however. At this point G cannot be followed since it represents a "serious infraction of the Jewish moral code" (Rosenberg, 247). Unfortunately, distinctions between groups and their manifestations are blurred in several ways in most modern versions.

Translation Proposals

Distinctions are neatly maintained in NRSV: "Then shall the young women rejoice in the dance, and the young men and the old shall be merry."

31.35

Textual Decisions

In the beginning of this verse, the Lord is first characterized as the one who gives the sun for light by day and then, according to M, as the one who (established) חֻקֹּת, "the laws" of moon and stars for light by night. This plural "laws" in M is only attested by S. The editions, it is true, only have the singular reading ܪܬܕ̈ܘܡܐ, "and the course," but manuscript Ambrosianus puts the plural marker on this word. Respecting the consonants of M, Aq has read a singular: ἀκρίβειαν, "precision," V: *ordinem*, "the (regular) order," and T: גזירת, "decree."

On the other hand, חֻקֹּת has not been rendered by G. It is also lacking in Kennicott's manuscript 681, but the value of this witness is insignificant.

The committee considered the singular reading in most versions as due to a translational initiative and the omission in G as the result of an assimilation to the preceding context. M received a B evaluation.

Evaluation of Problems

From Knabenbauer to recently, Bright, Holladay and McKane, חֻקֹּת has frequently been considered to be an intrusion from the next verse and as overloading the sentence. Many commentators therefore adopt the minus of G as the primitive text. Of modern versions, NAB and NEB do the same, according to their textual notes. Mainly because of semantic disturbance or redundancy many recent versions (GNB, CEV, FC, GN, GrN) follow the minus of G on translational grounds.

On the other hand, Volz (287), followed by Rudolph (204), emended חֻקֹּת to חֹקֵק, "who regulates," parallel to the preceding participle נֹתֵן, "who establishes." On just such a conjecture the rendering of NJB is based. Translators may want to produce such a rendering for translational reasons and not on the base of textual emendation. It could be considered a slight undertranslation of M.

In fact, M indicates the complex mechanism of the phases of the moon and the movements of the stars with its choice of the word חֻקֹּת, "laws." It is only possible to express this when a stylistically acceptable minimal paraphrase is found.

Translation Proposals

For a slight undertranslation of M, NIV can be quoted as a model: "he who appoints the sun / to shine by day, / who decrees the moon and stars / to shine by night."

REB can be cited for a minimal paraphrase of M: "Who gave the sun for a light by day / and the moon and stars in their courses / for a light by night."

31.40A

Textual Decisions

M starts with the difficult information וְכָל־הָעֵמֶק הַפְּגָרִים וְהַדֶּשֶׁן, "The whole valley of the dead bodies and the ashes."

The whole statement is confirmed by Th and the additions of the recensions of Origen and Lucian; the last two words are confirmed by Aq and Josephus. The Greek transcription of the third word as φαγαρείν, with its variants, makes the phrase unintelligible, however. It is attested by V: *et omnem vallem cadaverum et cineris*, "and the whole valley of the corpses and ashes." Indirectly, it is supported both by the paraphrase of S: "the whole valley in which one throws dung and ashes," and by the midrash of T: "and the whole valley where the corpses of the army of the Assyrians fell."

On the other hand, all of this information is lacking in G (38.40).

Since the next discourse in M also starts with וְכָל, the committee considered it probable that the omission in G was accidental and caused by *homoioarcton*, the eye of the translator having shifted from the first occurrence of וְכָל to the second. M therefore received four A and two B votes.

Evaluation of Problems

Both NEB and REB render M as follows: "All the valley (and every field)." Referring to "the valley," NEB notes that this is the reading of the Septuagint and that the Hebrew adds: "the corpses and the buried bodies." This is wrong, since "all the valley" is not present in G. This kind of selective use of textual data is of course unacceptable. REB drops the wording of NEB, replacing the reference to G with "probable reading" and admitting the conjectural character of its translation.

In spite of modern commentary support for this conjecture, translators are advised to follow M, with most recent versions.

The problem of interpretation remains. Through comparison with Arabic and Ugaritic vocabulary, van Selms (II, 84) "to his great relief [gets] rid of all the corpses and ashes," but translators will have to retain them. "Corpses" could be either human or animal in origin, whereas "ashes" could refer to the fatty ashes of the sacrificial victims. Many commentators find an allusion to human sacrifices to foreign gods, and they identify the valley with the valley of Hinnom. The proper name "Valley of the Corpses and Ashes" in NJV may stand for the valley of Hinnom. Some translations go so far as to introduce the "Hinnom Valley" into the text (CEV). There is good reason, however, to be reluctant with regard to this kind of overt identification in translation.

Translation Proposals

For a neutral translation, Moffatt may be used as a model: "The very valley of the dead, where the altar refuse is thrown."

31.40 B

Textual Decisions

In M, geographical directions are twice indicated by the preposition עַד, "toward," the first time in עַד־נַחַל קִדְרוֹן, "toward the Kidron Brook," or "as far as the Kidron Valley." The preposition is confirmed by all the extant ancient versions: G, V, S, and T.

Kennicott's manuscript 150, on the other hand, reads the preposition עַל, "above," "beside." According to the third apparatus (Medieval Bible Manuscripts) of HUB, Kennicott manuscript 30 (13th century A.D.) supports this reading as well. According to Kennicott himself, manuscript 150 is characterized by an abundance of variants (1780, 83).

The committee considered this manuscript alone to have no weight in comparison with the witness of the ancient versions, and an A evaluation was assigned to M. The additional witness of manuscript 30 would not have changed this evaluation.

Evaluation of Problems

Referring to Kennicott manuscript 150, Volz was the first to introduce this correction into M (284), followed by Rudolph (206), Bright (278), and Holladay (2.155). It has been taken over by NJB: "and all the ground beside the ravine of the Kidron," which in its note does not consider עַל to have a textual base, but a "conjecture." The same reading is provided in W and GrN without textual note. Likewise without textual annotation, GNB: "and all the fields above Kidron Brook" could also be suspected of having no textual base.

Although M will have to be rendered, translators will have to respect the directional system of the receptor language.

Translation Proposals

For a literal translation, NRSV could serve as an example: "all the fields as far as the Wadi Kidron, to the corner of the Horse Gate toward the east," and for a functional equivalence type of translation, CEV: "the eastern slopes that go down from Horse Gate into Kidron Valley."

32.11

Textual Decisions

This verse deals with a sealed deed of purchase and with an unsealed copy of it. The first one has been explained in M in the following terms: הַמִּצְוָה וְהַחֻקִּים, literally: "claim and obligations," or in paraphrase: "containing the terms and conditions." M is directly attested by the insertion of the Greek recensions of Origen and Lucian: τὴν ἐντολὴν καὶ τὰ δικαιώματα, "the order and the legal rights," which manuscripts Barberini and Marchalianus further attribute to all hexaplaric columns, with the exception of G. M also has the direct support of V: *stipulationes et rata*, "stipulations and regulations." M is indirectly confirmed by the "Oriental" variant found in manuscript Petrograd of the Prophets and manuscript JThS 232: ואת המצוה והחקים, "and with the claim and obligations," by S: ܘܒܦܘܩܕܢܐ ܘܒܢܡܘܣܐ, "with precepts and with ordinances," and by T: כהלכתא וכדחזי, "according to the halakhah and according to what is right."

As has been correctly determined by Rahlfs, the Old Greek (39.11) has the reading τὸ ἐσφραγισμένον καὶ τὸ ἀνεγνωσμένον, "the sealed one and the public one (read aloud)," therefore omitting the two words of M under discussion.

The committee regarded the prepositional variants found in the Oriental form of M and in S and T to be the result of syntactical facilitation. The omission in G was seen as due to ignorance regarding legal terminology. The form of M was judged to be proto-Masoretic and received a B evaluation.

Evaluation of Problems

Between Stade (1885, 176) and McKane (840), several commentators adopted G as the primitive reading, and they were followed by NEB and REB: "I took my copies of the deed of purchase, both the sealed and the unsealed." A uniquie position is taken by NJB which keeps M, putting the translation within brackets, indicating therewith its character as a gloss.

Other commentators such as Volz (306) and Rudolph (208) keep M but move the two words preceded by the preposition עַל, "according to," to the end of verse 10, where it originally belonged, according to them. This type of restructuring did not have much following among translators.

It should be noted, moreover, that NJV is unique in moving M to the end of verse 11 and in noting that the force of the two Hebrew words is uncertain: "I took the deed of purchase, the sealed text and the open one—according to rule and law—."

In CTAT (694) reference is made to the duplicate documents Mur 21, 23, and 28 found in the caves of Murabbaʿat, in which the sealed part of the document contained the essentials of the deed and the open part its entirety. It is not impossible that the two words of M refer to the data contained in the sealed document.

Translation Proposals

For a rendering of M, NRSV presents the following example: "I took the sealed deed of purchase, containing the terms and conditions, and the open copy."

32.26

Textual Decisions

In this brief introductory verse in M, the word of the Lord is addressed אֶל־יִרְמְיָהוּ, "to Jeremiah," a reading confirmed by Aq and Sym according to Codex Barberini, by the recension of Origen, and by V, S, and T.

G, on the other hand, has the rendering πρός με, "to me."

The committee considered this rendering the result of assimilation to a first-person singular context, and it gave a B evaluation to the more difficult reading of M.

Evaluation of Problems

From Giesebrecht (179) to Holladay (2.205), many commentators preferred G on textual grounds. This can only mean that they considered an original אֵלַי, "to me," to have been misunderstood as an abbreviation of (רמיהו)אל־י, "to Jeremiah." They do not apply their theory very consistently, however, because there are two other instances (42.12 and 43.1) in which G provides the same translation for the same reading in M (35.12 and 36.1). Commentators, however, were not tempted to adopt G there. NJB is the only modern translation to adopt G (and the Old Latin).

Translations of the literal or philological type simply reproduce M (RSV, NRSV, NIV, NAB, NEB, REB). Translations of the functional equivalent type mostly reproduce G, not for textual but for translational reasons (FC, GNB, GrN, GN).

Translation Proposals

For a literal (philological) type of translation, NIV can be followed: "Then the word of the Lord came to Jeremiah," and for a functional equivalent type of translation, GNB: "then the Lord said to me."

33.2

Textual Decisions

Verse 2a reads as follows in M: כֹּה־אָמַר יְהוָה עֹשָׂהּ, "Thus says the Lord who made it," verse 2b adding: יְהוָה יוֹצֵר אוֹתָהּ, "the Lord who formed it." It is the last word of the first sentence and the first word of the second one that have created problems. The second occurrence of the name of the Lord is confirmed by the Origen recension of G (40.2) as well as by V and T, but it is lacking in the first or second hand of 11 Hebrew manuscripts and in G and S. The reading עֹשָׂהּ, "who made it," is attested by Aq, V (if the reading *quae* of the manuscripts of Cava and Toledo is taken as original), and T. G has, however, the rendering ποιῶν γῆν, "who made the earth," whereas S presents second-person singular suffixes everywhere: "the Lord, who made you and formed you."

The committee considered the omission of the second occurrence of יְהוָה to be a stylistic abbreviation; it took the peculiar reading of G to be the result of an internal Greek deformation (ΓHN as a deformation of AYTHN), and the second-person object renderings of S with their reference to Jeremiah as an assimilation to verse 1. The deviating renderings of the versions being facilitating, M received a B evaluation.

Evaluation of Problems

In view of their readings and textual notes, there can be no doubt that the vast majority of modern versions follow G. In most cases, it remains obscure whether they do so on the authority of G itself or on the basis of a presupposed Hebrew Vorlage האדמה, "earth" (so Houbigant, 1753, 298) or (ה)ארץ (Cornill and others). Only NAB clearly states the last form without the definite article. Volz (312) presupposed a different Hebrew Vorlage, (ה)כל, "everything," a conjecture which was only taken up in the last revision of the Luther Bible.

However, any postulated Hebrew Vorlage is purely imaginary. Even Spohn's theory of Greek deformation, accepted by the committee, can be questioned. Weiser's observation that G only presents a clarification of the uncertain suffix of the verb עשה may be correct. Translators, if they agree with this interpretation of G, could certainly provide the same rendering without any textual note.

There are, however, other interpretational options. For Kimchi and others, the ambiguous suffix is referring to Jerusalem. And for others such as Ehrlich (327), the verbs used probably refer to planning and execution. Translationally, the first of these options has not found any followers, but the second has (NJB, GN).

Translation Proposals

If an interpretation along the lines of G is chosen, translators could follow NIV in translation and absence of footnoting: "This is what the Lord says, he who made the earth, the Lord who formed it and established it."

If the latter of the two different interpretations mentioned above is preferred, translators could take NJB as a model: "Thus said the Lord who is planning it, // the Lord who is shaping it to bring it about."

33.5

Textual Decisions

Verses 4–5 present many interpretation problems on the word and syntax level. In addition, verse 5 contains two textual problems, the first one related to the first occurrence of the particle אֶת: אֶת־הַכַּשְׂדִּים, "the Chaldeans"; the second problem is related to the third-person masculine plural suffix of וּלְמַלְאָם, "to fill them."

Regarding the first problem, אֶת has the support of the Lucianic recension of G (40.5) with its rendering μετὰ (τῶν Χαλδαίων), of V: *cum* (*Chaldaeis*), of S: ܟܠ, and of T: עַם. On the other hand, the first or second hand of 14 manuscripts of de Rossi as well as the first edition of the Prophets (Soncino, 1486) and the Soncino Bible of 1488 read the preposition אֶל, "with." Such a reading may also be the basis for the Old Greek, which renders πρὸς (τοὺς Χαλδαίους). No difference in meaning is involved.

With regard to the second problem, the verbal suffix of M is confirmed by the Origen recension of G and by V, S, and T. The rendering of G: καὶ πληρῶσαι αὐτήν, "and to fill her," seems, however, to presuppose reading וּלְמַלְאָהּ as referring to the city.

In the first case, the committee assigned a B evaluation to M, considering a Vorlage אֶל as an assimilation to the twofold occurrence of the same preposition in the preceding verse. In the latter case, M was evaluated in the same way, since G was regarded as belonging to a different literary tradition.

Evaluation of Problems

Cornill, and in his footsteps Giesebrecht and Oort, proposed omitting אֶת altogether, and they have been followed in this by RSV and NRSV, making it possible to take the Chaldeans as the subject of the sentence: "The Chaldeans are coming in to fight." NEB even omits "the Chaldeans," speaking only about "attackers." They possibly even adopted the old thesis of De Dieu and Schnurrer that אֵת introduces a nominative case here. There is no grammatical argument in favor of the latter thesis, and the committee decision prohibits an omission.

In the second case, with most modern translations, the suffix will have to be taken as referring to "the houses." Corpses would have been disposed of in the demolished houses, since the cemeteries outside the city could no longer be reached. There is no compelling reason to follow G, as done in NJB: "only to fill the city with corpses," although such a reading may be footnoted in projects with Orthodox participation.

The rendering of both verses will heavily depend on the interpretation of הַסֹּלְלוֹת in verse 4. Are these defensive installations for which materials coming from deliberately razed houses were used? Or is the word referring to siege works made by the Chaldeans?

Translation Proposals

NIV may present a useful model: "For this is what the Lord, the God of Israel, says about the houses in this city and the royal palaces of Judah that have been torn down to be used against the siege ramps and the sword in the fight with the Babylonians: They will be filled with the dead bodies of the men I will slay in my anger and wrath." Translators may want to mention in a footnote that the meaning of the Hebrew is uncertain.

33.6

Textual Decisions

The indirect object of the first Hebrew verb of this verse in M is לָהּ, "to her," "I am going to bring her (relief and healing)." This third-person feminine singular pronoun suffix of M is confirmed by G (40.6): αὐτῇ, by V: *ei* (according to the edition of Weber and Gryson), and by S: ܠܗ. On the other hand, a third-person masculine plural pronoun suffix seems to have been read by the Codex Alexandrinus of G: ἐπ' αὐτούς, "to them," in a number of editions of V: *eis*, and by T: להון. Since this plural reading is the product of a facilitating contextual assimilation to the following third-person masculine plural suffixes, the more difficult reading of M received a B evaluation.

Evaluation of Problems

Grätz (1883, 345) was the first to propose correcting the Hebrew text to read להם, "to them," and he has been followed by many commentators, recently by Holladay (2.221). This reading has also been adopted by BHS. Of modern translations, only NJB translated "I shall bring them," undoubtedly for textual reasons.

It is clear that the singular suffix in M refers back to the city of Jerusalem in verse 5. It is not so clear to what the plural suffixes refer. They could either refer to the inhabitants of Jerusalem or to its houses (McKane, 857). The latter interpretation is preferred by Cornill and Barthélemy (702). The literal translation of the Hebrew would then be: "I am bringing it recovery and healing, and I will heal them." Although the hyperbole "healing" for "rebuilding" is not impossible, it may be easier to have the plural suffixes refer to the inhabitants of Jerusalem, as has been done in FC. Some translations seem to think in terms of a wider circle: "my people" (NIV), "Judah and Israel" (NEB, REB) in anticipation of verse 7.

Some languages will require a certain degree of assimilation. In view of the textual decision above, assimilation of the plurals to the singular for translational reasons only could be considered preferable.

Translation Proposals

If the plural suffixes are taken to refer to the inhabitants, GNB could be quoted: "But I will heal this city and its people and restore them to health."

33.9

Textual Decisions

This verse starts with the following sentence: וְהָיְתָה לִּי לְשֵׁם שָׂשׂוֹן, literally: "And she shall be to me to a name of joy." M has the support of the Lucianic version of G (40.9): καὶ ἔσται μοι εἰς ὄνομα εὐφροσύνης, "and she shall be for me to a name of joy," a rendering which the Barberini manuscript attributes to Aq. M is also confirmed by T: ויהון קדמי לשום דחדוא, "and they shall become before me a name of rejoicing." Finally, in the Cairo manuscript the classical Tiberian reading is protected by a *masorah parva* which notes the unique character of the sequence of the two last words of the sentence.

On the other hand, Kennicott manuscripts 150 and 187, the first hand of his manuscript 195, and the first hand of de Rossi's manuscript 2 have the reading לששון, "to a joy." With the addition of a connective particle, this also is the reading of V: *et erit mihi in nomen et in gaudium*, "and it will be for me to a renown and to a joy," and of S: ܪܚܡܬܐ ܕܠ ܐܝܟܪܐ ܘܠ ܪܚܡܬܐ, "and she will be for me to a reputation and a delight." G (40.9) renders the whole sentence only with καὶ ἔσται εἰς εὐφροσύνην, "and it shall be for a joy," reading also לששון, "for a joy," but omitting לי לשם.

The committee considered it most likely that G testifies to a syntactical facilitation and a stylistic abbreviation, whereas V and S were only attempting syntactical facilitation. M was not judged to have suffered a textual accident. If M was not primitive, it underwent a literary development. The committee concluded with a B rating for M.

Evaluation of Problems

Houbigant (1753, 299) had already proposed adding a ל before the last word, whereas Giesebrecht (184) suggested that לשׁם contained the remaining part of an original reading ירושלם, "Jerusalem." The combination of both corrections was accepted by Rudolph (214) and others and, among recent translations, by NAB: "Then Jerusalem shall be my joy."

Most recent versions make either Jerusalem (NJB, GNB, GN) or "this city" (RSV, NRSV, NIV, NEB, REB) explicit for translational reasons, regarding it as the implicit subject of the verbal form וְהָיְתָה, "and she shall be." This is one interpretational option. The other is to take the feminine singular as a neutral form which alludes to all the divine interventions which have been announced in verses 6–8.

Finally, translators may have to make some stylistic adaptations in the receptor language, as was done in the ancient versions.

Translation Proposals

For the first interpretation, REB could be a model: "This city will win me renown and praise . . . ," and for the second one, RL: *Und das soll mein Ruhm und meine Wonne . . . sein*, "And that will be my renown and my joy."

33.20

Textual Decisions

This whole verse is a dependent, conditional clause, and the textual problem involves the verb. M has תָּפֵרוּ, "you break," "if you (plural) could break my covenant." In the absence of the Old Greek, which lacks verses 14–26, this reading of M is supported by the Origen recension: εἰ διασκεδάσετε τὴν δια- θήκην μου, "if you break my covenant," by Sym according to manuscript Marchalianus: ἐὰν διασκεδάσητε, "if you break," and by S: ܐܢ ܬܫܪܘܢ ܩܝܡܝ ܕܥܡ ܐܝܡܡܐ, "if you could bring my rule to an end."

On the other hand, a reading תֻּפַר, "be broken," could be presupposed to have been the basis of the Lucianic recension of G: εἰ διασκεδασθήσεται ἡ δι- αθήκη μου, "if my covenant could be broken," of V: *si irritum fieri potest pactum meum*, "if it could happen that my covenant would be without effect," and of the long paraphrase of T: "Just as it is impossible that my covenant which I made should be abolished."

The committee considered these latter renderings as facilitating assimilations to the form תֻּפַּר, "be broken," in verse 21 and it preferred the biting irony of the second-person plural of M, giving it a B rating.

Evaluation of Problems

Correcting M with תֻּפַּר was first proposed by Grätz (1883, 345) and Giesebrecht (186), and it has recently been proposed again by McKane (862) and Holladay (2.227). On the basis of V it entered into the German translations of Zwingli and Luther, and it is still to be found in RL: *Wenn mein Bund (mit Tag und Nacht) aufhörte*, "If my covenant (with day and night) would come to an end," and in EÜ. With the same appeal to V, NEB renders: "If the law that I made (for the day and the night) could be annulled."

There is no problem with a passive transformation as long as it is based on translational and not on textual grounds.

The Hebrew rhetoric of verses 20–21 may have to be formulated in such a way that the impossibility of the conditional action is brought out.

Translation Proposals

One of the ways in which the stipulations as formulated above may be met is phrased by REB: "It would be as unthinkable to annul the covenant that I made for the day and the night, . . . as to annul my covenant with my servant David. . . ."

33.25

Textual Decisions

In this verse, M speaks about בְּרִיתִי יוֹמָם וָלָיְלָה, "my covenant with day and night," an expression which syntactically should be considered the object of the double-duty verb שַׂמְתִּי, "I have established," at the end of the verse: "If I have not established my covenant with day and night." In the absence of the Old Greek, this syntactical constellation is confirmed by the Lucianic recension of G (40.25) and by S; furthermore, M is clearly presupposed by the Origen recension and by V. T, on the other hand, paraphrases in the same way as in verse 20: "Just as it is not possible that my covenant which I established (דאקימית) with the day and with the night should cease." However, the committee considered T to be filling out M and assimilating to verse 20, and it gave M a B evaluation.

Evaluation of Problems

Houbigant (1753, 299) was the first to propose a correction of M's בְּרִיתִי, "my covenant," with בָּרָאתִי, "I created." This verb, which was supposed to have been present in the first sentence originally, would have been assimilated by M to the three occurrences of בריתי, "my covenant," in verses 20 and 21. This suggestion was accepted by some, including Rudolph (218) and Holladay (2.227), who stressed the necessity of a parallel verb. It has been adopted by NJB: "If I have not created day and night," which in a textual note correctly describes the rendering as a conjecture. NEB gives the rendering: "If I had not made my law for day and night," referring to T (Brockington, 210). It should be clear, however, that T can hardly function as a textual base.

Translation Proposals

Translators may, of course, insert a parallel and synonymous verb in the first sentence, but only for stylistic reasons. An example of this can be found in REB: "If there were no covenant for day and night, and if I had not established a fixed order in heaven and earth."

34.7

Textual Decisions

Verse 7 states, according to M, that the army of the king of Babylon was fighting against Jerusalem וְעַל כָּל־עָרֵי יְהוּדָה הַנּוֹתָרוֹת, "and against all the cities of Judah that were left." This sentence is confirmed by V, S, and T. G (41.7), on the other hand, only has καὶ ἐπὶ πόλεις Ιουδα, "and against the cities of Judah," not rendering כָּל, "all," and הַנּוֹתָרוֹת, "that were left." Only the Origen recension inserts πάσας τάς, "all," before πόλεις, a reading which the Barberini manuscript attributes to Aq and Sym; both the Origen and Lucianic recensions add τὰς καταλελειμμένας, "that were left," after the last word of G.

Although M could have resulted from glossing (Janzen, 66), it would have been a matter of literary initiative, and not of textual accident. The committee considered it more likely, however, that G omitted the two words because of their redundancy. M therefore received a B evaluation.

Evaluation of Problems

Among recent commentators, both McKane (870) and Holladay (2.233) propose omitting כָּל, "all," with G. They are followed by TOB and NEB, according to their textual notes: "and the remaining cities of Judah, (namely Lachish and Azekah)." However, there seems to be no sufficient textual basis for doing this.

RSV and NRSV, on the other hand, render M: "and against all the cities of Judah that were left, Lachish and Azekah," without shying away from the incongruity of "all" and "two."

Translators should certainly be guided by the stylistic criteria of the receptor language in their decision to respect or to disregard certain redundancies of the base text.

Translation Proposals

As an example of a translation that keeps stylistic criteria in mind, then, REB could be a useful model: "and the remaining towns in Judah, namely Lachish and Azekah, the only fortified towns left there."

34.14

Textual Decisions

According to the three initial words of M: מִקֵּץ שֶׁבַע שָׁנִים, the liberation of slaves had to take place "after a period of seven years" or "in the seventh year," a reading which has the support of Aq, Sym, V, S, and T. On the other hand, G has the unique rendering ὅταν πληρωθῇ ἓξ ἔτη, "when six years are accomplished" (41.14). The committee judged (with Spohn) that G did not have a different Hebrew Vorlage, but had only expressed itself in a different way. M therefore received a B rating.

Evaluation of Problems

In view of the following שֵׁשׁ שָׁנִים, six years," Ehrlich (331) proposed changing the "seven" of M to the "six" of G. Translationally, he has been followed only by RSV: "At the end of six years."

It is more likely that the "seven" of M has to be understood as a rounded number, in the same way that French "fifteen days" means two weeks, and that G "corrected" the text out of concern that the phrase "at the end of seven years" would be taken too literally (Holladay II, 237).

Therefore, although rendering "at the end of seven years" (NJB, TOB) is possible, it should not be taken to mean "after seven years" (compare Deuteronomy 15), and it may be wiser to render M, with the vast majority of modern versions, in a broader way.

Translation Proposals

"In the seventh year" (NJV), "within seven years" (NEB, REB), and "every seventh year" (NRSV, NIV, NAB, GNB) are all examples of a broader rendering.

34.18

Textual Decisions

The first part of this verse in M ends with לְפָנַי, "before me," and the second part begins with הָעֵגֶל, "the calf." It is the sequence of these two words which has created particular problems. This sequence in M is formally attested by G (41.18): κατὰ πρόσωπόν μου τὸν μόσχον, "before me, the calf . . . ," by V: *in conspectu meo vitulum* (the same), and S and T: קדמי עגלא and מדבח קדמי עגלא, with the same meaning. Only Aq seems to have vocalized the first Hebrew word as לִפְנֵי and therefore rendered the sequence ἐνώπιον τοῦ μόσχου, "before the calf." The committee considered the rendering of Aq as syntactically facilitating, and it was divided between a B and a C rating for the reading לְפָנַי of M. Since the textual tradition with regard to הָעֵגֶל is entirely coherent, M received an A evaluation in this case.

Evaluation of Problems

Ehrlich (331) seems to have been the first to correct M הָעֵגֶל with כָּעֵגֶל, "like a calf." This would lead to this interpretation: "I will make the men who transgressed . . . like the calf which they cut in two." This conjecture has only met with a small amount of very hesitant approval (Volz, 320; Rudolph 224) and it has only been unambiguously stated as a base text by NAB.

A number of commentators, including recently Holladay (2.242), have solved the syntactical problem without conjecture by taking הָעֵגֶל as a second object of the initial verb וְנָתַתִּי, "I will give/make," "I will make the men who transgressed . . . the calf," which would be tantamount to "I will make the men . . . like the calf." This was Luther's interpretation in his translations of 1532 and 1545, and it has remained the interpretation of all successive Luther revisions up to the last one. It has also been the interpretation of the vast majority of modern translations, whether literal or functional equivalent.

It should be noted, however, that the double-accusative interpretation is not without difficulty, and that verses 18 and 19 could also be regarded as a long, involved, sentence which is resumed by means of the same verb, וְנָתַתִּי, at the beginning of verse 20. This interpretation, presupposed by G, could be taken into account in projects with Orthodox participation. It would, however, require some restructuring of verses 18 and 19.

Translation Proposals

NIV is an example of the majority interpretation: "The men who have violated my covenant and have not fulfilled the terms of the covenant they made before me, I will treat like the calf they cut in two and then walked between its pieces."

FC follows the other interpretation, with restructuring: *Les autorités de Juda . . . avaient conclu un accord solennel avec moi, en partageant le veau du sacrice et en passant entre les deux moitiés de l'animal. Mais ces gens ont violé l'accord, ils n'ont pas tenu leurs promesses. Je les livrerai donc à ceux qui désirent leur mort.* "The authorities of Judah . . . have made a solemn agreement with me, cutting the sacrificial calf in two halves and passing in between them. But these people have violated the agreement; they did not keep their promises. Therefore, I will hand them over to those who seek their lives."

35.4

Textual Decisions

According to M, Jeremiah brought the Rechabites into the house of the Lord, and, more precisely, into the room of בְּנֵי חָנָן, "the sons of Hanan." The plural reading "sons" has the support of the first part of the plural/singular doublets in Codexes Sinaiticus and Vaticanus of G (42.4), considered by Rahlfs and Ziegler to be the original text. The plural is also supported by V: *filiorum Anan*, and by S: ܕܟܒܢ ܣܒ. It also has the support of manuscript Urbinates 1 of T and the Yemenite manuscripts used by Sperber in his edition of T.

On the other hand, de Rossi signals that the first hand of his manuscript 211 of the Prophets (13th century) reads בן חנן, "the son of Hanan." This singular reading is also attested by Lucianic manuscript 449: υἱοῦ Ανανίου, by the last part of the plural/singular doublets in Codexes Sinaiticus and Vaticanus (considered by Barthélemy to be the primitive reading), and by the rendering בר חנן, "son of Hanan," in Codex Reuchlianus of T.

Finally, Codex Alexandrinus of G, the Coptic versions, and the Montefiore manuscript of T all omit the first word entirely.

The committee assigned a B evaluation to the more difficult and firmly attested reading of M.

Evaluation of Problems

Volz (324) was the first to propose the reading בן חנן or (with a different division of characters) the correction בֶּן־יְחָנָן, "Ben Johanan," combining the well-attested singular reading "son" with the reading יוֹחָנָן that occurs in manuscript Urbinates 2. Curiously, this is also the rendering of NJB, although the detailed textual evidence cited in the footnote is hardly correct. Furthermore, only NEB includes the variant reading "the son of Hanan," in a footnote.

Even though translators would have to favor the plural reading, the interpretational problem of whether "sons" is a reference to members of one family or to disciples of the prophet Hanan still remains. Since this problem is difficult to solve, most modern versions prefer to give a literal translation of the Hebrew. The metaphorical interpretation "disciples" is only given in translations of the functional equivalence type (GNB, CEV, GN, FC, TILC).

Translation Proposals

For the first interpretation, see NIV: "I brought them into the house of the Lord, into the room of the sons of Hanan, son of Igdaliah." A footnote could contain the variant interpretation.

36.16

Textual Decisions

In this verse the officials turned to one another in alarm and, according to M, they said to "Baruch," אֶל־בָּרוּךְ, "We certainly must report all these words to the king." The addressee of M is confirmed by the Origen and Lucianic recensions of G (43.16) as well as by V, S, and T. However, it is missing in G, where the officials talk to each other. The omission may have been caused by the fact that there is no "turning to one another in alarm" in G but a "taking counsel one with the other," συνέβουλεύσαντο, instead.

The committee discerned that either the addressee of M was original and had been omitted by G or that the addressee was due to a redactional gloss in M, with G being the original. In view of the smoothing style of the Greek translator in the whole context, the comittee was rather inclined to accept the first hypothesis. M, not being the result of a textual accident, therefore received a B rating.

Evaluation of Problems

Commentators generally agree that Baruch as the addressee of M seems awkward. Some modern versions firmly state in their textual notes that they follow G, as for example NAB: "they were frightened and said to one another . . . ," and NEB: "they turned to each other trembling and said. . . ."

An impressive number of older and newer translations, however, present the same kind of rendering (LV, LB, REB, CEV, GrN) without basing it on G. They may therefore have left the addressee of M implicit. In fact, Baruch was present, even if the words were not addressed to him directly (van Selms II, 138).

In view of the remaining uncertainties about the textual traditions, leaving the addressee implicit may be a wise translational procedure.

Translation Proposals

A literal translation of M would run, as in NRSV: "When they heard all the words, they turned to one another in alarm, and said to Baruch." REB can be taken as an example of an implicit addressee: "When they had listened . . . , they turned to each other in alarm and said. . . ."

36.17

Textual Decisions

This verse ends in M with: מִפִּיו, "from his mouth," "How did you write all these words from his mouth?" This reading is also attested by the asterisked addition of the Origen recension of G: ἐκ στόματος αὐτοῦ, "from his mouth," a rendering which the Barberini manuscript attributes to all the columns of the Hexapla with the exception of the G column. It is also present in V, S, and T; however, it is lacking in the Old Greek.

The committee considered G an assimilation of the end of verse 17 to the end of verse 16, and it credited M with four B and two C votes.

Evaluation of Problems

Most commentators consider מפיו to be an interpolation in M from verse 18, and they therefore consider G original. The only noteworthy defense of M comes from Holladay (2.258).

This being the case, a great number of modern translations (NAB, NEB, REB, NJB, GN) follow G, according to their textual notes. On the other hand, most modern versions which follow M seem (on the heels of Venema) to render the word under discussion as a sentence: "Was it at his dictation?" (RSV, NRSV, GNB; compare also NIV). Such a translation, however, sounds like an anticipation of the answer in verse 18. It also seems to be an overtranslation of the Hebrew expression. The question in verse 17 is asking who has taken the initiative, Baruch himself or Jeremiah. A low-profile translation as in NJV or one which leaves the information of M implicit may be the best approach.

Translation Proposals

NJV: "Tell us how you wrote down all these words that he spoke," may be a workable model for translation.

38.10

Textual Decisions

According to M, Zedekiah ordered the Cushite Ebed-Melech to take שְׁלֹשִׁים אֲנָשִׁים, "thirty men," with him to lift Jeremiah out of the cistern. This number "thirty" is confirmed by all other witnesses of M, as well as by G: τριάκοντα ἀνθρώπους (45.10), V, S, and T. Only Kennicott manuscript 96, as correctly presented in the second apparatus of HUB, has the reading שלשה, "three." However, this manuscript, which is preserved at St. John's in Cambridge, dates to the end of the fourteenth century, and it has no textual authority at all. Therefore, an A evaluation of the reading of M was unavoidable.

Evaluation of Problems

An impressive number of commentators nevertheless changed the "thirty" of M to "three." Two arguments for this correction have been put forward: (1) the construction שְׁלֹשִׁים אֲנָשִׁים would be ungrammatical and שְׁלֹשִׁים אִישׁ would have been expected (Giesebrecht, 206); (2) such a large number of men would not be required for the task. These arguments seem to have influenced quite a number of translations, such as RSV, NRSV, and GNB, and others (NAB, NEB, REB), based on their textual notes, seem also to be based on the one Kennicott manuscript 96.

It should be noted, however, that the first argument can easily be refuted, as even Rudolph (240) admits, and that the large number could be explained by the king's anticipation of an attempt at resistance on the part of the prophet's enemies (Isaiah da Trani).

In the almost total absence of textual evidence in support of the reading "three," translators are invited to render M, as done in NJV, NIV, NJB, CEV, FC, GN, and other recent versions.

Translation Proposals

NJV can be quoted as an example: "Then the king instructed Ebed-melech the Ethiopian, 'Take with you thirty men from here, and pull the prophet Jeremiah up from the pit before he dies.' " As has been done in NJV and CEV, the reading "three" in the one Hebrew manuscript could be mentioned in a footnote.

38.11

Textual Decisions

According to M, Ebed-Melech went אֶל־תַּחַת הָאוֹצָר, "to the-place-under-neath the treasury/storeroom" in order to get worn cloths and rags.

The word תַּחַת, used in M in its sense of a noun: "what is underneath," has been read and interpreted as a preposition by G, as far as the first part of the construction ὑπό(γαιον), "under(ground)," is concerned (45.11). The preposition "under" is confirmed by Aq and Sym according to the Barberini manuscript: ὑποκάτω, by V: *sub*, S: ܬܚܝܬ, and T: לתחות. The last word, וּצָר הָא, "the treasury/storeroom" is attested by Aq, Sym, V, S, and T.

The text can only come into question with regard to the second part of the construction (ὑπό)γαιον in G since G seems to be based on a permutation of the characters in the reading האוצר, producing the reading הארץ, "the earth": "under the earth," "underground."

The committee, however, concluded that the rendering of G would pre-suppose a Vorlage תחת האדמה, "under the ground." In view of the additional support of Aq and Sym for M, M received a C evaluation.

Evaluation of Problems

Already in 1901, Ehrlich proposed changing M's אֶל־תַּחַת to מֶלְתַּחַת, "wardrobe," referring to the occurrence of this word in 2 Kgs 10.22. Perles (1922, 17f.) noted that the word *eltâḥ* in Ethiopic means "cloth," and, staying closer to M, he suggested the emendation אֶלְתַּחַת with the same meaning "wardrobe." Since then, many commentators have adopted this emendation. It thus crept into a large number of recent versions (RSV, NRSV, NAB, NJB, NEB, REB, FC, GN, etc.). Since, however, "a wardrobe of the storehouse" sounds rather redundant, many translators do not render the last word, הָאוֹצָר.

With McKane (955), M should be preserved. Ehrlich's argument that אֶל־תַּחַת, if original, should be followed by the preposition לְ before the next noun, can be refuted by many examples (Lev 14.42; Judg 6.19; 1 Sam 21.5; Jer 3.6; Zech 3.10). Moreover, there is nothing strange in the fact that unused cloths would be thrown into a kind of lumber room in the basement.

Translation Proposals

A model for translation can be found in Moffatt's rendering: "he got some torn, tattered rags out of a lumber-room below the treasury."

38.23

Textual Decisions

After the announcement to Zedekiah: "you shall be seized by the king of Babylon," M continues with the rather enigmatic statement: and this city (= Jerusalem) תִּשְׂרֹף, "you will burn" with fire. This rendering of M has the unique support of one Yemenite manuscript of T (BMOr. 1474): תוקיד.

On the other hand, Kennicott manuscript 224 vocalizes the Hebrew consonant form as a *nifal*: תִּשָּׂרֵף, "(this city) shall be burned (with fire)," a vocalization also found in, for example, three de Rossi manuscripts. This vocalization is presupposed by the rendering of G (45.23): κατακαυθήσεται, "shall be completely burned," by the rendering of S: ܬܐܩܕ, and by T: תתוקד, "shall be burned." It could also be presumed by the rendering of V: *conburet*, "he (= the king of Babylon) will burn up (this city)," but this is more likely due to a contextual harmonization.

The majority of the committee judged that the active vocalization of M was erroneous and was caused by the failure to recognize a nominative introduced by the particle אֶת, normally used as the direct-object marker. So 4 C votes were given to the *nifal* vocalization and only two C votes to M.

Evaluation of Problems

The classical exegesis of M has always taken the enigmatic statement to mean: "and you shall cause this city to be burned with fire" (Freedman and Rosenberg, 258), irresponsible acts being implied. Because this exegesis is too subtle, however, it has not even been followed in any modern Jewish version (BR, NJV, Chouraqui); instead, the *nifal* vocalization, which according to Ibn Ezra (Sephat Jether, §104) had already been defended by Judah ben Qoreish, clearly seems to be preferred.

A few recent versions (SR, FC) use the active voice of V for translational reasons. This example can be followed in languages that lack passive forms.

In all other cases, the almost universal use of the passive can be adopted. Depending on the principles and the readership of the translation, a textual footnote may be desirable.

Translation Proposals

FC can serve as a model for active voice: *le roi de Babylone te fera prisonnier et il détruira cette ville par le feu*, "the king of Babylon will take you as a prisoner, and he will destroy this city with fire." For the majority reading see, for example, CEV: "you will be taken as a prisoner to the king of Babylon, and Jerusalem will be burned down." The informative textual note of CEV can also serve as an example.

38.28

Textual Decisions

M reads in 28b: וְהָיָה כַּאֲשֶׁר נִלְכְּדָה יְרוּשָׁלָ֑ם, "And it happened when Jerusalem was taken," after the marker of a new paragraph, the *setumah*. The presence of this whole sentence is attested by the recensions of Origen and Lucian, the Greek text of which has been attributed to Th by the Marchalianus manuscript. It is also confirmed by V and T.

On the other hand, according to new collations of a certain number of Kennicott manuscripts for HUB, the sentence is as a whole lacking in manuscripts 89, 93, and 96, as well as in S. Moreover, it can also be noted that verse 28b and verses 1–2 of the next chapter are absent from the Würzburg palimpsest (Ranke, §312) which is the only witness of the Old Latin.

The first two words of 46.1: καὶ ἐγένετο, "and it happened," in G should be considered a rendering of the first word of 38.28b in M: וְהָיָה which served as an introduction to 39.1.

The committee judged the omission of the sentence in some Hebrew manuscripts and in S as due to homoioteleuton, the last two words of 28b being the same as the last two words of 28a. It took G to be an abbreviation for the purpose of not giving the impression that 39.1 (46.1) would provide the date of the event alluded to in 28b. Observing that the problems of M were problems of literary criticism and exegesis, it attributed a C evaluation to M.

Evaluation of Problems

Among modern versions, only NEB, REB, and GN entirely omit verse 28b. In GN this could have been done for translational reasons; in the first two, a textual appeal was made to G, overlooking the presence of the first word in this version.

Since the problems are exegetical in nature, M can be interpreted in two ways: (1) 28b is considered to be part of the preceding information, as done by Menaḥem de Posquières, who inserted שָׁם, "there," after the verb וְהָיָה as a reference to the presence of Jeremiah. This option is followed by, for example, NJB: "And he was there when Jerusalem actually was captured"; (2) 28b is considered part of the following information, either as a heading of the next literary unit (so NIV, SR, FC) or (as seen by Grotius) as belonging to verse 3 after a parenthesis of 39.1–2 (so RSV, NRSV, GNB, CEV). The latter part of the second option seems to be most in harmony with the syntactical structure of the discourse.

Translation Proposals

If 39.1–3 are taken together, verse 3 can be introduced, as in CEV, by "After Jerusalem was captured." A footnote can state that this phrase is from 38.28.

39.3

Textual Decisions

Following the first name, Nergal-sharezer, M reads סַמְגַּר, "Samgar," a word connected by means of a *maqqef*, a hyphen, to the following נְבוֹ־, "Nebu." The form סַמְגַּר was read by the Origen recension of G: Σαμαγαρ, by V: *Semegar*, and by T.

G (46.3), however, has the transliterated Σαμαγωθ, which presupposes the reading of a final *dalet*. So S: ܣܡܓܪܬܢܒܘ. Moreover, S distinguishes itself by the insertion of the connecting *waw* and by the unification of the two items that are separated by a *maqqef* in M.

The committee judged it very likely that an equivalence can be established between Nergal-Šarri-uṣur amêlu Sîn-magir, the second name on the list of Babylonian court officials published by Unger, and Nergal-sharezer Samgar in 39.3. It further discerned that the Greek reading of Codex Alexandrinus (apart from the *resh-dalet* confusion): ΝΗΡΓΕΛΣΑCΑCΑΡΕΙCCΑ-

ΜΑΓΑΘ, could reflect a Vorlage נרגל שראצר איש סמגר, "Nergal-sharezer, the man (from) Simmagir," which could be identical with the Neo-Babylonian name. The committee reasoned, however, that a translation according to the Babylonian list would lead translators into the prehistory of the biblical text and would force them to disconnect "Samgar" and "Nebu," which would leave them with the probably corrupt form "Nebusarsekim." Considering M to be less corrupt than the other variants, it accredited it with a B evaluation.

Evaluation of Problems

Most modern versions are in agreement with transliterating M. The result is usually "Samgar-nebo" (RSV, NRSV, NJV, NJB, GNB, FC, etc.).

It should be noted, however, that the decision to what extent the prehistory of a Hebrew text will be taken into account depends mainly on the principles of a translation project. If it is permitted to make use of data concerning the prehistory of the text, one still must decide whether "Sîn-magir" or "Simmagir" is a place-name: "Nergal-sharezer of/from Simmagir," or a title: "Nergal-sharezer the Simmagir." Von Soden (86–90) has defended the latter hypothesis, and he is followed by Barthélemy (727–28). Unger and McKane are in favor of the first hypothesis. Because the genitive construction is ambiguous, one also must decide whether Simmagir is the place of origin or the area over which the prince in question had authority.

The long discussion in McKane (974–76) clearly shows that we have no means of deciding between the two options. The title can only be transliterated, since we are unable to discern its function. No wonder, therefore, that the modern translations that used the Babylonian sources opted for the place-name (NEB, REB, NIV, NAB, CEV).

Translation Proposals

If one decides to use the place-name, "Nergalsarezer of Simmagir" (REB) would be an appropriate rendering, maintaining the ambiguity of the genetive construction. In a note, one could state that the names are found in a Babylonian inscription and that the person concerned became king of Babylon as successor to his brother-in-law Evilmarduk.

39.4

Textual Decisions

After the use of two verbs in third-person plural, M ends this verse with a verb in third-person singular: וַיֵּצֵא, "he set out," and this without the introduction of a new grammatical subject. This difficult reading is only attested by T: ונפק, "and he went out."

On the other hand, 12 manuscripts of Kennicott and de Rossi read the plural ויצאו, "and they went out," a reading confirmed by the recensions of Origen and Lucian, based on Th: καὶ ἐξῆλθον, further by V: *et egressi sunt*, and S: ܐܢܦܩܘ, all translating with third-person plural. The Old Greek is lacking verses 4–13.

The committee rationalized that the singular reading of the verb in the parallel text, 2 Kgs 25.4, proved on a literary level the authenticity of M in this verse. With regard to textual criticism, it preferred the more difficult reading of M to the contextual assimilation in most versions, with a B vote for M.

Evaluation of Problems

Most modern versions automatically make what they consider to be a necessary contextual assimilation, without even signaling the textual problem. Only NJB conscientiously notes that its reading, "and (they) made their way towards the Arabah," is based on S and that M reads "(he) made."

All modern Jewish versions (BR, NJV, Chouraqui), as well as NAB, adopt the reading of M, and, in view of the textual decisions taken, such a procedure must be seriously taken into consideration. There can be no doubt that the third-person singular form refers back to Zedekiah, king of Judah, mentioned in the beginning of the verse. But the contextual implications are important. This decision would imply that, in the course of his flight from Jerusalem, Zedekiah was at some stage separated from his soldiers. This would be in agreement with the exclusive focus on King Zedekiah in the following verses (Volz, 346; McKane, 978) and it would not necessarily be contradicted by the fact that the Chaldean troops pursued *them* in 39.5.

Translation Proposals

NJV can be quoted as an example. After a semicolon, it reads: "and he set out toward the Arabah." In the footsteps of Vatable in his annotations on the Bible of Estienne (1545), translators may prefer to make "the king" explicit as the agent.

39.8

Textual Decisions

The first object burned by the Chaldeans is the house of the king, the second according to M: וְאֶת־בֵּית הָעָם, "and the house of the people." This singular reading of M has the support of the Origen recension: καὶ τὸν οἶκον τοῦ λαοῦ (a rendering attributed to Th), of V: *et domum vulgi*, and of T: וית בית עמא.

The Lucianic recension of G, however, has a plural: "and the houses of the people," καὶ τοὺς οἴκους τοῦ λαοῦ, just like S: ܪܬ ܕ ܪܬܒܠܐ. As indicated in the preceding case, verses 4–13 are lacking in the Old Greek.

The committee assigned a B evaluation to the more-difficult and well-supported reading of M.

Evaluation of Problems

Rudolph (245) has proposed, based on the parallel text in Jer 52.13, inserting the following between the two nouns of M: יְהוָה וְאֶת־בָּתֵּי, "(the house of the king and the house) of the Lord and the houses (of the people)," information which would have been accidentally omitted from 39.8. According to Brockington (211), NEB adopts this suggestion when it translates this way: "The Chaldeans burnt the royal palace and the house of the Lord and the houses of the people." So still REB (compare also the note in NJB). No textual evidence exists for this correction, however, and in the parallel text the temple is mentioned before the palace.

It seems more correct, therefore, to identify "the house of the people" in 39.8 with "all the houses of Jerusalem" in 52.13, both following the reference to the palace. Ehrlich's original proposal to see a reference to the temple in the words "the house of the people" is weakened by the last argument of the above paragraph, although it is defended by Landsberger (152) and is found in a footnote of CEV, which proposes a variant translation.

NAB bases its plural rendering on a conjecture, and NJB uses S as a basis for its plural. These justifications may be unnecessary. Since Kimhi, the singular בית has often been analyzed as a collective noun. This legitimates a plural rendering, even without textual note, as in the majority of modern versions.

Translation Proposals

A rendering "houses of the people" could be footnoted, as in NJV: "Taking Heb. singular as collective, with Kimhi."

39.9

Textual Decisions

In M: וְאֵת יֶתֶר הָעָם הַנִּשְׁאָרִים, "and the remnant of the people that were left," the first and the last group of those who are exiled are literally the same. This repetition of information in M is supported by all the extant textual witnesses: Th, the Origen and Lucianic recensions of G, V, S, and T. The only difference is the presence of some stylistic variation in the Greek and Latin witnesses. As in the preceding cases, G is missing the verse.

Because all witnesses agree, M received an A evaluation.

Evaluation of Problems

From Giesebrecht (210) to, recently, McKane (979) and Holladay (269), it was commonly proposed to correct הָעָם, "the people," according to the parallel text in Jer 52.15, as הָאָמוֹן, "the artisans," reading thus: וְאֶת יֶתֶר הָאָמוֹן, "and any remaining artisans." This is what has been done in a number of recent versions, such as NEB, REB, NAB, NJB, and FC, which define the third group in this way. In fact, these translations assimilate to the parallel text as a whole, since הַנִּשְׁאָרִים, "that was left," which is present in 39.9 but not in 52.15, also remains untranslated. A correct description of the textual problems is found only in the footnote of NJB.

Although the result of this kind of intervention may be more satisfactory logically, assimilation should be avoided because it is devoid of any textual support.

In dealing with M, two translational possibilities exist: (1) apply a certain degree of stylistic variation as done in some ancient versions (so also RSV, NRSV, NIV, NJV); (2) consider M's repetition redundant and therefore omit it (GNB, CEV, GN, GrN).

Translation Proposals

Stylistic formulation of the repetition may, for example, take the form of the rendering in TOB: *bref, ce qui restait de la bourgeoisie,* "in short, what remained of the citizens."

Leaving the repetition implicit because of redundancy may lead to minor modifications, as in CEV: "led away everyone from the city as prisoners, even those who had deserted to Nebuchadrezzar." This rendering does justice to the focus on the information that is at the center of the chiastic construction.

39.11

Textual Decisions

According to M, Nebuchadnezzar gave an order concerning Jeremiah בְּיַד, "through," literally "through the hand of," Nebuzaradan, the captain of the guard.

The semi-preposition בְּיַד is attested by Th: ἐν χειρί, "through the hand (of)," a rendering adopted by the Origen recension of G. It is also confirmed by T.

However, according to the Syro-Hexapla, Sym has the order given directly to Nebuzaradan, and Sym also seems to have been the source of the rendering with a dative in the Lucianic recension of G: Ναβουζαρδαν τῷ ἀρχιμαγείρῳ, "to Nabuzaradan, the chief of the royal guard." The same translation is found in V: *Nabuzaradan magistro,* "to Nebuzaradan, the commander," and in S: ܠܢܒܘܙܪܕܢ, to Nebuzaradan." G is lacking verses 4–13.

The variant in which Nebuzaradan is directly addressed was not thought to be based on a different Hebrew Vorlage. It was instead taken to be the result of syntactical facilitation. M therefore received a B evaluation.

Evaluation of Problems

NEB and REB appeal exclusively to V in rendering "sent orders . . . to," according to their textual notes. It is clear, however, that V is a rendering of M. A literal rendering which tries to match the semi-preposition בְּיַד with the preposition "through" (RSV, NRSV, NAB, NIV) may be impossible in many languages. For an acceptable translation, therefore, the meaning of M has to be analyzed better.

The Hebrew semi-preposition indicates that Nebuzaradan was the person who was responsible for the execution of the order (Barthélemy, 735; McKane, 980) and at the same time extends the chain of command beyond Nebuzaradan (Rudolph, 245). Sym, V, and S (and so, for example, NJV, FC) emphasize the first implied meaning of בְּיַד; GNB focuses on the second, leaving Nebuzaradan's responsibility implied.

Translation Proposals

A paraphrase that does justice to all of the meaning components of בְּיַד is found in TOB: *Au sujet de Jéremie, Nabuchodonosor, roi de Babylone, prit des dispositions dont il confia l'exécution à Nebouzaradan, chef de la garde personelle, lui enjoignant,* "Nebuchadrezzar, king of Babylon, made arrangements concerning Jeremiah and he entrusted the execution of those to Nebuzarradan, commander of his body guard, ordering him. . . ."

GNB is a model that stresses the chain of command but leaves the self-evident responsibility of the captain of the guard implicit: "But King Nebuchadnezzar commanded Nebuzaradan, the commanding officer, to give the following order."

40.5

Textual Decisions

There are two major textual problems in this verse, the first consisting of the first two words: וְעֹדֶנּוּ לֹא־יָשׁוּב, "and he will still not return," and the second consisting of the following word: וְשָׁבָה, "and go back."

Regarding the first case, M does not seem to be supported by any witness. Although Ziegler puts G: εἰ δὲ μή ἀπότρεχε, "but if not, run away," at the beginning of verse 5 (47.5), it seems more correct to state that G is lacking. The phrase εἰ δὲ μή seems to summarize the first 6 words of the 22 in Hebrew between וְאָם in verse 4b and the last word of our first problem, and ἀπότρεχε apparently is a rendering of the last word of verse 4. With regard to the extant witnesses, Th reads: καὶ ἕως ἐμοῦ ἔτι οὐκ ἐπιστρέψεις, "and to me you will no longer return," a rendering which may have influenced V: *et mecum noli venire*, "and do not come with me." Sym has the rendering καὶ πρὶν ἢ ἀπαλλαγῶ ἐγώ, "and before I depart," whereas S reads ܐܡܪ ܠܗ ܐܢ ܬܩܘܐ, "and he said to him: if you remain." The consonantal text of T reads ואם לית את צבי למתב. The original text of T is probably represented by the manuscripts and editions which vocalize the last word as לְמִתַּב, "but if you do not want to stay." However, three manuscripts, including Codex Reuchlinianus, vocalize לְמֶתָב, "but if you do not want to return."

The committee judged that the attempt of the versions to insert the sentence into the discourse of Nebuzaradan is the reason for their great divergence, but they judged that none of them permits reconstructing a Hebrew Vorlage to compete with M. For this reason, M received a C evaluation.

Concerning the second case, וְשֻׁבָה, "and go back," M is attested by G: καὶ ἀνάστρεψον, and T: ותוב. However, V has the rendering *sed habita*, "but dwell," and S ܬܒ, "dwell." These renderings presuppose a different vocalization, וּשְׁבָה. According to the Syro-Hexapla, Sym would have had a double translation: ܦܘܩ ܘܬܒ, "return, stay."

The committee decided in this case that the vocalization of V and S unnecessarily anticipates the imperative וְשֵׁב, "and stay," which follows and that the use of distinct prepositions in M confirms the correctness of its vocalization. It therefore assigned a C evaluation to M.

Evaluation of Problems

From Cappel (1684, 532) to recently, Bright (242), many commentators followed G in omitting the first three words of M, as a corrupt gloss. This opinion has had some influence on (mainly older) translations (NV).

Out of embarrassment, some recent versions (RSV, NRSV) preferred to render S: "If you remain, then return to Gedaliah," but it seems better to try to interpret M. In this respect, the gloss by Estienne in his Bible of 1557 explains M in the following way: *Adhuc enim ille non responderat se velle reverti*, "For until that moment, he had not yet answered that he wanted to return." Thus יָשׁוּב was analyzed as having an implicit object, דָּבָר, "word": "return a word," or "answer." Schleusner in his edition of the *Observationes* of Johann D. Michaelis (1793) had objected that this meaning would require a *hiphil* vocalization יָשִׁיב, but König (1897, §383b) admits the possible use of the *qal*. This interpretation has been the basis of NEB: "Jeremiah had not yet answered when Nebuzaradan went on, Go back to Gedaliah," and of REB: "Before Jeremiah could answer, Nebuzaradan went on, 'Go back to Gedaliah.'" It has also been adopted by SR, GNB, and GrN.

It is also possible, however, to understand M literally: "before he left," as a kind of parenthesis by the redactor of the book of Jeremiah, as has been done in NJV, NIV, NJB, NAB, and FC.

Translation Proposals

For the last option, NIV can be taken as a model: "However, before Jeremiah turned to go, Nebuzaradan added, 'Go back to Gedaliah.'" As in NIV, translators could propose the variant translation in a footnote: "Or: Jeremiah answered."

40.8

Textual Decisions

Among the leaders who met with Gedaliah at Mizpah, M mentions וְיוֹחָנָן וְיוֹנָתָן בְּנֵי־קָרֵחַ, "Johanan and Jonathan, the sons of Kareah." Both names and the plural "sons" are attested by the Origen recension of G (47.8), V, and S, as well as by the most important witnesses of T. However, two manuscripts of Kennicott (145 and 154) and the first hand of three de Rossi manuscripts (20, 409, and 596) do not read וְיוֹנָתָן, "and Jonathan," and they therefore read the singular בֶּן, "son." This reading is also confirmed by the Old Greek and by Codex Reuchlinianus of T. It should further be noted that the Lucianic recension of G reads καὶ Ιωαναν υἱὸς Καρηε καὶ Ιωναθαν, "and Johanan, son of Kareah, and Jonathan," and that it is followed by the first editions of V: *& Iohanan filius Caree & Ionathan.*

The committee considered it possible, on the one hand, that the Old Greek could have preserved the original state of the text but, on the other hand, did not exclude the possibility that the variants were the result of an assimilation to the form "Johanan, son of Kareah," found in the parallel 2 Kgs 25.23 and in Jer 40.13–16; 41.11–16; 42.1, 8; 43.2, 4, 5. It also noted (with Rudolph, 248) the other abbreviations in the parallel of Kings. The B vote for M was in fact intended to avoid the assimilation of a rare reading to the form in one of its parallels.

Evaluation of Problems

From Giesebrecht (213) to Holladay (271), commentators frequently regarded M as a conflate text (Janzen, 17), and therefore they eliminated the plural and corrected the grammar. Some recent versions apparently have done the same, speaking only of "Jonathan son of Kareah" (RSV, NRSV, GNB, NAB) but, with the notable exception of NAB, they give no textual justification for this rendering.

Rudolph (248) has correctly observed that G could also have omitted "Jonathan" through haplography of . . . ויו and that the parallel text in 2 Kgs 25.23 has little authority in view of the elimination of other names in the list. It therefore seems appropriate to render M, with the majority of modern translations. In projects with Orthodox participation, the translation of G can be footnoted as a variant translation, as is done in NEB.

Translation Proposals

With the majority of translations, the rendering of the text should be: "Johanan and Jonathan, the sons of Kareah."

5

JEREMIAH 41-50

41.1

Textual Decisions

According to M, Gedaliah received a visitor named "Ishmael, son of Nethaniah, son of Elishama," after which M continues: מִזֶּרַע הַמְּלוּכָה וְרַבֵּי הַמֶּלֶךְ וַעֲשָׂרָה אֲנָשִׁים, "of royal blood and chief officers of the king and ten men." The third and the fourth Hebrew words, וְרַבֵּי הַמֶּלֶךְ, have been literally rendered by V: *et optimates regis*, "and the best men of the king," S: ܘܪܘܪܒܢܐ ܕܡܠܟܐ, "and the royal princes," and T: ורברבי מלכא, "and the princes of the king." M is also attested by the Origen recension of G: ἀπὸ γένους τοῦ βασιλέως καὶ τὰ παιδάρια τοῦ βασιλέως, "of the family of the king and the children of the king," and by the Lucianic recension: ἀπὸ γένους τῆς βασιλείας καὶ τὰ παιδάρια τοῦ βασιλέως, "of royal family and the children of the king." The peculiar translation τὰ παιδάρια, "the children," may have been due to a misinterpretation and a reading of Aramaic (א)רבי, "youth" (see also HUB). The Old Greek, however, only has: ἀπὸ γένους τοῦ βασιλέως, "of the family of the king."

The committee considered that G probably had been victim of *homoioarcton* (identical beginning of two words), the eye of the translator having shifted from the second word to the fourth word in M, as cited above. Since the presence of the two words in M cannot be explained as a textual accident, M received a B evaluation.

Evaluation of Problems

Most scholars from Giesebrecht (214) to Holladay (II, 272) pronounced themselves in favor of the omission of וְרַבֵּי הַמֶּלֶךְ, "and chief officers of the king," with G. This position influenced several older translations, such as Moffatt, LV, and W, and among recent versions it influenced NEB and REB, according to their textual notes.

Although a rendering of M should be preferred, the ambiguous syntax of the source text allows four different interpretations: (1) Ishmael is of royal blood, and the chief officers of the king form a separate group; (2) Ishmael is of royal blood, and the chief officers of the king consist of ten men; (3) Ishmael is of royal blood and belongs to the group of the chief officers of the king; the ten men form a distinct group; (4) Ishmael's grandfather Elishama was of royal blood, and a leading royal official and the ten men are separate.

The last interpretation was defended by Ehrlich (1912, 345) and Richter (123f.) and is preferred by Barthélemy (743), but it did not clearly enter into any translation. The first interpretation was adopted by SR and NJB but, although some of the ambiguity of the original is carried over in literal translations and makes an analysis difficult, the vast majority of modern versions seem to have adopted the third, probably preferable, interpretation. In projects in which unintentional ambiguities of the source text should not be reproduced in translation, an unambiguous formulation of relationships imposes itself.

Translation Proposals

For a translation preserving the ambiguity, see NIV for an example. A transparent formulation of the third interpretation is found in CEV: "But in the seventh month, Ishmael . . . came to Mizpah with ten of his soldiers. He had been one of the king's officials and was a member of the royal family." If the first interpretation is preferred, NJB can be cited as an example: "In the seventh month, however, Ishmael son of Nethaniah son of Elishama, who was of royal descent, came with officers of the king and ten men to Gedaliah son of Ahikam at Mizpah."

41.9

Textual Decisions

After the information "the cistern into which Ishmael had thrown all the bodies of the men," M proceeds with אֲשֶׁר הִכָּה בְיַד־גְּדַלְיָהוּ, "whom he had struck down by the hand of Gedaliah." The textual problem concerns the last two words, which make little sense.

G (48.9) has the rendering φρέαρ μέγα, "a large cistern" which seems to presuppose a different Hebrew Vorlage, בור גדל. The Origen recension, keeping the Old Greek rendering, adds: ἐν χειρὶ Γοδολίου, "by the hand of Gedaliah." This reading of M is also supported by T: ביד גדליה.

In order to facilitate the interpretation of M, the Lucianic recension, also keeping the Old Greek, inserts: μετὰ Γοδολίου, "with Gedaliah," taking some liberty in the rendering of the preposition. The same freedom is taken by S: ܥܡ ܓܕܠܝܐ, "with Gedaliah," and V: *propter Godoliam*, "because of Gedaliah" or "next to Gedaliah."

It is true that de Rossi found the reading ביד in his manuscript 226, but this manuscript from the 12th century was not copied very carefully, and it is difficult to build an argument upon a ר/ד and ו/י confusion.

In view of the difficulty in ascribing a satisfactory meaning to ביד in M, the committee as a whole adopted the Vorlage בור of G with a C evaluation. Two members also endorsed the Vorlage גדול, "large," of G with the same evaluation. The other four members, convinced by Ehrlich's argument (346) that the reconstruction of such a Vorlage is inadequate because of the lack of definite articles, maintained M for the second word: "the cistern of Gedaliah," that is, the cistern in which the body of Gedaliah had been thrown.

Evaluation of Problems

Although a majority of scholars correct M according to G, a number of modern versions (BR, Chouraqui, NJV, NIV, SR, NEB) still retain M. Some of these interpret the questionable preposition as "along with" (NIV, BR) which is lexically still possible. Others, such as NJV: "in the affair of," or NEB: "by using Gedaliah's name," interpret it in a more questionable way. The only consideration these translations have in common is that Gedaliah was the ultimate cause of the slaughter of the 80 men (McKane, 1020).

It should also be noted that Ehrlich's arguments about Hebrew grammar and the sound reasoning that there is no need to state that a cistern is great when 100 corpses have been dumped into it convinced the majority of the committee but none of the translators! It seems acceptable, with a minority of the committee, to follow G, especially in projects with Orthodox participation. In interconfessional translations, the reading of M should be mentioned in a footnote.

Translation Proposals

REB can be taken as a model of the above-mentioned textual choice: "The cistern in which he threw all the bodies of those whom he had killed was the large one which King Asa had made."

41.16

Textual Decisions

The first part of the verse in M states that Johanan, son of Kareah, took all the rest of the people אֲשֶׁר הֵשִׁיב מֵאֵת יִשְׁמָעֵאל, "whom he recovered from Ishmael." This relative sentence: "whom he had brought back from Ishmael," is confirmed by G (48.16): οὓς ἀπέστρεψεν ἀπὸ Ισμαηλ (which after this, however, omits the following ten words in M): *quas reduxerat ab Ishmahel*, by S: ܐܝܟܢܐ ܕܐܦܢܝ ܡܢ ܐܝܫܡܥܐܠ, and by T: דאתיב מלות ישמעאל.

M, being attested by all textual witnesses, received an A evaluation.

Evaluation of Problems

From Hitzig to, recently, Holladay, the emendation אֹתָם שָׁבָה אֲשֶׁר, "whom (Ishmael) had taken captive," was proposed, and this conjecture has been adopted by many recent versions (RSV, NRSV, GNB, NAB, NJB). There is no textual justification for doing so, and a rendering of M should be preferred.

It is true that the redaction of this particular verse is very confusing and overcharged. This is most likely the reason that G omitted the following ten words in M, which are a source of semantic disturbance. The following comple- ment, מִן־הַמִּצְפָּה, "from Mizpah," especially causes problems. Some translations have tried to solve these problems in putting this complement after the first verb, "took": "Johanan . . . took from Mizpah all the survivers whom he had rescued from Ishmael . . ." (so NEB and REB and, as far as construction is concerned, NIV). However, they created other problems in doing so! Barthélemy (746) sup- poses that "from Mizpah" is in fact shorthand for a longer paraphrase: "he (= Ishmael) having taken them away as prisoners from Mizpah." Semantically, the result is the same as that of the emendation. Although the possibility of such an extended amount of implicit information could be questioned, this nevertheless seems to be a possible way to deal with the problem.

Translation Proposals

NAV is an example of this kind of textual treatment: *Joganan seun van Kareag en al die leëraanvoerders by hom het al die mense saamgeneem wat oor was, al die mans, die soldate, die vrouens, kinders en ontmandes wat hy by Gibeon bevry het en wat deur Ismael seun van Netanja weggevoer was uit Mispa*, "Johanan, son of Kareah, and all the army officers with him had taken all the people which remained, all the men, the soldiers, the women, children, and eunuchs whom he had rescued at Gibeon and who had been taken away by Ishmael, son of Nethaniah, from Mizpah."

42.1

Textual decisions

After having mentioned all the commanders of the forces, and Johanan, son of Kareah, M adds the name וִיזַנְיָה בֶּן־הוֹשַׁעְיָה, "and Jezaniah, son of Hoshaiah," also attested by V, S, and T.

G (49.1), however, has καὶ Αζαρίας υἱὸς Μαασαίου, "and Azarias, son of Maasaeas," as in the parallel text, 43.2 (50.2). The recensions of Origen and Lucian have the double reading καὶ Ιεζονίας υἱὸς Ανανίου καὶ Αζαρίας υἱὸς Ωσαίου (Lucian: Ιωσαίου), "and Jezaniah, son of Ananiah, and Aza- riah, son of Hoshaiah."

The committee considered it possible that the Greek recensions had the following Hebrew Vorlage: ויזניה בן חנניה ועזריה בן הושעיה, "and Jezaniah, son of Hananiah, and Azariah, son of Hoshaiah," and that the text of M was the result of an accident of homoioarcton, the eye of a scribe having shifted from the first occurrence of בן, "son," to the second. However, it judged the two Greek recensions to be insufficient basis for a high degree of certainty. It also considered it hazardous to take G as grounds for the assimilation of the name to the one presented in 43.2. Taking into account the further versional support for M, the committee gave it a C evaluation.

Evaluation of Problems

Most scholars join Ewald by replacing the name Jezaniah in M with the name Azariah from G, and the vast majority of modern versions (with or without a textual note) do the same. This is rather surprising since the same scholars, with the notable exception of Ehrlich (347), refuse to assimilate the rare proper name Hoshaiah of M, which otherwise occurs only in Neh 12.32, to the frequently used proper name Maaseiah, as done by G in 42.1 and 43.2. Moreover, it should be noted that Jezaniah is also a relatively rare proper name (only six occurrences) in comparison with the recurrently used proper name Azariah (47 times).

For all of these reasons, it seems more prudent to render M with a minority of recent translations (NJV, NIV, CEV, SR, BR).

Translation Proposals

The rendering "Jezaniah, son of Hoshaiah," could have a footnote containing the complete rendering of G. It could further be stated that the original Hebrew text may have read: "and Jezaniah, son of Hananiah, and Azariah, son of Hoshaiah."

42.12A

Textual Decisions

In M, after having said: וְאֶתֵּן לָכֶם רַחֲמִים, which could mean: "And I will grant you mercy," or "And I will grant you (to arouse) mercy," the Lord continues: וְרִחַם אֶתְכֶם, "and he will have mercy on you," in which "he" apparently refers back to the "king of Babylon," mentioned in the preceding verse. This third-person singular of the verb only has the support of T: וירחים עליכון, "and he will have mercy on you." All the other extant versions read a first-person singular: "and I will grant you mercy," G: καὶ ἐλεήσω ὑμᾶς, V: *et miserebor vestri*, and S: ܘܐܪܚܡܟܘܢ.

The committee gave M a B evaluation considering the assimilation to the first person in the last three versions to be due to a misunderstanding of the ambiguous preceding sentence in M.

Textual Problems

Houbigant (1753, 238) proposed correcting M, but he had very few followers, Delitzsch (1920, par 58b) being one of the rare exceptions. In the domain of translation, the situation is the same. Many medieval translations, such as the Middle Dutch translation of 1384, rendered first person because they were based on V. It was under the influence of V that Luther, in his 1545 Bible, kept the first person: *und* (*wil*) *mich über euch erbarmen,* "and I will have mercy upon you." It is less understandable that the last Luther revision (1984) has literally followed the text of the Luther Bible, which was abandoned by other versions such as EÜ and GN.

M will have to be rendered with the quasi totality of recent translations, and care must be taken to interpret and render the preceding sentence correctly. This could be paraphrased: "And I will grant you (to arouse) mercy," namely, in the king of Babylon.

Translation Proposals

NJV can be quoted as an example of such an interpretation: "I will dispose him to be merciful to you: he shall show you mercy."

42.12B

Textual Decisions

The second part of the verse in M starts with the verb וְהֵשִׁיב, "and he will bring back," "and he will bring you back to your own land." As in the preceding case, M is only supported by T: ויתיב, "and he will restore," "and he will restore you to your own land."

All other versions agree in using a verb in first-person singular, but only G (49.12) corresponds to M's derivation from the root שׁוּב, "return": καὶ ἐπιστρέψω ὑμᾶς, "and I will bring you back." Aq, rendering according to the Syro-Hexapla ܐܘܬܒܟܘܢ, "and I will cause you to dwell," S, with the same, and V: *et habitare vos faciam,* "and I will make you live," all render their Hebrew Vorlage as a derivative from the root ישׁב, "to dwell."

The committee considered it possible that all versions read the same Hebrew consonants, interpreting them as an infinitive absolute and attaching them either to the root שׁוּב, "return," or the root ישׁב, "dwell." The first-person rendering was judged to be a contextual assimilation, as in the preceding case, the first one making the second obligatory. The committee regarded the rendering of M to be meaningful, and it opted for M, with a C vote.

Evaluation of Problems

The first-person rendering of most ancient versions has in the case of modern translations only had a self-evident influence on Luther and RL (see the preceding case).

The issue which has divided commentators and translators alike is the root from which the Hebrew consonantal form must be derived. J. D. Michaelis already proposed the vocalization וְהֹשִׁיב, "and he will let you stay," from the root יָשַׁב, and he was followed by many commentators, including recently McKane (1034f.), and by a number of translations, such as RSV, NEB, REB, and LB. Other commentators, with (Rudolph, 254) or without arguments (Bright, 251; Holladay II, 274), defend the vocalization of M, and so do most modern versions.

Against a derivation from שׁוּב, "return," it has been argued that the fugitives were still in Judah. That they were at the border between Judah and Egypt, fleeing to Egypt, is a counterargument. So Jeremiah's assurance that the king of Babylon authorized their "return" to the country makes sense. Here, as in other cases, the *hiphil* הֵשִׁיב implies the meaning "to authorize somebody to do something."

Translation Proposals

M can be rendered as in NJV: "he shall show you mercy and bring you back to your own land."

43.10

Textual Decisions

According to M, after having said: "I am going to send and take my servant, King Nebuchadrezzar of Babylon," God continues: וְשַׂמְתִּי, "and I will set," "and I will set his throne above these stones." This first-person reading of the verb "I will set" is attested by Aq with his rendering ܐܣܝܡ according to the Syro-Hexapla, by V: *et ponam*, and by T: וֶאֱשַׁוֵּי, both: "and I will place."

In opposition to this reading, G: καὶ θήσει, S:ܢܣܝܡ, and Codex Amiatinus of V: *et ponet*, have a rendering of the third-person singular: "and he will place," referring to the king of Babylon as the agent.

The committee noted that the following verb also has a different grammatical person in G. Hence, they supposed that there was a literary remodeling of the text at the initiative of either M or G. In order to avoid a tainting of one literary state by the other, the committee decided to assign a B evaluation to M.

Evaluation of Problems

From Giesebrecht (219) to McKane (1056), the third-person reading was largely preferred by commentators and translators: RSV, NRSV, GNB, NEB, REB, NAB, and NJB. Sometimes even a different Hebrew Vorlage, וְשָׂם אֶת־, "and he set" + direct object marker, was reconstructed (Rudolph, 258; BHS; and Brockington for NEB) against all probabilities, hinting at a possible textual accident! Only occasionally was the warning sounded that M was not impossible (Bright, 259 and Holladay II, 277).

McKane (1056) in his recent discussion, in which the data of the Final Report were taken into account, paid no attention to the real motivations of the committee in their judgment of M and G. The committee did not deny that G could be original rather than M; they only stated that they were rejecting a decision by which one literary tradition would contaminate another.

Translation projects in which this rejection has been adopted as a principle will therefore follow M with a minority of recent versions (NJV, NIV, CEV, SR, FC, RL, GN). A compromise between M and the variants is nevertheless possible, similar to the way that CEV has rendered the text.

Translation Proposals

Either NIV: "and I will set his throne over these stones," or (in the spirit of the compromise signaled above) CEV: "I will . . . have him set up his throne . . . over these stones," can be quoted as a translational example.

43.12

Textual Decisions

M starts this verse with וְהִצַּתִּי, "and I will set," "and I will set fire," and this first-person verb is followed by four verbs in third-person masculine singular referring to Nebuchadrezzar. The first person of M is protected by a *Masorah parva* which signals six occurrences of the verbal form and which, according to Ginsburg (*Masorah* IV 518, §543), stems from one of the oldest Masoretic lists. The reading is also attested by Aq and Sym as stated in the Syro-Hexapla: ܐܘܩܕ, "I will kindle," and by T: ואדליק, "and I will kindle."

On the other hand, G (50.12) renders the third-person singular of the verb: καὶ καύσει, "and he will kindle." So do V: *et succendet*, "and he will kindle," and S: ܘܢܘܩܕ, "and he will set (a fire) to."

The committee considered it obvious that the third-person rendering of G, V, and S was simply the result of an assimilation to the third-person singular readings of the verbs in the context. A majority B evaluation was therefore assigned to M.

Evaluation of Problems

Ever since Houbigant, almost all commentators have adopted the third-person singular rendering. Some of them (Rudolph, 258; McKane, 1050; Holladay II, 277; BHS) do so on the basis of a presupposed Hebrew consonant Vorlage והצית. Such a Vorlage would only differ from M in the transposition of *yod* and *taw*. However, no commentator discusses whether an accidental or an intentional metathesis is concerned or in which direction. The majority position of the commentators has nevertheless influenced recent translations considerably (RSV, NRSV, NEB, REB, NAB, NJB, FC). Even translations that traditionally adhere to M, such as NIV, agree with that position, banishing M to a variant reading in a footnote.

However, as in the preceding case, M makes excellent sense in stressing the fact that Nebuchadrezzar is only acting as God's agent (Freedman and Rosenberg, 281). The opening reference to God in first person and the implied reference to Nebuchadrezzar in the following verbs emphasize this fact again through the sequence of events in the text. Therefore, M can be selected, as done in NJV, GNB, GN, NAV, and GrN. The implicit relationships between agents can also be spelled out, as in CEV.

Translation Proposals

NJV: "And I will set fire to the temples of the gods of Egypt," or CEV: "I will have him set Egypt's temples on fire," could be a translation example. If the first option is chosen, a footnote may state the reading of G, as done in NJV.

44.9

Textual Decisions

After the crimes of the kings of Judah, M mentions the crimes נָשָׁיו, "of his wives." This reading of M, difficult with regard to the pronominal suffix, has the support of Aq: αὐτοῦ, "of him," and of Sym, according to Field but not according to Ziegler: ἑκάστου αὐτῶν, "of each of them." It is also attested by V: *uxorum eius*, and T: נשוהי, both: "of his wives."

On the other hand, the Lucianic recension of G (51.9) has the logically expected plural pronoun αὐτῶν: γυναικῶν αὐτῶν, as do S: ܢܫܝܗܘܢ, and some of the Vulgate editions: *uxorum eorum* (Froben, Gadolo, and the Alcala polyglot), all meaning: "of their wives."

Finally, in G no wives of kings are mentioned at all, but τῶν ἀρχόντων ὑμῶν, "of your princes."

The committee considered the rendering of G to be an assimilation to parallels such as 8.1, 44.17, and 44.21 and the plural pronominal suffix rendering of some recensions and versions to be a translational facilitation. It took the singular suffix reading of M to be a reference to only one of the kings of Judah, Solomon, who would not have been mentioned by the author, out of a sense of decency. M was therefore approved by a majority of B votes.

Evaluation of Problems

According to Houbigant, G reflects a Hebrew Vorlage with שָׂרָיו, "his princes," which he considered to be original. Some commentators, most recently Ehrlich (350), followed him in this judgment. It had little impact upon modern translation, however, NJB and FC being the only notable exceptions.

On the other side, the interpretation of M defended by the committee seems to be rather forced (so also McKane, 1092), and the lack of any translation proposal in CTAT is not surprising. However, the singular suffix of M can be understood as having a distributive sense: "of the wives of every one of them." In fact, this was Sym's interpretation already, and it became the classic through Radaq and Zwingli. It is also one of the possible renderings proposed in the Preliminary Report (290). Should such an emphasis be judged superfluous, translators could follow (with all other modern translations) the facilitation of some of the ancient versions.

Textual footnotes are only necessary in projects with Orthodox participation because of the distinct literary tradition of G.

Translation Proposals

NIV is one of the examples that could be followed: "Have you forgotten the wickedness committed by your fathers and by the kings and queens of Judah."

44.15

Textual Decisions

Among those contesting the oracle of Jeremiah, M mentions "(all the people who lived in the land of Egypt) in Pathros": בְּפַתְרוֹס, therefore locating Pathros within Egypt. This reading of M is also attested by G, V, and T. Only S: ܘܒܦܬܪܘܣ, "and in Pathros," and two manuscripts of V distinguish the two separate locations, by means of the preceding conjunction.

The committee considered this variant to be due to syntactical facilitation, and it allotted an A evaluation to the asyndeton of M.

Evaluation of Problems

Stade (1886, 296) omitted the whole sentence "and all the people living in Egypt, in Pathros," considering it a later addition. He has been followed by some more recent commentators (Rudolph, 260; Bright, 261), but only by one modern version: NEB.

The rendering with conjunction is based on the insight that "Mitsrayim," or "Egypt," stands for Lower Egypt (or Northern Egypt) and Pathros for Upper Egypt (or Southern Egypt). This insight was already noted by Bochart (Phaleg 276, 22) and it has been repeated by Holladay (2, 279). It has been adopted with a correct textual annotation by NAB: "all the people who lived in Lower and Upper Egypt," without textual note in CEV: "Jews from both northern and southern Egypt," and with a wrong textual footnote in NIV, stating: "Hebrew *in Egypt and Pathros.*"

However, the evidence in Ezek 29.14, which deals with the "Egyptians" brought back to their home country, the land of Pathros, shows that the inhabitants of Pathros could be called "Egyptians."

This evidence, combined with the A evaluation of M, would make a strong point for a rendering of M, with most modern versions (RSV, NRSV, NJV, REB). For reasons of comprehensibility, geographical indications could be modernized translationally.

Translation Proposals

For a literal translation, NRSV: "all the people who lived in Pathros in the land of Egypt," can be taken as an example and for a functional type of translation, GNB: "including the Israelites who lived in Southern Egypt."

44.19

Textual Decisions

This verse begins in M with וְכִי, "And when," as a continuation of the speech which started at the beginning of verse 16. This expression in M is confirmed by G (51.19): καὶ ὅτι, Th: καὶ ὅτε, Sym: εἰ δὲ καί, V: *quod si,* and T: וארי, all meaning: "and when."

However, the recensions of Origen and Lucian have the following insertion before the beginning of the verse: καὶ αἱ γυναῖκες εἶπον, "And the women said."

A somewhat different insertion is found in S: ܘܥܢܝ ܟܠܗܝܢ ܢܫܐ ܘܐܡܪܝܢ, "And all the women answered and said."

The committee considered the agreement between M, G, and V with regard to the shorter reading as well as the disagreement between the insertions in the Greek recensions and in S to be decisive in voting for M with a majority B evaluation.

Evaluation of Problems

A number of commentators regard the longer text as original, and only their reconstructed Hebrew Vorlage differs, depending on whether Lucian/Origen (Rudolph, 260; BHS) or S (Stade 1886, 297) has been taken as the basis for the reconstruction. Many modern versions (RSV, NRSV, NEB, REB) follow the longer reading, providing textual informations in a footnote. These notes are not sufficiently transparent, however, for the reader to discover the textual judgment of the translators.

Other commentators have correctly considered the insertion to be an exegetical supplementation (van Selms, II, 210; McKane, 1076), and some recent translations such as NAB, and NJV simply render M, apparently judging that "our husbands' approval" later in the verse is an adequate indication of who the speakers are. Only NJB, not absolutely sure that this information does not come too late, adds a footnote after the word "besides" that states: "The women speak at this point."

In fact, for the sake of clarity it may be necessary to follow the example of the Greek recensions and S and make this information explicit straight away at the beginning of the verse. The information should not necessarily take the form of the versions, however, and it should not be accompanied by a textual footnote.

Translation Proposals

A brief introduction, as in NIV: "The women added," illustrates this requirement.

44.23

Textual Decisions

After having stated why this disaster has befallen the Judeans, this verse ends in M with the expression כַּיּוֹם הַזֶּה, "as (at) this day." These words are lacking in G (51.23), but they are present in all other columns of the Hexapla as well in the recensions of Origen and Lucian: καθὼς ἡ ἡμέρα αὕτη, "as this very day." The expression is also confirmed by V: *sicut et die hac*, "as also this day," S: ܐܝܟ ܝܘܡܐ ܗܢܐ, "as this very day," and also by T: כיומא הדין, "as this day." The omission in G was explained as an effort to avoid the burdensome repetition of the same words, already present at the end of the preceding verse. Their presence in M was therefore not considered to be the result of a textual accident, and M received a majority A evaluation.

Evaluation of Problems

Only more recent commentators (Holladay, II, 279 and McKane, 1078) prefer the shorter text of G, judging the presence of this expression in M at the end of verse 23 to be distinctly superfluous. NEB seems to be alone among modern versions in omitting the statement for textual reasons. It is true that it is also absent in some other translations such as CEV, but the absence of a footnote suggests that this omission is to be explained by translation considerations, as in G.

The repetition in two successive verses of M can be taken as a rhetorical device in order to create impact (CTAT, 758). This impact is produced in some cases by verbatim repetition (NJV, RL, SR) and in others by stylistic variation. Examples of the last can be found in NJB, NIV, and REB.

Translation Proposals

When verbatim repetition is chosen, NJV with its refrain "as is still the case" presents a good example. For stylistic variation, see REB with "as it still is" (verse 22) and "The disaster you *now* (my italics) suffer" (verse 23).

44.25A

Textual Decisions

The addressees of this oracle are, according to M: אַתֶּם וּנְשֵׁיכֶם, "you and your wives." They are the same in the Greek recensions of Origen and Lucian (51.25): ὑμεῖς καὶ αἱ γυναῖκες ὑμῶν, in V: *vos et uxores vestrae*, S: ܐܢܬܘܢ ܘܢܫܝܟܘܢ, and T: אתון ונשיכון—all of these versions having the same meaning as M.

The Old Greek, however, has only the women as adressees: ὑμεῖς γυναῖκες, "you, women."

The committee considered M to be the more difficult reading, the verb following the address being feminine plural, whereas the foregrounded addressee, אַתֶּם, "you," is masculine plural. Because of the coherence of the proto-Masoretic text, M received a majority B evaluation.

Evaluation of Problems

The correction of M to אַתֵּנָה הַנָּשִׁים, "you women," as the presupposed Hebrew Vorlage behind G, first introduced by Giesebrecht (223), has been widely followed by modern commentators. It has, nevertheless, been of little consequence for modern translations, since the Greek has only been adopted in NEB and REB.

The more difficult reading has to be retained by translators. The broken syntax of M probably is the result of a synthesis of arguments formulated by both men and women, as was the case in verses 16–19. In many languages this kind of syntax cannot be reproduced to the same semantic effect, and some harmonization may be necessary.

Translation Proposals

For a useful translation model, see NJB: "You and your wives, what your mouths promised, your hands have indeed performed!"

44.25B

Textual Decisions

At the end of the verse, twice M has the reading אֶת־נִדְרֵיכֶם, "your vows," "confirm your vows and perform your vows." The second occurrence of this word is only confirmed by the Greek recensions of Origen and Lucian: τὰς εὐχὰς ὑμῶν, by T: נדריכון, and S: ܢܕܖ̈ܝܟܘܢ, all: "your vows."

The repetition of the object is absent in the Old Greek (51.25), whereas in V it is reduced to the demonstrative pronoun *ea*, "these," referring back to *vota*, "vows."

On the other hand, the first or second hand of seven manuscripts of Kennicott and de Rossi (226, 228, 250, 380, 211, 554, and 663) do not repeat the word, but read instead נִסְכֵּיכֶם, "your libations." This is also the rendering of T, according to manuscript Urbinates I and according to the first and second Rabbinic Bible and the London Polyglot.

It can be noted that, according to the Aleppo Codex and the *Masorah* edited by Ginsburg (נ, §121), the repetition of M is protected by a *masorah*, which states that the word occurs four times in the Bible, twice in this particular verse. Further, it can be stated that M is supported directly by the Greek recensions of Origen/Lucian, S, and T and indirectly by V with *ea*, and even by G, where the object is left implicit.

This case has been treated in CTAT (759–60), but it was not submitted to the judgment of the committee.

Evaluation of Problems

Following Janzen (58), Holladay adopted the omission of the repetition, with G (II, 280), but this omission has only been followed by literal translations which have chosen the Old Greek as their exclusive base text.

On the other hand, the correction נִסְכֵּיכֶם, "your libations," has been proposed by Volz (367) and it has found approval by a number of recent commentators. Its effect on modern translations remains very limited. It is manifestly endorsed by NRSV, but without any textual justification. It is also selected in TOB which refers to the above-mentioned Hebrew manuscripts.

However, McKane (1079) is no doubt correct in considering this variant an "improvement" of M rather than a witness to an original text. Therefore, M should be preferred in translating. If a literal repetition would be cumbersome in the target language, acceptable stylistic variation could, of course, be introduced, but the stress implied in the repetition of the source language should be expressed.

Translation Proposals

Many recent versions present examples of stylistic variation. Compare NAB: "Very well! keep your vows, carry out your resolutions!" and NJB: "Very well, keep your vows, perform them punctiliously!"

46.9

Textual Decisions

In verse 9b, after having evoked כּוּשׁ וּפוּט תֹּפְשֵׂי מָגֵן, "Cush and Put, that are grasping the shield," M terminates the verse with וְלוּדִים תֹּפְשֵׂי דֹּרְכֵי קָשֶׁת, "and the Ludim who are grasping, drawing the bow." The textual problem has been connected with the repetition of the verbal participle תֹּפְשֵׂי, "who are grasping," in the second half-line at the end of the verse.

M is literally confirmed by Aq and Sym according to the Syro-Hexapla: ܡܣ, and by V: *arripientes*, both: "grasping." With the only difference being that the participle has been rendered by a plural imperative, M is also attested by G (26.9), if Ziegler's emendation ἀναλάβετε, "take," proposed by Spohn, is accepted. All extant Greek texts read ἀνάβητε, "go up," however, no doubt by assimilation to the occurrences of this Greek verb in the preceding context.

T, translating the second verb "who smite," renders the first participle with דנגדין, "who draw," which seems to be an assimilation to the related Targumic text of Isa 66.19. S takes this and the following participle together: (ܒܩܫܬܐ) ܠܡܫܕܐ ܝܕܥܝܢ, "who know to shoot (with the bow)."

The committee considered the repetition of a verbal form to be a normal phenomenon in Jeremiah. The juxtaposition of two plural participles in the construct state was deemed to have several parallels. Combined with the strong textual support, this resulted in a B vote for M.

Evaluation of Problems

From Houbigant to, recently, McKane (1116), the deletion of the second occurrence of תֹּפְשֵׂי, "who are grasping," because of dittography was generally defended by commentators. It is also reflected in many modern translations, sometimes with an accompanying footnote (NAB, NJB, NRSV), sometimes without (NIV, GN). In view of the fact that the textual tradition has unanimously read two verbs in the second half of verse 9b, the omission of "who grasp" can only be considered a conjecture.

The character of the Hebrew text nevertheless remains unsatisfactory for translators. They have to choose between an almost literal rendering of M (NJV,

SR) or some kind of paraphrase (RSV, NEB, REB, GNB). With the last choice, a qualifying paraphrase of the type already found in S may be preferred.

Translation Proposals

For an almost literal translation, NJV can serve as an example: "And the Ludim who grasp and draw the bow," and for a paraphrase, RSV: "men of Lud, skilled in handling the bow."

46.12

Textual Decisions

In the beginning of this verse, the grammatical object of what the nations have heard, is according to M: קְלוֹנֵךְ, "your shame." The same object is found in: τὴν ἀτιμίαν σου, "your disgrace," a version which the Greek Barberini manuscript attributes to Sym and the Syro-Hexapla attributes to Aq and Sym. M is also supported by V: *ignominiam tuam*, by S: ܒܗܬܟܝ, and T: קלניך, all: "your shame."

G (26.12) however, has the rendering φωνήν σου, "your voice" and a rendering τὴν φωνήν σου has been ascribed by the Barberini manuscript to both Th and Aq.

As seen above, there is a discrepancy between the Barberini manuscript and the Syro-Hexapla regarding the rendering attributed to Aq. The committee considered it more likely that Aq would confirm the reading of M. It further took G to be an assimilation to "your cry" in the second half-line. M therefore received a B vote.

Evaluation of Problems

From Cappel (1684, 533a) to, recently, McKane (1120), many scholars preferred the rendering of G, assigning it to a Hebrew Vorlage קוֹלֵךְ, "your voice." Translators seem not to have been particularly impressed by their arguments, since only NEB and REB adopted G.

There is no doubt that G presents the easier reading and M the more difficult one (Holladay, II, 322). And, although the textual evidence in favor of G could be somewhat stronger than suggested by the vote of the committee, M should be rendered, with the overwhelming majority of modern translations. In projects with Orthodox participation, the rendering of G should preferably be displayed in a footnote.

Translation Proposals

For the whole line NJB can be taken as example: "The nations have heard of your shame, / your wailing fills the world."

46.15

Textual Decisions

In M the first half-line of this verse runs as follows: מַדּוּעַ נִסְחַף אַבִּירֶיךָ, "Why is (are) your mighty one(s) overthrown?" However, there are important textual problems with the second and the last word.

The verbal root of M has been retained by S: ܐܬܬܚܪܒܘ, "(Why) are (your mighty ones) overthrown?" Sym: συνεψήσθη, "swept away," seems to be based on the Hebrew root סחב, since this Hebrew verb is rendered with συμψάω by G in 22.19, by G and Sym in 49.20, and by Aq in 50.45. V renders the verb *conputruit*, "has become putrid," as has been done in 38.11. The origin of T: אתברו, "have been broken," can only be a matter of guesswork.

G (26.15), on the other hand, has the rendering (διὰ τί) ἔφυγεν ὁ Ἄπις, "(Why) has Apis fled?" For Ἄπις certain manuscripts read ὀπίσω, "backward," whereas manuscript Vaticanus has Ἄπις, preceded by a doublet ἀπὸ σοῦ, "from you." These readings apparently are inner-Greek corruptions. The Greek translator did not read נסחף, but two words: נס and חף, the first one vocalized as נָס, "he fled," the second as חָף, Ḥp, the Egyptian name of the God Apis, the mighty bull-calf. It is to this Hebrew Vorlage of G that the committee attributed a B vote, arguing that the reading of M was the result of cultural ignorance.

As to the last word אַבִּירֶיךָ, the classical Tiberian text has the plural orthography: "your mighty ones," which is supported by S and T. However, de Rossi attributes a singular orthography אַבִּירְךָ to 60 Hebrew manuscripts, including 89 and 93 and the second hand of 150 (HUB). A singular is also presupposed by G: ὁ μόσχος ὁ ἐκλεκτός σου, "your choice calf," by Sym: ὁ δυνατός σου, (so also "the three," Aq, Sym, Th) and by V: *fortis tuus*, both: "your mighty one." The same B vote was attributed by the committee to the singular reading and/or interpretation. The plural of M was seen as an assimilation to the following verse.

Evaluation of Problems

Cappel (1684, 533a) was the first to suggest the base of G and Kennicott (1780, par 45) was the first to consider G as original. With the exception of Volz and Rudolph, this judgment is shared by modern commentators and most recent translators. Only NJV, BR, Chouraqui, and SR provide a rendering of M without any annotation, whereas NIV follows M in the text but presents, at least in its Study Bible, a translation according to G as an alternative.

However, the correction of M should be favored. It should be noted that אַבִּיר in a number of texts designates the "bull" and that it is also here an appropriate designation of the bull-god Apis. Moreover, in verses 14 and 19 mention is made of Memphis or Noph, a center of the Apis cult.

Translation Proposals

A translational model could be found in REB: "Why does Apis flee? Why does your bull-god not stand fast?" For certain translations, the cultural information provided in NJB might serve as a footnote.

46.16

Textual Decisions

In M this verse starts with the enigmatic sentence: הִרְבָּה כּוֹשֵׁל, literally: "He increased one stumbling." The construction of M is also attested by Aq according to the Syro-Hexapla: ܐܤܓܝ ܠܗܘ ܕܡܬܬܩܠ, "he multiplied the one who stumbled," V: *multiplicavit ruentes*, "he has multiplied those who tumble down," and by T: אסגיאו מתקליהון, "They have increased their stumblings." The differences are only in number and person, partly depending upon previous options taken in the context.

G (26.16), however, renders this sentence as follows: καὶ τὸ πλῆθός σου ἠσθένησε, "and your multitude has stumbled," translating the second word as a third-person singular verbal form, punctuating כָּשַׁל, and taking the first word as its grammatical subject. The same has been done by S: ܣܘܓܐܗܘܢ ܐܬܬܚܬܝܘ, "most of them (lit., their multitude) have been cast down." Both G and S could have vocalized the first Hebrew word as הָרֻבָּה.

For the committee, G and S were the product of translational liberty, and M was retained with a B vote.

Evaluation of Problems

Since Giesebrecht (229), the revocalization כָּשַׁל, "he has stumbled," has become commonplace among commentators. For the first word, opinions are divided. Some propose a revocalization of הָרַבָּה, others הַרְבֵּה, and still others propose the conjectural reading עֵרְבְךָ "your mixed company." In recent versions, both RSV and NRSV note that they follow G in translating: "Your multitude stumbled." Although there are no textual notes in NEB and REB, they seem to do the same with their rendering "The rabble of Egypt stumbles."

It must be noted, however, that M is not devoid of meaning. The classic interpretation since Kimchi has been to take the Lord as the subject of the first verb: "He has multiplied," and to consider the singular participle כּוֹשֵׁל a collective: "the stumbling ones," "He has caused many to stumble." This, based on their meaning, is what NJV, NJB, and SR have done.

Another possible interpretation would be to take Apis as subject and to ascribe to the *hiphil* of רבה the meaning "to do frequently" the action expressed by the following verb כשל: "to stumble frequently." The participle of the next verb, כּוֹשֵׁל, would then have the value of an infinitive (so Wernberg-Møller 1959, 65). This interpretation can be found in NAB and NIV.

Translation Proposals

For the first interpretation, see NJV: "He made many stumble"; for the second, NAB: "he stumbled repeatedly."

46.17

Textual Decisions

This verse begins in M with (פַּרְעֹה) קָרְאוּ שָׁם, "They exclaimed there (Pharaoh)." The difficult reading of M is unequivocally confirmed by T: זמינו לתמן, "They have summoned there (Pharao)."

G (26.17), however, has the rendering καλέσατε τὸ ὄνομα, "Call (imperative plural) the name (of Pharaoh)," which is based on a different vocalization of the same Hebrew consonants: קְראוּ שֵׁם. This different Vorlage is also presupposed by *vocate nomen*, "Call the name," the rendering of V.

For the second word, S has a double translation: ܬܡܢ ܫܡܗ (ܐܝܟܐ), "there his name." It should, nevertheless, be observed that Ephrem only quotes the second word of this doublet in his commentary and that he interprets the first word, ܐܝܟܐ, as an imperative. S therefore seems to be based on the same reading as G and V.

The concordance of G, V, and S as well as the absence of any variant in the Greek tradition was for the committee an indication that the vocalization tradition of M had not been firmly established in the proto-Masoretic period. It further judged that the vocalization of the Vorlage of G, V, and S better suited the Hebrew consonantal text, and a majority gave it a C vote. It was considered possible that the interpretation of M in the Babylonian Talmud (*Moed Katan* 16a), "one has convocated Pharaoh," had constituted a kind of *al tiqre* which would have eliminated the older vocalization maintained in the major versions.

Evaluation of Problems

Once Cappel (1684, 533a) noted the different vocalization of the Vorlage of G, almost all commentators adopted the correction of M. Most translators have done the same, without any justification in a footnote (RSV, NRSV, NEB, REB, GNB, CEV), or with justification (NAB, NJB, FC, GN).

A particular case is BR, where the plural imperative correction is rendered for the first word, but the second word is kept according to M. In BJ the opposite is done: the vocalization of M is retained in the first word and the second is corrected. Such hybrid translational procedures are certainly not recommended.

Only a few recent versions (NJV, NIV, NAV, SR, Chouraqui) translate M, but not always in a convincing way. It should be observed that קָרָא שֵׁם followed by a genitive is the normal way to express the idea of giving a name to somebody, and that a perfect contrast is created with the "King, whose name is the Lord of Hosts," in the following verse. Therefore, the reading of G should be adopted and duly noted.

Translation Proposals

For a meaningful rendering, see GNB: "Give the king of Egypt a new name—'Noisy Braggart Who Missed His Chance.'"

46.20

Textual Decisions

After having compared Egypt to a beautiful heifer, M states that a gadfly from the north בָּא בָא, "is coming, is coming." This repetition of the verb is found in the Aleppo Codex, the Cairo Codex, and in manuscripts New York JThS 232, Petrograd, and Reuchlin of the Prophets, as well as in many others. In the Ben Chayyim Bible and in a number of manuscripts, the sequence of these identical words is protected by a *masorah parva*, noting its unique character.

However, the first hand of manuscripts 89, 93, and 150 as well as the first or second hand of 104 other codexes of Kennicott and de Rossi read בא בה, which could mean "is coming upon her." This is also the rendering of all the versions: G (26.20): ἦλθεν ἐπ' αὐτήν, V: *veniet ei*, S: ܡܠܟ ܐܬܐ, and T: ייתון עלה, the Targum meaning: "(nations) will come against her."

The committee noted that none of the Hebrew manuscripts reading בה has a *mappiq* in the word-final ה, which could mean that the scribes considered בה to be an unusual orthography of בא. It observed, moreover, that the repetition of the verb might intend to stress the incessant attacks of the gadfly. Since the reading בָּא בָה apparently is a syntactical facilitation, a C evaluation was assigned to M.

Evaluation of Problems

The reading בא בה has traditionally been preferred by both commentators and translators. Only NAB: "from the north a horsefly lights upon her," and NEB: "but a gadfly from the north descended on her," bother to provide a textual note, justifying their translation. A comparable rendering without note is presented by RSV, NRSV, NJB, NIV, FC, GN, etc. In fact, they may have dismissed the reduplication and provided an object for translational reasons. Many of their colleagues may feel obliged to do the same. Already Menaḥem de Posquières, although reading בא בא, presupposed the ellipsis of עָלֶיהָ, "upon her," the restoration of which he judged to be necessary for the comprehension of the sentence.

As Menaḥem indicates, the reading בָּהּ seems to be rather unsatisfactory; one would expect either עָלֶיהָ or לָהּ (Luzatto; Schwally 1888, 193, note 3; Ehrlich, 354). If, in addition, incessant attacks would be implied in the repetition, M could be rendered, either literally or freely, as has been done in NJV, NAV, Chouraqui, BR, and SR.

Translation Proposals

If literal repetition has the required rhetorical function, NJV can be taken as an example: "A gadfly from the north is coming, coming," or SR: *Le taon vient du nord, il vient,* "The gadfly comes from the north, it comes." Stress can sometimes be obtained by different foregrounding, as in NAV: *maar daar kom 'n blindevlieg uit die noorde,* "but there comes a gadfly from the north."

46.22

Textual Decisions

The first half-line of this verse in M runs as follows: קוֹלָהּ כַּנָּחָשׁ יֵלֵךְ, "Her sound is like a snake as (it) goes." The textual problem is especially connected with the last word יֵלֵךְ, "it goes."

M has the literal support of Aq and Sym according to the Syro-Hexapla: ܢܐܙܠ, "it will go," and it certainly is the basis for the more specific renderings of S: ܕܪܚܫ, "which creeps," and T: זחלין, "creeping (serpents)."

The rendering of G (26.22) remains debatable. All the witnesses of G have the rendering συρίζοντος, "hissing": φωνὴ ὡς ὄφεως συρίζοντος, "(their) voice as of a hissing snake." In 1821, Schleusner (V, 228) and in 1824 (in the posthumous publication of his commentary), Spohn proposed emending G and reading σύροντος, "creeping," which would bring G close to S and T and which would make the presupposition of a different Hebrew Vorlage for the Old Greek unnecessary. Ziegler (1958, 24) rejected this conjecture, arguing that nobody could have reasonably changed an original σύροντος into συρίζοντος. However, φωνή, "voice," in the immediate context, could have inspired the rendering συρίζοντος, "hissing." V, anyway, with its rendering *sonabit*, "will sound," seems to provide a generic translation of G: συρίζοντος, "hissing."

The committee noted that in Dan 11.26 Ziegler follows Schleusner (III, 266) and Field in conjecturing κατασύρειν, "to carry off," for G, instead of reading κατασυρίζειν, a rare word only attested in the passive voice. The committee endorsed Schleusner's conjecture, considering συρίζοντος to be the result of internal textual corruption. The weight of the witnesses made it possible to assign a B evaluation to M.

Evaluation of Problems

All reconstructions of a different Hebrew Vorlage, including those trying to restore an original behind G, are highly speculative and even less convincing than M. From Ewald to Bright (304), a correction to שֹׁרֵק, "hissing," was most frequently proposed. According to Brockington (213), this also is the basis for the rendering of NEB: "Hark, she is hissing like a snake." But apart from NJB, which bases its translation "Hear her hissing like a snake" on G, all other translations pretend to render M.

In a rather confusing way, some modern versions seem to qualify the "sound" translationally as "hissing." So, for example, REB has: "Egypt is hissing like a fleeing snake," and NIV, GNB, GN, and GrN are comparable. It is questionable, however, whether this explicit statement is really implied by the text. And, if the intention is to present a translation that is a compromise between different text traditions, the intention is invalid and should be avoided.

As Tremellius has already seen, the noise, made by a snake gliding away, is probably minimal, and its flight is almost a silent one.

Translation Proposals

NJV can serve as a model: "She shall rustle away like a snake."

46.23

Textual Decisions

At the end of the first line of this verse, M reads the third-person singular of the *nifal* imperfect יֵחָקֵר, "be searched out," "(for) it can(not) be searched out," "it" referring back to the forest mentioned in the first half-line.

The singular is also attested by Aq according to the Syro-Hexapla: ܢܬܒܥܐ (דרל), "for it can(not) be sought out," and by V: (*qui*) *supputari* (*non*) *potest*, "(which) can(not) be counted." G (26.23) also respects the singular: (ὅτι οὐ μὴ) εἰκασθῇ, "(for it cannot) be guessed," but it associates this verb with the next one: πληθύνει, "it exceeds," also put into the singular.

The first hand of de Rossi manuscript 345, however, has the plural reading יֵחָקְרוּ, "they (cannot) be searched out," which could refer back to the "trees" in verse 22, standing for the Egyptians, or to the "woodcutters" in the same verse or even to the Babylonian soldiers. The plural is also confirmed by S: ܗܢ ܕܝܠ ܗܘܡܣܐ ܠܝܠ ܩܡܠ, "(because) there is (no) summing up of them," and by T: אָרֵי לֵית לְהוֹן סוֹף, "although there is no end to them." In T the plural refers back to her great men," that is, "the great men of Egypt," made explicit as the subject of the preceding verb.

For the committee, the late medieval manuscript 345 had no authority. It was further noted that G assimilated the following verb to the one under discussion and that S and T had made the opposite assimilation. M was therefore considered the starting point of opposite assimilations, and its more difficult reading received a B vote.

Evaluation of Problems

Volz (401) corrected M on the basis of manuscript 345 of de Rossi and was followed by Rudolph (270) and by the apparatus of BHS. Without textual notes, the plural was adopted in REB: "for they cannot be numbered," and RL. In spite of syntactical incoherences in these two modern versions, the back reference is to the Babylonians.

In view of the textual decisions, it will be clear that M has to be rendered with the overwhelming majority of modern translations, and that either the boundless character of the forest or its density (that which cannot be searched) should be marked in translation. Furthermore, translators will have to be particularly careful to render the images and objects of the comparisons coherently, even if no interpretation can offer an entirely satisfactory explanation of the singular-plural transitions (McKane, 1134).

Translation Proposals

NIV presents a coherent model of translation for the whole verse: " 'They will chop down her forest,' declares the Lord, 'dense though it be. They are more numerous than locusts, they cannot be counted.' "

47.5

Textual Decisions

In the second line of this verse M characterizes Gaza and Ashkelon as עִמְקָם (שְׁאֵרִית), "(remnant) of their valley." M is only attested literally by V: (et reliquiae) vallis earum, and it may have been the base of the paraphrase of S: ܩܐܡܕܚܘ (ܛܘܚܙܪܟܙ ܠܗܐ), "(and all that remains) of their inhabitants." T with its interpretation: תוקפהון (שאר), "(the remnant) of their strength," could have been influenced by the meaning of עמק in Samaritan (so Castle, 2800; HALAT, 803a for Ugaritic).

Sym and Aq, on the other hand, have the rendering τῶν κοιλάδων, "of the lowlanders," which agrees with the reading ascribed to "the Hebrew" in the Syro-Hexapla. This translation seems to presuppose a Hebrew Vorlage עֲמָקִים, "lowlanders," since this is the word which indicates the inhabitants of the Jordan Valley in 1 Chr 12.16.

G (29.5), however, renders with (καὶ οἱ κατάλοιποι) Ενακιμ, "(and the remnant) of the Anakim," presuming therefore a Hebrew Vorlage עֲנָקִים.

With a C decision, the committee considered the Vorlage of G to represent the original text and M to be the result of a *nun/mem* confusion. The Hebrew text behind Sym and Aq was regarded as a transitional form between the Vorlage of G and M.

Evaluation of Problems

From Grotius and Houbigant (IV, 341) to McKane (1151), almost all commentators defended the same point of view as the committee.

It is true that a number of recent versions (NJV, NIV, NJB, SR) render M, but the obscurity of the resulting translations only underlines the graphical error of M. Only NEB with its rendering "Poor remnant of their strength" and REB with its clearer translation "the remnant of the Philistine power" seem to spell out G. G. R. Driver's thesis (1950, 61) that M has to be interpreted in the light of Akkadian *emuqu* and Ugaritic ʿmq as "strength," "power." It remains unclear, on the other hand, how the footnote in NRSV can state that the comparable translation "O remnant of their power" is based on G.

"Remnant of the Anakim" as a designation for the inhabitants of Gaza, Gath, and Ashdod is a literary parallel to "remnant of the isle of Caphtor," which is a designation for the Philistines in verse 4. And Jer 47.5 can best be understood in the light of Josh 11.22: "No Anakim were left in the land taken by the Israelites; they survived only in Gaza, Gath and Ashdod." There is no doubt that a translation of G must be preferred.

Translation Proposals

"O remnant of the Anakim" (RSV) or "The Anakim who survive" (CEV) are possible translations. The reading of M could be stated in a footnote which could also provide some cultural information with regard to the Anakim.

48.4

Textual Decisions

The last word of this verse in M has a *ketiv* צעוריה and a *qere* צְעִירֶיהָ, "her little ones," "her little ones let a cry be heard."

The *qere* is rendered by Aq: οἱ μικροὶ αὐτῆς, "her little ones," and by Sym: οἱ νεώτεροι αὐτῆς, "her young ones." The same is done by V, no matter whether the reading of the Cava manuscript: *parvuli*, "little ones," or the dative case of the editions: *parvulis*, is considered to be original. The *qere* is certainly behind the interpretation ܡܚܝܠܝܗ̇, "its poor ones," of S as well. It could be behind the interpretation of T: שלטונה, "her rulers," according to the Montefiore and Urbinates manuscripts or שלטוניהון, "their rulers," according to the Sperber edition, if Radaq is correct in considering T an antiphrasis.

However, Spanish de Rossi manuscripts 26 and 187, the Reuchlin manuscript of the Prophets, and manuscript New York JThS 232 have a *ketiv* reading צעורה. This is also at the root of G (31.4): εἰς Ζογορα, "as far as (in)
Zoar."

With a C evaluation the committee considered this *ketiv* צעורה behind G
to be primitive and the *ketiv* of M צעוריה (with prefinal *yod*) to be corrupted
by the *qere*.

Evaluation of Problems

Cappel (1684, 534a) was the first to note the basis of G, which since then
has been adopted by almost all scholars.

Nevertheless, most recent translations (NRSV, NIV, NJB, CEV, GNB,
NJV, RL, GN, etc.) render the *qere*, and only NJV mentions the rendering of
the *ketiv* in a footnote, in spite of the fact that the Hebrew evidence is characterized as an emendation.

However, the probability that the *ketiv* צעורה is original is certainly favored by the context. In the next verse, the place-names Luhith and Horonaim
are mentioned. Isa 15.5b or its source, in which mention is made of Zoar, Eg-
lat-shelishiyah, Luhith, and Horonaim, is being alluded to here. With the exception of Luhith, all these place-names turn up again in Jer 48.34. This
reading should be rendered, following RSV, NAB, NEB, REB, and FC, especially in projects with Orthodox participation.

Translation Proposals

NAB presents an example for translation: "their outcry is heard in Zoar."
It may be helpful to provide a rendering of the *qere* in a footnote in which,
moreover, information about the Moabite town of Zoar could be supplied.

48.5A

Textual Decisions

The second half-line of verse 5a reads in M: בִּבְכִי יַעֲלֶה־בֶּכִי which could
be understood to mean "with weeping shall go up weeping." The last word especially has been problematic.

M is literally confirmed by Sym, according to the Syro-Hexapla: ܒܒܟܝܐ
ܣܠܩ ܒܒܟܝܐ, "with weeping goes up weeping (noun)."

G (31.5), in spite of different syntax, has the following corresponding elements: ἐν κλαυθμῷ ἀναβήσεται κλαίων, "with weeping, one goes up weeping," which are also found in V: *plorans ascendet in fletu*, "weeping, one goes
up in tears." T produces the following paraphrase: כד בכן יסקון בכן, "while
they weep, they go up weeping."

Only S does not render the last word: ܚܕ ܚܕܝ ܢܣܩܘܢ, "while they weep, they go up."

The committee argued that G, V, and T interpreted the last word as a participle and that they therefore had a Vorlage like M. S was regarded an elusive abbreviation. Wanting to prevent an assimilation to the parallel in Isa 15.5, the committee assigned a B evaluation to M.

Evaluation of Problems

Ehrlich (356) took בְּכִי to be the result of dittography because of the following כִי and therefore omitted the last word, obtaining the same result as S. No modern translation seems to have followed the omission.

Houbigant, on the other hand, suggested that בכי originated from reading בו, "on it," and dittography, because of the next כִי. He therefore proposed reading בו, as in the parallel in Isa 15.5. This conjecture has been favored by many scholars. According to the note in NJB: "lit. 'they climb it,'" it is the basis of its rendering: "Up the slope of Luhith, weeping they go." So also TOB and, probably, RSV.

Since assimilation is not recommended, translators will have to determine the meaning of the repetition of בכי. The repetition could express a certain insistence, stressing either a continual weeping (so NJV) or an intensive one (NRSV and others). It is true that because of the *maqqef* the verb could be interpreted as a *hiphil*: "For ascending Ludith makes tear rise on tear."

Whatever interpretation is chosen, some form of translational adjustment will have to be applied.

Translation Proposals

REB provides the following model of translation: "on the ascent to Luhith / they go up weeping bitterly."

48.5B

Textual Decisions

The last half-line of the verse runs as follows in M: צָרֵי צַעֲקַת־שֶׁבֶר שָׁמֵעוּ which has been interpreted to mean either "the enemies, a cry of destruction they have heard," or "disasters (announced by) a cry of destruction they have heard." The word which causes the problem, צָרֵי, is, according to the Syro-Hexapla, attested by Sym with the rendering ܒܥܠܕܒܒܐ, "enemies," as well as by the translation *hostes*, "enemies," in V.

According to the edition of Sperber, the presence of צָרֵי is also confirmed by T, where it is understood as "the distressed," מעיקי, "the distressed utter the cry of those broken in war." This reading is, uniquely, found in manuscript Or 2211 in the British Library.

The presence of the word under discussion can certainly be detected in the insertion κίνδυνον, "danger," or "distress," in the recensions of Origen and Lucian, taken from Th, and in the rendering ܪܘܠܐ, "distress," "calamity," in S.

G (31.5), however, in its translation κραυγὴν συντρίμματος ἠκούσατε, "a cry of destruction you have heard," does not render צְרִי. The same can be stated for the original text of T.

The committee considered the omission in G and T to be an elusive abbreviation and gave a B evaluation to the more difficult reading of M.

Evaluation of Problems

Since Ewald, the general tendency among scholars has been to omit צְרִי as a later gloss. This is also the opinion of RSV: "They have heard the cry of destruction," NAB, and FC.

No doubt much is to be said in favor of such a point of view. It is true that the traditional rendering of M, still present in KJV: "the enemies have heard a cry of destruction," and in some modern translations such as SR, is grammatically, syntactically, and contextually hardly possible. It is also correct that צְרִי as a plural of צַר with the value of an absolute state would be unique in Biblical Hebrew (McKane, 1160). Nevertheless, if M is maintained with the majority of modern versions, its understanding would be based on the connective chain "distress of a cry of destruction," which would have to be reformulated. The only other possibility would be an elusive omission of the word under discussion on translational grounds.

Translation Proposals

The reformulation, noted above, has developed the following rendering in REB: "an anguished cry of destruction is heard."

48.6

Textual Decisions

The second half-line of this verse contains the problematic expression: כַּעֲרוֹעֵר, like Aroer" in M: "and be like Aroer in the desert," reading a place-name.

A place-name is also involved in the transcription of Sym: ὡς Ἀροήρ, "like Aroer," and in the paraphrase of T: "and be like the tower of Aroer."

According to the Barberini manuscript, Aq has the rendering ὡς μυρίκη, "like a tamarisk." Most witnesses of V have the same rendering: *quasi myrice*, some reading the plural: *quasi myricae*, such as Josephus: αἱ μυρῖκαι. These translations could be either based on a homonym עֲרוֹעֵר or on a Vorlage of

כְּעַרְעָר. S with its free rendering ܐܝܟ ܥܪܥܪܐ, "like a root," is in line with the interpretation of a tree.

G (31.6), on the other hand, presents the translation ὥσπερ ὄνος ἄγριος, "like a wild ass," which presupposes a Hebrew Vorlage כְּעָרוֹד. According to the Syro-Hexapla this would also be the rendering of Aq: ܥܪܕܐ, "a wild ass." The committee considered G to be a contextual assimilation, an association of ideas between "wild ass" on one side and "desert" on the other. It judged M to be the result of an assimilation to verse 19: "you inhabitant of Aroer." The majority of the committee assigned a C evaluation to a correction to כְּעַרְעָר with the meaning "juniper."

Evaluation of Problems

Very occasionally, scholars from Rosenmüller to van Selms (III, 28) have preferred the reading of G. Modern translations in particular have been tempted to follow G, probably because it facilitates translation (so RSV, NRSV, GNB, CEV, NJB, NAB, FC). Rare are the recent versions which render M as a place-name. Even among Jewish translations, NJV stands out as an exception.

However, in spite of its sense, the first reading cannot be accepted; nor can the second reading be accepted, since it is devoid of sense.

Other recent versions hesitate between a generic indication, such as "bush" (NIV, RL, GrN), and a specific one, such as "juniper" (BR, Chouraqui, SR, GN).

A functional equivalent translation of the last image is provided in REB: "and become like one destitute in the wilderness." In view of the evidence presented in CTAT (779–80), however, a specific rendering may be preferred.

Translation Proposals

The variant translation in the footnote of REB could serve as an example: "and become like a juniper in the wilderness."

48.7

Textual Decisions

In M this verse states the following about Moab: "(you trusted) in your works and in your treasures": בְּמַעֲשַׂיִךְ וּבְאוֹצְרוֹתַיִךְ.

For these two words, G (31.7) has only one phrase: ἐν ὀχυρώμασί σου, "in your strongholds." According to the Hexapla, this Greek expression would correspond to the first word in M. This can be concluded from Aq and Sym's correction of G to ܒܥ̈ܒܕܝܟܝ ܠ, "in your works," in the Syro-Hexapla and from Origen's recension which has the asterisked addition ἥξουσι θλίψεις σου, "your troubles will come," attributed to Th in the Barberini manuscript. The last rendering agrees with the second word in M when divided into two words: וּבָאוּ צָרוֹתַיִךְ, a clear graphical error.

It seems far more likely, however, that G's rendering matches the second word of M, read as בְּצוּרוֹתַיִךְ (so Cappel 1684, 534a and Schleusner, *Lexicon* 4, 154). The frequent translation of the root בצר with the root οχυρ- in G would likewise point in this direction.

Both V: *in munitionibus tuis et in thesauris tuis*, "in your fortifications and in your treasures," and S: ܠܟ ܣܡܬܕ ܡܚܠ ܘܠܟܝܢ ܕܡܢ, "in your fortresses and in your treasures," seem to have made the same wrong identification as the Hexapla.

T with its rendering באוצרך ובבית גנזך, "in your treasures and in your treasure houses," provides a double translation of the last word, omitting the first one, like G.

The committee was of the opinion that the false identification of the "minus" in G means that the Greek recensions, V, and S could not have been testifying to the proto-Masoretic text. The first item is only directly confirmed by Aq and Sym and indirectly by the fact that Th, adding the translation of the second word, indicates that a first word has already been translated. The omission in G and T could be due to the difficulty of determining the precise meaning of the word. Since all the consonants of the second word are confirmed by Th and no variant is offered for the first, M received a C evaluation.

Evaluation of Problems

Apart from some modern translations of G, no recent version has rendered its shorter text. According to their notes, however, some of them have substituted the first Hebrew term with the Greek rendering, keeping M for the second. So RSV and NRSV: "Surely, because you trusted in your strongholds and your treasures." In the light of the textual relationships, this procedure is unacceptable.

The absence of textual notes seems to indicate that NEB and REB (compare also RL and GN) render M in their translation: "(Because you trust) in your defences and arsenals," probably using a suggestion made by Janzen (19–20) that the first Hebrew word could mean "(defensive) works." There is, however, no convincing evidence for such a meaning.

M should certainly be rendered, with most translations (NAB, NIV, NJB, BR, SR, etc.) but, instead of using a generic term such as "works" or "deeds," the result of efforts may be stressed in translation (König 1936, 238a).

Translation Proposals

For this kind of focus, two possible models can be cited: NJV: "Surely, because of your trust / in your wealth and in your treasures," and FC: *tu te fiais / à tes réalisations, à tes réserves*, "you trusted in your accomplishments, in your reserves."

48.9

Textual Decisions

The first line of this verse in M presents two main problems, mainly inter-pretational in nature: (a) the meaning of the item that must be given to Moab, which is written ציץ, and (b) the meaning of the infinitive absolute plus finite verb combination: נָצֹא תֵּצֵא.

Concerning (a), the meaning "flower" for Hebrew ציץ has been rendered by Aq: ἄνθος, and by V: (*date*) *florem* (*Moab*), "(give) a flower to (Moab)." Both S: ܟܠܝܠܐ and T: כתרא enlarge the flower to "a crown." Sym with a ren-dering βλάστημα, "shoot," remains in the same semantic domain. Only G (31.9) has the variant reading σημεῖα, "signs," "signals." For Volz (409), G was based on the Hebrew Vorlage צִיּוּן, "tombstone." Barthélemy (783) noted, however, that the meaning of the only other occurrence of צִיּוּן, in Jer 31.21, was not understood by the Greek translator, who provided a transcription. It is therefore more likely that G interpreted ציץ. In spite of its evident importance for translators, this case was not submitted for the judgment of the committee.

Concerning (b), the combination of verbal forms in M is rendered by Aq: ἀνθοῦσα ἐξελεύσεται and by V: *floriens egredietur*, both: "flourishing, he will go forth." Sym: εξόδῳ ἐξελεύσεται, "in going, he will go out," and T: מגלא תגלי, "he shall surely go into captivity," seem to have assimilated the first verb to the second יָצֵא, "to go out," whereas S: ܢܬܚܒܠ ܡܬܚܒܠܘ, "he will be totally ruined," seems to have assimilated the second verb to the first, נָצֹא, "fall in ruin." G: ἀφῇ ἀναφθήσεται, "with kindling, he will be set ablaze," seems to be based on an interpretation of M. The similar translation of תֵּצֵא with ἀναφθῇ in 21.12 also points in this direction.

The committee gave M a C evaluation.

Evaluation of Problems

The flower interpretation in most ancient versions, void of sense in the context, is only found in translations based on V. This may explain the relative success of the contextually coherent rendering of both G and its presupposed Vorlage. Examples of the latter can be found in GNB: "Set up a tombstone for Moab," NAB, GN, and FC; examples of the former, in NEB: "Let a warning flash to Moab" and REB: "Give a warning signal to Moab." The presupposed Vorlage of G is most uncertain, however, and the "warning signal" is inappo-site in the context.

For this reason Moran (70) proposed, on the basis of Ugaritic *ṣṣ*, interpreting M as a homonym with the meaning "salt," "salt marsh." This suggestion has been used in recent scholarship and in some modern versions, such as NIV: "Put salt on Moab," NRSV: "set aside salt for Moab," and others. This symbolic act would indicate that Moab's farmland would become barren.

This procedure may be farfetched, but the only other possibility is to adopt the classical meaning of צִיץ as "wing," still to be found in the dictionaries of Buxtorf (1907), Gesenius-Buhl (682b), König (387a), and BDB (851b). The infinite absolute נָצֹא could then, with Menaḥem ben Saruq, be given the meaning "to fly," and, as in other cases, one could have a figure in which the infinitive and the following finite verb are from different roots but stylistically bound together through assonance. The meaning of the whole line would then be: "Give wings to Moab, for with powerful wing beats she will go (namely: into exile)." The sarcasm contained in these sentences would have to be matched in translation. The wing metaphor, adopted by RSV, NJV, NJB, BR, Chouraqui, and SR, has the advantage of being more frequent than the salt metaphor.

Translation Proposals

For the last interpretation, see NJB: "Give Moab wings / so that she can fly away," and for the salt metaphor, NIV: "Put salt on Moab, / for she will be laid waste." Whatever the choice in the text may be, the possible variant translation could be provided in a footnote.

48.31

Textual Decisions

In M after two verbs in first-person singular: "I wail" and "I cry out," the verse ends with a verb in third-person masculine singular: יֶהְגֶּה, "he moans," "for the people of Kir-heres he moans."

M is supported by 2Q, by the Origen recension of G (31.31): καὶ μελετήσει, "and he shall moan," attributed by the Barberini manuscript to Th, and by the Lucianic recension of G: καὶ μέλος ἐρεῖ, "and a lamentation he shall utter," attributed by the same manuscript to Aq and Sym.

On the other hand, manuscript Kennicott 180 (= manuscript Hamburg 27) and manuscript de Rossi 737 have the first-person singular reading אֶהְגֶּה, "I moan." This also is the *qere* reading that the Petrograd manuscript ascribes to the Babylonians.

V: *lamentantes*, "lamenting," S: ـܝ ـܐܐܡܠ, "they are anxious," and T: דוון, "they (that is, the Moabites) lament," all seem to paraphrase; thus, no first-person singular appears.

G (31.31) renders: βοήσατε ἐπ' ἄνδρας Κειρ Αδας αὐχμοῦ, "cry out against the men of K.A. . . ." The word αὐχμοῦ has been a desperate case for interpreters. It has generally been concluded that the genetive case of αὐχμός, "drought," in no way corresponds to the verb in M. It therefore seems correct to note, with HUB, that the verb is lacking in G.

The committee judged that M was sufficiently confirmed by 2Q, Th, Aq, and Sym to receive a B evaluation for its more difficult reading.

Evaluation of Problems

Most modern versions (RSV, NRSV, REB, GNB, NIV, NJB, RL, FC) do not signal any textual problem in connection with their first-person singular rendering. They simply assimilate to the other first-person readings for translational reasons, as they so often do. Only a few recent translations (NJV, NEB, NAB) judge some kind of justification in a footnote to be necessary. Translators can be easily convinced by McKane's argument (1184): "Even if one were to agree that on strict text-critical grounds יהגה is to be preferred, אהגה would be desiderated in respect of sense."

One could agree that some of the explicit interpretations of the third-person singular are farfetched, as for example "my heart": "my heart shall mourn for the men of Kir-heres" (KJV; compare also LB). It would be possible, however, to interpret the third-person singular as a neutral "one" (SR, NAV), or to see in the neutral statement a reference to either the Moabites (Radaq) or the people of Kir-heres (GN).

Translation Proposals

In the case of a neutral interpretation, NAV can be taken as a model: *en kerm die mense oor die manne van Kir-Geres*, "and people moan for the men of Kir-heres."

48.32

Textual Decisions

After having said about the vineyards of Sibmah: "Your branches crossed over the sea," M notes that they reached as far as יָם יַעְזֵר, "the sea of Jazer." The repetition of the word יָם, "sea," has created a problem.

According to the Syro-Hexapla: ܥܕܡܐ ܠܝܡܐ ܕܝܥܙܝܪ, "until the sea of Jazer," the reading of M is attested by Aq and Sym. It is also confirmed by S, which has exactly the same rendering, by V: *usque ad mare Iazer*, "until the sea of Jazer," and by T, which just copies M.

On the other hand, יָם is missing in the first hand of Kennicott manuscripts 30 and 93 (HUB), rather late manuscripts with no particular textual authority.

According to the rendering of G, the branches reached πόλεις Ιαζηρ, "the towns of Jazer" (31.32). For Ziegler (1958, 104), πόλεις in G represents a Hebrew Vorlage עָרֵי. It is more likely, however, that G read עָרִים instead of עַד יָם (so also HUB).

The committee considered G to be due to a graphical error, and the omission of יָם in the two Hebrew manuscripts as an assimilation to the parallel text of Isa 16.8. Since M is almost universally attested, even indirectly by G, it received a B rating.

Evaluation of problems

Modern scholars have, in spite of the textual evidence, globally eliminated the repetition of יָם as erroneous, and they have been followed by the vast majority of modern translations. When they do this based on textual evidence (so RSV, NRSV, NAB, NEB, REB, FC, GN), they are not very convincing. They are more credible when they do so without textual justification (NAV, GNB, NJB, CEV, RL, GrN).

Rare are the translations that reproduce M. Only NIV, SR, and NJV can be mentioned. The first two run into difficulties with their rendering "the sea of Jazer." The word יָם is certainly a reference to the Dead Sea, and Jazer is not located on the shore of the Dead Sea. The attempts of Delitzsch, Keil, and Nägelbach to give a restricted meaning to יָם are entirely artificial and the statement that the redactor was not concerned about topography is not very helpful. Only the different division of the text in NJV: "Reached to the sea, to Jazer," may bring out a possible hyperbolic character of M. But the meaning is not very different from that of a translation based on an omission.

Translation Proposals

If M is maintained literally, NJV can be accepted as a model for verse 32b: "Whose tendrils crossed the sea, / Reached to the sea, to Jazer." If a different translational approach is followed, GNB can function as an equivalent model: "whose branches reach across the Dead Sea and go as far as Jazer."

48.33

Textual Decisions

The last two sentences of this verse read as follows in M: לֹא־יִדְרֹךְ הֵידָד הֵידָד לֹא הֵידָד, "one shall not tread (with) a shout, a shout not a shout." (The Hebrew word הֵידָד is an onomatopoeia.) Textual problems have arisen with regard to the last word of the first sentence, הֵידָד, and with the last sentence as a whole.

(a) Concerning הֵידָד, M is confirmed by the transcription ηδαδ, found in Aq and Sym. The testimony of G remains uncertain. If the conjecture of Cappel (1684, 535a) and Ziegler is followed: οὐκ ἐπάτησαν αιδεδ, "they did not tread (with) a shout," G would attest M.

On the other hand, Babylonian manuscript Oxford Bibl. Bodl Heb d 26, edited by Yeivin (1973, IV, 246), has the reading הַדֹּרֵךְ, "the treader," which also is at the base of both S: ܟ̈ܕ̈ܟܐ, and T: עיצורין, "the treaders."

Nothing can be deduced from the global paraphrase of V: *nequaquam calcator uvae solitum celeuma cantabit*, "by no means he who treads the grapes will sing the usual song."

(b) Regarding the last sentence as a whole, M would have the support of G if Ziegler's conjecture is adopted: αιδεδ οὐκ αιδεδ, "a shout not a shout." It certainly is confirmed by Aq and Sym in their rendering ηδαδ οὐκ ἔστιν ηδαδ, "a shout is not a shout."

As seen above, the last sentence has been paraphrased by V. The same is done by S with: ܘܠܐ ܢܥܢܘܢ ܘܠܐ ܢܐܡܪܘܢ, "and they will not answer and they will not say: 'hurrah, hurrah,'" and T: ולא ירימון בקלהון, "and they shall not lift up their voice."

The committee considered the variant reading in (a) to be an assimilation to the parallel text of Isa 16.10. It noted the support of Aq and Sym and possibly G for the reading of M in both textual cases. In order to preserve the textual form of Jeremiah from an assimilation to the form in Isaiah, the committee assigned a majority B rating to M.

Evaluation of Problems

From Grätz (1883, 396) to Holladay (II, 344), the variant reading הַדֹּרֵךְ was adopted by many commentators and by some translations: NAB, RL, FC, and NJB: "the treader of grapes treads no more."

In addition, Rudolph (282) proposed reading an unattested verbal form, יְהֵדַּד, "shouted," for the last occurrence of הֵידָד, a conjecture which has been adopted by NJB (see textual note): "the joyful shouting has ceased." Moreover, Ehrlich (358) proposed deleting the last sentence, as a gloss, and some recent versions (for example, TOB) have followed this suggestion.

There are, however, no valid textual grounds for adopting any of these proposals. In the last sentence, the meaning of M might be that the cry of war has replaced the shout of joy. Compare BR: *ein Hussa, nicht ein Heissa ists nun!* Otherwise, a restricted paraphrase must be used.

Translation Proposals

Two possible paraphrases can be considered: NRSV: "no one treads them with shouts of joy; the shouting is not the shout of joy," and REB: "and the shouts of those treading the grapes / will echo no more."

48.39

Textual Decisions

This verse starts in M with the following statements about Moab: אֵיךְ חַתָּה הֵילִילוּ, "How it is broken! Wail!" or: "How they wail!" The textual problem is connected with the last verbal form.

This form is attested by Th and Sym in their rendering ὀλολύξατε, "wail," according to the Barberini manuscript. It is also confirmed by the translation אֵילִילוּ, "they howl," in T. V: *et ululaverunt*, and S: ܐܠܝܠܘ, "and they wailed," are, of course, also witnesses of M, because the conjunction has been added for translational reasons.

More problematic is the evaluation of G. Ziegler has made a convincing reconstruction of the first three words of the text (31.39), proposing: πῶς Ατατ ἠλάλαξε, "How has Atat cried out." In this case, the second Hebrew word has been transcribed and the last word rendered in the singular, possibly on the basis of a Vorlage with הֵיליל. But it can in no way be stated that G does not testify to the presence of the last verbal form of M.

In spite of uncertainty whether the Vorlage of G read a final *waw*, the committee considered a B rating of M to be justified, the strong support of M being taken into account.

Evaluation of Problems

From Schleusner to Bright (318), the omission of הֵילִילוּ on the basis of G was frequently accepted. In modern translations, only NEB and REB, according to their textual notes, do the same. From the textual discussion above, it becomes evident that this procedure cannot be advised.

Occasionally, translations have followed their own conjectures, such as NAB, basing its rendering "How terror seizes Moab, and wailing!" on חַת וְהֵיליל. And recently a conjecture, much closer to M, has been proposed: חַתָּה וְהֵיליל ן . . . , "How terrified he is in wailing and . . ." (Holladay II, 344) which has not yet found any acceptance among translators.

Almost all recent translations adopt M, hesitating between a rendering of the Hebrew perfect tense, "How they wail" (RSV, NRSV, NIV, RL), and a translation of the imperative: "Wail" (NJV, NJB, GNB, BR, SR, FC, GN). In view of the existing parallelism with verse 20 of this chapter, the imperative interpretation may be preferred.

Translation Proposals

GNB can be used as a model: "Moab has been shattered! Cry out!"

48.45

Textual Decisions

After having stated that a fire has gone out from Hesbon, M affirms in the parallel half-line of verse 45b that a flame has gone out מִבֵּין סִיחוֹן, "from the midst of Sihon."

Verses 45–47 are lacking in G.

The prepositional phrase in M is only confirmed by V: *de medio Seon*, "from the midst of Sihon," and by T's transcription: מבין.

A fragment from Cave 2 of Qumran (Baillet, DJD III, 68) reads, however, מקרית, "from the town of," the reading of the initial *mem* being uncertain. This is also the rendering of Th: ἐκ πόλεως, "from the town," and of S: ܡܢ ܓܘ, "from the (walled) city."

Finally, the reading מְבֵית, "from the house/palace of," is found in Kennicott manuscript 2, de Rossi manuscript 26, and in the first hand of de Rossi manuscript 1252.

The committee regarded the last reading as an apparent facilitation and the Qumran reading מקרית as an assimilation to the parallel text in Num 21.28. The more difficult reading of M received a majority C vote.

Evaluation of Problems

Among recent commentators and translators, no one seems to have been tempted to follow the older, Qumran evidence on textual grounds. On the other hand, most commentators adopted the textually irrelevant reading מבית, found in a few medieval manuscripts. It is therefore not surprising that a number of translations do the same either by rendering "from the house of Sihon" (NAB) or "from the palace of Sihon" (NJB, NEB). The textual base for this kind of rendering has been shown to be very weak.

It is true that a few translations such as NJV, NIV, and REB, render M either as "from the midst of Sihon," or "from within Sihon." Such a translation is only plausible if Sihon is taken as the name of another town, mentioned after Hesbon, as suggested already by Movers (15) and Hitzig. There can be no doubt, however, that the reference is to the Amorite king Sihon, who had Hesbon as his capital city. Therefore, the textual problem seems to be irrelevant for translators, who will be obliged to provide the explicit information "town" or "palace" for translational reasons anyway. The absence of textual footnotes in many recent versions (RSV, NRSV, GNB, FC, GN) is fully justified.

Translation Proposals

NEB, without textual justification, can be taken as an example: "flames have shot out from the palace of Sihon."

49.1

Textual Decisions

In the last line of this verse, M reads מַלְכָּם, "their king," "Why has their king taken possession of Gad?" For this reading M has the support of T only: מלכהון, "their king."

The Origen recension of G (30.1) transcribed this as the proper name of the chief god of the Ammonites, Μολχομ, and the Lucianic recension as Μελχομ. V with *Melchom* and S with ܡܠܟܘܡ have done the same. All of these versions presuppose a base text vocalization מִלְכֹּם. In fact this form also is the basis for the transliteration Μελχολ of the Old Greek. Cappel (1684, 535) thought that the final *lambda* had its origin in the fact that no Greek word ends with a *mu*. Since a *lambda* also cannot stand at the end of a Greek word (H. W. Smith, §133), this argument loses its value.

The committee assigned a B rating to the vocalization מִלְכֹּם, and it concluded that the change of vocalization in M was of a theological nature, aiming at the elimination of the name of an idol. The same applies to the identical textual case of verse 3.

Evaluation of Problems

This is one of the few cases in which the global opinion of scholars coincides with that of the committee. Taking into account the editorial character of the superscription "concerning the Ammonites," it should, moreover, be noted that the third-person plural suffix ם-, "their," in M cannot be related to any antecedent of the context.

Almost all modern Jewish and Christian translations opt for the correction. For the rendering of M, apart from KJV, only SR and the footnoted variant translation of NIV can be quoted. The transcription of M "Malkâm" in Chouraqui seems to follow the practice of Calvin, Zwingli, and Luther (!).

Translators working on projects in which M in its vocalized form has been defined as the base text, will have to provide a textual footnote along the lines of, for example, FC.

Translation Proposals

NJB: "Why should Milcom have inherited Gad and his people have settled in its towns?" with its extensive note could serve as a model for translators.

49.3A

Textual Decisions

After the initial imperative: "Wail, O Heshbon," M gives the motivation: כִּי שֻׁדְּדָה־עַי, "for Ai is laid waste." In particular, the place-name Ai has caused problems.

M is confirmed by the transcription Γαι in the Old Greek (30.3), although it is true that this reading is one of the uncials attested only by Codex Marchalianus, that it is lacking in Codex Vaticanus, and that it is transformed into καί in Codex Alexandrinus. However, Codex Marchalianus is an extremely important witness, and the transcription of ʿ*ayin* with a *gamma* is a sign of antiquity. M furthermore has the support of V, with its transcription *Ahi*, and of S and T, which reproduce the form of M.

The only variant is the reading עֹז, "strength," found in the Soncino Bible edition of 1488, a reading copied into Kennicott manuscript 253 in 1495. It is rather surprising that this reading coincides with the rendering ἡ ἰσχύς, "the strength," found in Sym.

The variant reading and Vorlage of Sym עֹז was considered by the committee possibly to be due to assimilation to Num 21.24. The strongly supported text of M received a B rating.

Evaluation of Problems

The problems are, in fact, not of a textual but of a contextual nature. An address to the Moabite town of Heshbon in a context dealing with the Ammonites is extraordinary, and a town with the name Ai in Ammon or Moab is not otherwise known. Ai has only been identified as a town close to Bethel.

For this reason Grätz (1883, 397) proposed correcting with עָר, Ar being known at least as a Moabite town (Num 21.28). This correction has been adopted by NJB without textual note and mentioned in a footnote by GN.

For the same reason, Volz (415) suggested emending שֻׁדְּדָה עַי to שֹׁדֵד עָלָה, "a despoiler has advanced," a suggestion adopted by NAB: "for the ravager approaches." These conjectures are too speculative, however, to be recommended to translators.

If one does not want to make another conjecture "without great conviction" (McKane, 1207), the consonantal text of M could still be interpreted in two different ways: (a) as a place-name and (b) as the common noun עִי, "ruin." Venema (1084) was the first to suggest this vocalization, which has recently been adopted by Holladay (II, 366). This solution has been endorsed by BR, NAV, and CEV. Against the interpretation "ruin," it can be said that contextually a place-name is expected instead. In favor of the first interpretation, it can be modestly noted that our present knowledge of the ancient topography of Transjordan is not without lacunae. The majority of recent versions are apparently of the same opinion (RSV, NRSV, NJV, NEB, REB, NIV, FC, RL, etc.).

Translation Proposals

For the traditional interpretation, NIV can be quoted as an example: "Wail, O Heshbon, for Ai is destroyed," and for the second interpretation, CEV: "Cry, people of Heshbon; your town will become a pile of rubble."

49.3B

Textual Decisions

The second line of this verse in M ends with this very difficult sentence: וְהִתְשׁוֹטַטְנָה בַּגְּדֵרוֹת, "and run to and fro (second-person feminine plural imperative) in the hedges." The main textual problem is with the last word.

M is confirmed by the rendering of Sym: καὶ περιέλθετε διὰ τῶν τριγχῶν (late form for θριγκῶν), "go around among the fences," by the asterisked addition of the Origen recension: καὶ διαδράμετε ἐν τοῖς φραγμοῖς, "run in the hedges," as well as by V: *circuite per sepes*, "go around along the hedges."

T, on the other hand, renders the sentence ואתהממו בסיען, "and make a loud noise in companies," the second word having been read as בגדדות, with a second *dalet* instead of a *resh*. S, by translating ܘܐܬܗܡܡܘ ܒܣܝܥܢ, "and roar one with another," seems to have done the same.

The sentence is lacking in the Old Greek.

The committee thought that G could have omitted the sentence because of its obscurity. The renderings of T and S were considered possible assimilations to 48.37. The rather well-supported reading of M obtained four B and two C votes.

Evaluation of Problems

No modern translation has adopted S and T's interpretations, but several of them accepted the conjectured textual base of בַּגְּדֵרוֹת, interpreting it in the sense of 48.37: "with gashes." It is true that the mention of another funeral rite makes excellent sense in the context. However, it is less clear how these translations deal with the verb. In fact, the verb is only kept in the rendering of NAB: "run to and fro, gashing yourselves," and in the translation of RL. NRSV: "and slash yourselves with whips," and NEB and REB: "and score your bodies with gashes," smooth over their emendations.

To smooth away the problems of M by rendering it as: "Run about in confusion" (GNB) does not seem to be acceptable either. And the kind of interpretation found, for example, in CEV: "You will turn here and there, but your path will be blocked," is too fanciful to be taken into consideration.

The only possible interpretation of M is that "among the hedges," "in the sheepfolds" (NJV), and "among the sheep-pens" (NJB) refer to a situation where civilized gatherings no longer exist. It is this situation which needs to be described in translation.

Translation Proposals

NJV could be taken as an example: "And run to and fro in the sheepfolds."

49.4

Textual Decisions

After having asked: "Why do you boast of your valleys?" M states זָב
עֲמָקֵךְ, "fruitful is your (singular) valley."

Although it has a different interpretation of the Hebrew participle זָב, this
sentence is directly attested by V: *defluxit vallis tua*, "your valley has passed
away," and probably by Sym, according to the Syro-Hexapla: ܗܝ ܪܥܡܩܟ ܕܝ,
"your valley has declined," although the plural reading "valleys" is not entirely impossible.

The plural is attested by the Greek recensions in their reading τὰ πεδία
σου, "your plains," the Origen recension having the transcription ζηβ for the
verb, and the Lucianic recension having the rendering διέρρευσε, "fell away."
The plural is also found in S: ܪܥܡܩܝܟ, "your valleys."

The presence of the sentence in T is confirmed by its paraphrase: חרובו
תוקפך: "destroyed are your strongholds."

This sentence has not been rendered in the Old Greek.

The committee theorized that the plural rendering was an assimilation to the
preceding plural noun, עמקים, "valleys," and it retained M with a B evaluation.

Evaluation of Problems

From Schwally (188, 200, note 2) to McKane (1203), most commentators
proposed omitting the sentence, as a marginal comment. A few recent versions do the same (RSV, NJB, REB) without noting the evidence of G.

Although (with most modern translations) a rendering of M should be
preferred, several interpretations of M remain open. In agreement with the ancient versions, a negative interpretation of the participle of the verb זוב, "to
pine away" (DCH III, 95a; HAL I, 255b, with question mark), could be given.
Notice also, in light of T, that the double use of עמק in M could reflect a play
on the homonyms עמק I: "valley," and עמק II: "strength," "stronghold." Most
of the recent versions that follow M (NRSV, NAB, NEB, NJV) combine the
negative meaning of זָב with the meaning of "strength": "Why do you boast in
your strength? Your strength is ebbing" (NRSV).

However, זוב in most occurrences in the Hebrew Bible, expresses the
concept of fertility which is very applicable to a valley. (Compare the expression "flowing with milk and honey," where the same verb is used.) With NIV,
RL, and GN, this interpretation may therefore be favored.

Translation Proposals

NIV is a suitable model for this: "Why do you boast of your valleys,
boast of your valleys so fruitful?"

49.11

Textual Decisions

According to M, the Lord addresses Edom with the imperative עָזְבָה, "Leave," "Leave your orphans, I will keep them alive." An imperative with the same meaning has been rendered by Aq, according to the Syro-Hexapla, and by S: ܫܒܘܩ, by Sym: κατάλειπε, by V: *relinque*, and by Josephus: ἔασον, "let alone."

Although Sym renders an imperative, he connects the information of verse 11 with the end of the preceding verse, particularly the last word, וְאֵינֶנּוּ, "and he is no more": καὶ οὐκ ἔστιν ὅς ἐρεῖ κατάλειπε τοὺς ὀρφανούς σου, "And there is no one who says: leave your orphans." A different speaker is therefore made explicit by means of the extra ὅς ἐρεῖ, "who says." The Lucianic recension of G (29.12), with ὁ λέγων, "who is saying," does the same.

Without any plus, G immediately connects verse 11 with verse 10: καὶ οὐκ ἔστιν ὑπολείπεσθαι ὀρφανόν σου, "and none of your orphans will be left (alive)."

In the paraphrase of T, the negation of verse 10 is present: וליתנון, "and are not," and is carried over into verse 11 as well, where the addressee is different: "You, O house of Israel, shall not (לא) be forsaken."

The committee explained the renderings of G and T as syntactical facilitations and as ways to solve the problem caused by the order to abandon the orphans. With a majority B vote, it conserved the reading of M.

Evaluation of Problems

No recent translator has adopted the interpretation of Sym, in spite of the encouragement of some modern commentators to do so, such as Rudolph (288). The only modern versions deviating from M are NEB and REB which take the first three consonants of עזבה with the preceding verse, vocalizing עֹזֵב (Brockington, 214) and giving the Hebrew root the meaning "to help." The last consonant ה is apparently taken as the interrogative particle and is prefixed to the next word of verse 11, as can be deduced from the renderings: "there is no one to help him. What! am I to save alive your fatherless children?" (NEB), and "there is no one to deliver him. Am I to keep alive your fatherless children?" (REB). These versions follow Driver's suggestion (1937/38, 125) that the meaning "help" of the Ethiopic cognate ʿâzzäbä should be assigned to the Hebrew root. But this comparative philological treatment, criticized by Barr (141), never gained general acceptance.

Translators will have to make a difficult choice between various interpretational options. If the Lord is considered to be the speaker and the Edomites the addressees, M must express bitter irony, and the translation must almost be the opposite of the surface form in the text, coming close to the interpretation of G.

If the statements are taken at face value, only the Israelites, as observed in Jewish exegesis, could be the addressees. In the Edomite context, however, this is unlikely.

A third option is to affirm that no neighbor will be able to make a statement such as in verse 11 (FC, GN), and this interpretation is not far from the one behind the rendering of Sym and the Lucianic recension.

It seems that only in literal types of translation can decision-making be avoided.

Translation Proposals

For a literal translation, NJB can be selected: "Leave your orphans, I shall support them."

For an interpretation along the lines of the third option, FC can be cited: *Pas un voisin ne pourra dire: "Quand vous ne serez plus là, je ferai vivre vos orphelins,"* "No neighbor will be able to say: 'When you are no longer there, I will keep alive your orphans.'"

49.23

Textual Decisions

After having noted that Hamath and Arpad are troubled, the text of M continues, stating בַּיָּם דְּאָגָה, literally: "on the sea of anxiety." The prepositional phrase "on the sea" is also attested by π': ἐν θαλάσσῃ, V: *in mari*, and S: ܒܝܡܐ.

However, more than 20 manuscripts of Kennicott and de Rossi have the reading כַּיָּם, "like the sea," whereas G (30.12) has nothing which corresponds to the prepositional phrase.

An uncertain position is held by T which lacks the prepositional phrase in its manuscripts (it is only present in the editions of the first and second Rabbinic Bible). However, the extensive paraphrase: "Behold, like those who go down to the sea, who are silent, they cannot rest," seems to be inspired by the variant form כַּיָּם.

Since the reading with *bet* clearly belongs to the proto-Masoretic text tradition and the reading with *kaf* can be judged to be a syntactical facilitation, the committee assigned a B rating to M.

Evaluation of Problems

Most modern translations (RSV, NRSV, NIV, NJB, NJV, NAB, REB) adopt the reading כַּיָּם and provide textual justification in a footnote. See, for example, the translation of NJB: "like the sea that cannot be calmed."

Volz (419) conjectured נָמוֹג) לְבָּם מִדְּאָגָה), "their heart (is convulsed) with anxiety," and HUB notes that לבם is read by the first hand of Kennicott manuscript 150; thus, this word loses some of its conjectural nature. This fact is ignored in CTAT (810). Volz's conjecture was more recently adopted by Bright (333), and it entered into some recent versions such as, for example, FC and RL.

Since translators are invited to render M, its meaning has to be determined. Some modern translations (BR, GN) seem to have taken the prepositional phrase literally, as in "at the sea" or "on the coast." One would then face a kind of tension, since neither Hamath nor—if the identification is correct—Arpad was located on the seashore. It is therefore more likely that "on the sea of anxiety" is a metaphor, an image provoked by the statement about agitation in the cities of Hamat and Arpad. Translationally, such a metaphor will often have to be presented as a comparison, so that no difference between a rendering of M and a translation of the variant will show up. Of course, in such a case, no textual information will be provided in a footnote.

Translation Proposals

Following the above procedure leads to a translation such as that of NIV: "(They are) troubled like the restless sea," or GNB: "Anxiety toils over them like a sea, and they cannot rest."

49.25

Textual Decisions

There are two textual problems in this verse in M: (a) the negation לֹא in the first sentence: אֵיךְ לֹא־עֻזְּבָה עִיר תְּהִלָּה, "How is *not* forsaken the glorious city," and (b) the reading מְשׂוֹשִׂי, "(the town of) my joy."

Concerning the first problem, the reading of M is attested by G (30.14), S, and T. The negation marker is only omitted in the rendering of V. Regarding the second problem, M only has the support of the Old Greek according to the reading of manuscript 534, selected by Ziegler: (κώμην) ἣν ἠγάπησα, "(the village) which I loved." All other versions render their Hebrew Vorlage with a noun, without adding the first-person singular suffix *yod*: Aq and Sym: εὐφροσύνης, "of merriment" (a rendering also attributed to Th by the Syro-Hexapla), V: *laetitiae*, "of delight," S ܕܚܕܘܬܐ, "of joy"; or, like T, with an adjective: חדאה, "joyous."

For the committee, M merited a B rating in both cases: in the first one because of strong versional support and in the second because of the facilitating omission of the *yod* in most versions and the backing of M by manuscript 534 of G.

Evaluation of Problems

Most modern versions (RSV, NRSV, NAB, NJB, RL, FC) omit both the negation and the first-person possessive suffix on textual grounds, rendering, for example, as in NRSV: "How the famous city is forsaken, the joyful town." NEB and REB, appealing to S, do the same in the second case: "the city (place) of gladness," but not in the first one, although at first sight the negation seems to be absent: "How forlorn is the town of joyful song." In fact, they keep the negation but attribute the meaning "to help" to the verb עזב, as in 49.11, so that "forlorn" is a gloss for "not helped."

It should be noted, however, that M makes excellent sense when the negation is combined with the meanings "desert," "evacuate," "abandon," for עזב: "Why has the city not been deserted?" (NJV, NIV; compare also CEV, GN). In the light of this interpretation, moreover, the relation of verse 25 to verse 26 becomes much clearer. The *yod* in the second sentence could be considered (with Grotius) "paragogic" and therefore needing no translation, as interpreted in most versions. However, if the *yod* is taken as a first-person suffix, one would have to determine both the speaker and the city referred to. The possibilities are: God and Jerusalem, God and Damascus, the prophet (speaking on behalf of God) and Damascus, or the prophet (speaking on behalf of the king and/or the population of Damascus) and Damascus.

Translation Proposals

The NIV can function as one model: "Why has the city of renown not been abandoned, / the town in which I delight?"

50.2

Textual Decisions

The second prophetic command in the verse in M appears in the following sentence: וּשְׂאוּ־נֵס הַשְׁמִיעוּ, literally: "and set up a banner, proclaim." The first two words have been rendered in the insertion of the Origen and Lucianic recensions as καὶ ἐπάρατε σημεῖον, "and lift up a standard"; the last word in the first recension is ἀκουστὸν ποιήσατε, "cause to be heard," and in the second recension is ἀκουτίσατε, "let hear." The sentence is translated literally in S and T, and it is also attested by V, the only difference being the nontranslation of the clause-initial *waw* (as correctly signaled in HUB). However, the clause is not attested in the Old Greek (27.2).

The committee pointed out that the Hebrew Vorlage of G could have fallen prey to homoioteleuton, the eye of the scribe having shifted from הַשְׁמִיעוּ to וְהַשְׁמִיעוּ. On the other hand, it did not exclude the possibility that M could have amplified an originally shorter text form such as the one attested by

G. In the latter case, the literary initiative would have occurred on the level of the proto-Masoretic text. For this reason, M was given three A and three B votes.

Evaluation of Problems

From Movers (13) to McKane (1252) and Holladay (II, 391), the clause in M was frequently regarded as an addition taken from parallel passages and was therefore omitted. In recent translations, only NEB and REB delete the complete sentence, whereas NAB only removes the first two words.

It seems preferable, however, to respect the literary tradition of M, especially since the amplifications could be a rhetorical feature, used to enhance the importance of the following oracle. The purpose of setting up a banner is to summon the people to hear the message, and for this signal a functionally equivalent gesture may have to be found.

Translation Proposals

GNB: "Give the signal and / announce the news!" and CEV: "Raise the signal flags; shout . . . ," are some ways in which the sentence in M could be rendered.

50.5

Textual Decisions

The second line of this verse in M begins with two verbal constructions, both of which have presented problems: בֹּאוּ וְנִלְווּ, "Come (plural imperative) and they will join themselves."

The imperative only has the support of S: ـܘ. G (27.5), with its rendering καὶ ἥξουσι, "and they shall come," seems to presuppose וּבָאוּ, whereas Aq with his translation ـܘܐܬܐ according to the Syro-Hexapla, V with its rendering *venient*, and T with יֵיתוֹן, all meaning: "they shall come," seem to imply a reading יָבֹאוּ.

The second verbal construction in M is attested by G: καὶ καταφεύξονται, "and they will flee for refuge," by Aq and Sym according to the Barberini manuscript: καὶ προστεθήσονται, by V: *et adponentur*, and by T: וְיִתּוֹסְפוּן, all: "and they will be joined to." Only S, by rendering ܢܬܠܘܐ, "let us join ourselves," seems to have vocalized the Hebrew form as a first-person plural imperfect of the *nifal*: וְנִלָּוֶה.

The committee regarded M as the more difficult reading and as the base from which the ancient versions had made differing opposite contextual assimilations. The imperative of M only received a C rating because of rather weak versional support. The second verbal construction of M, being better attested, was voted B. This decision was reinforced by the presence of a syntactical parallel in Joel 4.11.

Evaluation of Problems

From Giesebrecht (246) to Holladay (II, 391), correcting M with וּבָאוּ, based on G, was defended by several scholars. Among recent translations, NEB, NJV, and NRSV apply this correction with textual justification and NIV, FC, and CEV without. From Radaq (1862, 54a) to Bauer/Leander (322v), the second verbal construction of M was sometimes interpreted as a rare form of the *nifal* imperative: "(Come) and join yourselves to." This point of view, more widespread among translators in the sixteenth century (Pagnini, Estienne, Calvin), is not often shared by their modern colleagues, SR and Chouraqui being some of the exceptions.

Most modern versions, following Luther and KJV, prefer the Syriac model of combining imperative and first-person plural optative mood (RSV, NAB, NJB, REB, RL, GN). Only REB and NJB provide textual notes defending their renderings as based on S.

The proposed translation of CTAT (819): "Come and may one be united," in which the third-person plural imperfect is translated by an impersonal third-person singular optative, is not very practical, and even translators who base their work on M will have to make a linguistic adaptation along the lines of S.

Translation Proposals

NAB: "Come, let us join ourselves to the Lord," is therefore an acceptable model for translation.

50.9

Textual Decisions

In the last line of this verse, M characterizes the warrior as מַשְׁכִּיל, someone "who bereaves (people of children)." The reading with *shin* is found in 27 manuscripts, representing the classical Tiberian text, and in three editions. It is further supported by Aq: ἀτεκνῶν, "making childless," V: *interfectoris*, "of a murderer," and T: מתכיל, "who makes people childless."

Three Hebrew manuscripts and six editions, however, have a reading with *śin*: מַשְׂכִּיל, "skilled," which is also attested by G (27.9) and Sym: συνετοῦ, "intelligent," and by S: ܕܡܨܠܚ, "who succeeds."

The committee concluded that the *hiphil* participle מַשְׁכִּיל could have the meaning: "one who makes another person childless," and that the reading with *śin* certainly could be regarded as an assimilation to a more current form.

Therefore, the reading with *shin* collected three B votes and one C. Two B votes were nevertheless cast for the reading with *śin*.

Evaluation of Problems

From the end of the seventeenth century (de Dieu) to the present time, most commentators adopted the reading with *śin*. Only Holladay (II, 392) recently emphasized the fact that the reading with *shin* seems to be the more difficult one. The trend of modern translations, however, is to follow the reading with *śin*, mostly without even mentioning the presence of a textual problem. NAB is the sole version to provide textual justification for its rendering, which is "Their arrows are arrows of the skilled warrior."

Translators who do not want to endorse the reading with *shin*, following a few rare versions (Chouraqui, NAV, but the latter with a different interpretation), should at least footnote the variant pointing and provide a variant translation, as is done in NJV, CEV, and SR.

Translation Proposals

An example of the above recommendation can be found in NJV: "Their arrows are like those of a skilled warrior / Who does not turn back without hitting the mark," with a textual note: "So many mss., editions, and versions; other mss. and editions read 'a warrior who bereaves.'"

50.11

Textual Decisions

In the second line of this verse in M, the behavior of the Babylonians is compared with that of a heifer דָשָׁה, "threshing." This reading with *he* is the reading of the classical Tiberian text.

A number of Hebrew manuscripts, including the manuscript of the Prophets of Bern, manuscripts Paris BN hébr 2 and 6, and Urbinates 1 and 2, read a final *alef*: דשא. It is clear that this form, vocalized as דֶּשֶׁא, "grass," was read by G (27.11): (ὡς βοΐδια) ἐν βοτάνῃ, "(as calves) in the grass," by Aq: (ὥσπερ μόσχοι) χλόης, "(like calves) of tender grass," and by V: (*sicut vitulus*) *super herbam*, "(as a calf) on the grass."

The rendering of S: () , "(like) fattened (calves)," seems to be rather indeterminate with regard to its Vorlage. T with its rendering כעגלי) רבקא) would attest the same meaning as S (so HUB, with a mistake in the second Syriac character) if Levy's definition (II, 403a) is followed. Gesenius (Thesaurus 1260a) proves, however, that T translated the reading with *he*. In this case T would be the only witness of the classical Tiberian text.

In spite of this rather weak support, the committee considered the reading with *alef* a graphical error, and it credited the reading with final *he* with three B and three C votes.

Evaluation of Problems

A considerable number of recent versions (RSV, NRSV, NAB, NJB, RL, FC, Chouraqui) opt for the reading with final *alef*, but only occasionally (NAB, NJB) is a textual justification given. Its absence may be due to the traditional majority interpretation since the sixteenth century and/or to the conception that a *he/alef* confusion is a current grammatical phenomenon (Abulwalid 1886, 88.25–89.14).

Kimchi (1887, 36) explains at length, however, that the heifer, while it is threshing, is unmuzzled so that it can eat the whole day, and Anderlind (44) estimates that an average heifer absorbs 30 liters of wheat per day. Further cultural data provided by Bochart (I, 301f.) also show that a rendering of the Tiberian text is to be preferred, with REB, NEB, NIV, GNB, CEV, BR, NJV, and SR.

Translation Proposals

CEV: "and jumping around / like calves threshing grain," can serve as a model for translators. In some circumstances it may be useful to add a footnote stating that three ancient translations render "in a pasture."

50.21

Textual Decisions

In the last line of the verse, M starts with the following sentence: חֲרֹב וְהַחֲרֵם אַחֲרֵיהֶם, "Slay, and destroy after them." It is especially the prepositional phrase which has created problems.

M does not have the support of any primary witness. The prepositional phrase is lacking in G (27.21). It is true that it is present in the recensions of Origen and Lucian, taken from Th, but in the curious form ὀπίσω (Lucian: κατόπισθεν) αὐτῶν κακά, "after them evil." The addition of κακά which is, incidentally, lacking in the Armenian version, can hardly be explained.

S renders the last words ܘܩܛܘܠ ܐܢܘܢ, "and slay them with the sword," a rendering which could have found its origin in the reading וְהַחֲרִימֵם, "and destroy them." S could have omitted the prepositional phrase (as did G) and instead made a badly needed object explicit.

The translation of T: ייתון לגמרא שארהון, "let them come to destroy their remnant," could be based on the reading אַחֲרִיתָם, if it was not simply guided by the necessity to provide a meaningful translation.

The same can be said with regard to the rendering of V: *et interfice quae post eos sunt*, "and slay who are after them." For the committee, the difficult reading in M was the basis of the smooth renderings of V, S, and T, and its syntactical difficulty possibly was the reason for its omission by G. The intentional threefold sequence of *ḥet-resh* was another consideration for the B evaluation of M.

Evaluation of Problems

Giesebrecht (248) has proposed the correction אַחֲרִיתָם, according to the supposed reading of T, and this correction apparently is the basis for NJB's renderings: "and curse with destruction every last one of them," and of NRSV: "and utterly destroy the last of them." On the other hand, both NEB and GNB have the rendering "and destroy them," the latter translation referring to S as its base and the first to the presupposed Hebrew Vorlage of S: וְהַחֲרִימֵם (Brockington, 215).

It is true that M remains difficult. The vivid language which van Selms detects (III, 59): "With sword and ban after them!" unfortunately requires too many revocalizations. With some ellipsis, M may simply want to say: "destroy everything/everyone they have left behind them." For a smooth rendering, translators will have to apply the procedures followed in the ancient versions. These translational procedures will make textual footnotes superfluous.

Translation Proposals

REB: "put them to the sword and utterly destroy them," and CEV: "Kill them all! Destroy their possessions!" are possible ways to fill up the ellipsis of M.

50.28

Textual Decisions

At the end of this verse, M reads נִקְמַת הֵיכָלוֹ, "vengeance for his temple," as an apposition to "the vengeance of the Lord our God." The presence of this apposition is attested by the recensions of Origen and Lucian, according to manuscript Marchalianus by all the columns of the Hexapla; and by V, S, and T. It is only lacking in the Old Greek (27.28).

The committee considered the presence or absence of the apposition to be due to a literary initiative and not to a textual accident. In view of its presence in all proto-Masoretic witnesses, M received an A evaluation.

Evaluation of Problems

Movers (48) considered the apposition in M to be a later gloss, dating from after the destruction of the temple. Rudolph (302), Janzen (60), and

McKane (1280) proposed omitting it as an insertion from 51.11. Their advice is followed in the apparatus of BHS, in NEB and NAB. EÜ presents the translation in the text, but between square brackets, which is its device for marking an unauthentic text.

It has been observed, however, that the next verse ends with a similar kind of apposition, and this balanced rhetorical structure favors retaining the apposition here. "Vengeance for his temple" obviously is shorthand for "revenge for the profanation of his temple."

Translation Proposals

An example of an explicit rendering of the apposition has been given above. A more literal type of translation can follow a model such as REB: "the vengeance he takes for his temple."

50.38A

Textual Decisions

After five instances in the preceding three verses in which חֶרֶב, "the sword," has been evoked, M summons חֹרֶב, "a drought" in this verse, "a drought against her waters." This reading of M has the literal support of V: *siccitas*, and of T: שרבא.

In G (27.38) the word is lacking. The recensions of Origen and Lucian, however, have the addition μάχαιραν, "sword," presupposing therefore a Hebrew Vorlage with vocalization חֶרֶב. The same rendering ܣܝܦܐ is found in S.

The committee considered the omission of G to be deliberate, in order to avoid the problem presented by the reading חֹרֶב, and the renderings of the Greek recensions and S as assimilations to the five occurrences of חֶרֶב in the preceding context. It judged the rupture of M to be rhetorically acceptable and cast three B and three C votes for the reading of M.

Evaluation of Problems

From Ewald to McKane (1290), commentators regularly defended the correction of M with חֶרֶב. The instruction of the critical apparatus of BHS may also have pushed translators in the same direction. At least NAB and NEB (Brockington, 215) cite S as the basis for their translation "a sword upon (over) their waters," and FC in a note cites two ancient versions for its rendering: *Guerre à ses cours d'eau*, "War to his waterways." Other translations (REB, TOB, BR, EÜ) do not judge it necessary to footnote matters of vocalization.

Although a translation of M should be recommended, it should be observed that drying up the canals around Babylon is a military operation (van Selms, III, 61); thus, a close relationship between the two readings exists.

Modern versions that follow M can be divided into those which footnote the variant as an alternative translation (NIV, NRSV) and those which do not (Chouraqui, GNB, NJB, NJV, RL, RSV, SR).

Translators may want to note the play on sounds in the words *choreb* and *chereb*, as done in NJV. In some languages the staccato style of M will have to be abandoned in favor of a complete sentence.

Translation Proposals

TILC is a useful example: *La siccità colpirà i suoi fiume*, "Drought will affect their rivers."

50.38B

Textual Decisions

The last verb of the verse in M reads: יִתְהֹלָלוּ, "they are driven mad," "Through their dread images they are driven mad." This *hitpoal* reading of the root הלל III is not attested by any of the versions, but it has the almost complete support of the Masoretic tradition. In fact, de Rossi notes that his manuscripts 174 and 815 have the vocalization יִתְהַלְלוּ, "they glorify," "they glorify in their dread images," reading therefore the *hitpael* of הלל II. These two manuscripts are of no textual significance, however. Nevertheless, this kind of vocalization, with the meaning "they boast," was most likely what was rendered by G (27.38): κατεκαυχῶντο, and certainly by Aq: ἐγκαυχῶνται, Sym: καυχῶνται, V: *gloriantur*, S: ܡܫܬܒܗܪܝܢ, and T: מִשְׁתַּבְּחִין.

The committee ascertained that the *patah* vocalization in the versions was due to the interpretation of the preceding noun, "dread images," as a simple parallel to idols, in which one can glorify. However, M correctly signifies the nuance of "dreaded gods," and this, in turn, justifies its *holem* vocalization. Five C ratings were given to the latter vocalization. One C rating was given to the variant.

Evaluation of Problems

From Hitzig to Penna the variant was occasionally defended, but recent research is preponderantly in favor of M (McKane, 1291; Holladay II, 395). Modern translations are in harmony with this situation. In fact, only NEB and REB, with their common rendering: "(for it is a land of idols) / that glories in its dreaded gods," translate the variant reading. Brockington (215) claims the support of the two Hebrew manuscripts for the rendering of NEB, whereas REB does not enter into the details of vocalization.

In spite of the lack of external support, a rendering of M should clearly be preferred. The grammatical subject of the verb (they) does not have any "idols" in the preceding half-line to be the antecedent, and therefore a rendering such as that of NIV: "idols that will go mad with terror," is wrong. The subject of the verb is the people implied by the word אֶרֶץ, "land," at the beginning of the line.

Translation Proposals

The following can serve as a model for translation: "for it is a land of images driven mad by its dreaded gods" (McKane).

6

JEREMIAH 51–52

51.1

Textual Decisions

After Babylon M deals with the inhabitants of לֵב קָמָי, "Leb Qamai." Only Sym transcribes these words as a proper name, reading λεβ καβη or perhaps λεβ καμη. Most of the ancient versions provide a translation or a paraphrase for these words. So Aq: καρδίαν ἐπεγειρόντων, "the heart of those who have risen up," a rendering adopted by the Origen recension, V: *qui cor suum levaverunt contra me*, "who have lifted up their heart against me," and S: ܠܒ ܡܥܝܪ, "of the hardhearted."

G (28.1), however, has the rendering Χαλδαίους, "the Chaldeans," which could be based on an older Hebrew Vorlage with כשדים or on the Greek trans-lator's decoding of לב קמי as an original, so-called, "athbash," a cryptogram in which the first letter of the Hebrew alphabet was replaced by the last, the sec-ond by the next-to-last, and so on, resulting in כשדים.

The Lucianic recension combines decoding with the translation of Aq: Χαλδαίαν καρδίαν ἐπεγειρόντων, "Chaldea, the heart of those who have risen up." T combines decoding with this paraphrase: "(and against the inhabitants) of the land of the Chaldeans peoples, who kill, whose heart is high, and they are beautiful in stature."

With Bright (355), the committee judged it possible that the use of cryp-tograms was already current during the Babylonian exile as a means to protect the writers and that at a later stage of history this use would have lost its func-tion. This would explain the decoding in G and T. The "athbash" of M consti-tuting at least the proto-Masoretic text form, it therefore received a B rating.

Evaluation of Problems

Sarsowsky (150–51) conjectured קַמְבּוּל (the name of a Babylonian re-gion) based upon metathesis of M, but it did not receive any acceptance among commentators and it was only adopted by NEB: "and those who live in Kambul."

In fact, most translations transliterate: "Leb-kamai," explaining, however, in a footnote that the proper name is a cipher for Chaldea (so Chouraqui, NAV, NIV, NJB, NJV, NRSV, REB). A few modern versions, especially those of the German tradition (BR, RL, GN) provide a translation of M, as done by most of the ancient versions. A few others (RSV, NAB, CEV, EÜ) decipher the Hebrew in their text, the English versions producing at least a footnote explaining the reading.

Translators may follow any of these procedures as long as they make sure by translation or by means of a footnote that the modern reader does not face an unsolved cryptogram. In projects with Orthodox participation, decoding in the text may be preferred.

Translation Proposals

For the procedure of transliteration plus a footnote, REB is a model: "against Babylon and the inhabitants of Leb-kamai" (plus note: Leb-kamai: a cipher for Chaldea); for translation, use GN: *gegen die Stadt Babylon und gegen alle, die in diesem Zentrum des Aufruhrs gegen mich wohnen!* "against Babylon and against all who live in this center of revolt against me"; and for decoding, CEV: "(to destroy) the people of Babylonia," with a footnote: "the Hebrew text has *Leb-Qamai*, a secret way of writing 'Babylonia.'"

51.2

Textual Decisions

This verse in M begins with the statement that the Lord will send זָרִים, "strangers," against Babylon and that "they will winnow her": וְזֵרוּהָ. The reading זָרִים does not have the support of any version.

According to the Barberini manuscript, Aq and Sym have the rendering λικμητάς (καὶ λικμήσουσιν αὐτήν), "winnowers (and they will winnow her)." In other words, they have vocalized the Hebrew consonantal text as זֹרִים. The same vocalization and meaning are presupposed by V: *ventilatores* (*et ventilabunt eam*), and at least the same vocalization is presupposed by the interpretations of S: (ܡܢܕܪ̈ܢܐ) ܟܕܪ̈ܐ, and T: (ויבזונה) בזוזין, both meaning "plunderers (and they shall plunder her)."

G (28.2) yields the rendering ὑβριστάς (καὶ καθυβρίσουσιν αὐτήν), "and haughty men (and they will treat her contemptuously)." As already has been noted by Cappel (1684, 537b) and Schleusner (5, 359), G read a *dalet* instead of a *resh*, both in the noun and in the verb.

The committee considered the rendering of G to be due to a graphical error. It was inclined to regard the paranomasia or word-play of M as original and the rendering of the other versions as a contextual assimilation. In view of the weak attestation of M, only four C ratings were given to it, and two C ratings were assigned to the variant vocalization.

Evaluation of Problems

Scholars have been rather unanimous in their preference for the variant vocalization. Without mentioning any problem, most modern versions (EÜ, NEB, REB, RSV, NRSV RL, etc.) follow this reading. Only two translations, NAB and NJB, justify their rendering in a footnote, mentioning the reading of M.

M is not without advocates, however, as is shown by BR, Chouraqui, CEV, GN, GNB, NIV, and NJV. In fact, the word "foreigners" could be anticipating "the kings of Media," who are the major participants in the next discourse, section 11–14.

Whether translators opt for M or for the variant vocalization, some kind of annotation seems to be necessary.

Translation Proposals

NIV can be quoted as an example of M's rendering: "I will send foreigners to Babylon // to winnow her and to devastate her land," and for some editions NIV's footnote may be of interest: "The Hebrew for this phrase is an excellent example of alliteration and assonance."

For a rendering of the variant, see FC: *Je vais lâcher contre elle // des gens qui l'éparpilleront // comme la paille au vent*, "I will release people against her who will scatter her like straw in the wind."

51.3

Textual Decisions

This verse contains three textual problems. The first two concern the two particles with which the first two sentences of M begin: אֶל and וְאֶל; the third problem is the *ketiv* יִדְרֹךְ in the first sentence.

The first אֶל, "to," produces a rather difficult syntax: "To let him bend let him bend he who bends his bow." The *seghol* vocalization is found in the manuscripts which constitute the classical Tiberian text. Support from the versions, however, is debatable. G (28.3) renders the first sentence with τεινέτω ὁ τείνων τὸ τόξον αὐτοῦ, "let the archer bend his bow," and therefore does not translate אֶל. It is possible that the word did figure in his Vorlage but that he did not know how to translate it in this exceptional context. M is attested by T if the rendering לה, "it" (the bow), or "to her" (Babylon), found in the Babylonian manuscript Oxford Bibl Bodl Heb d 26 and in the Urbinates is taken to be original.

Contrariwise, a number of Hebrew manuscripts as well as the editions of Soncino (1488) and of Brescia (1494) have a *paṭaḥ* vocalization, reading therefore אַל, "not," "let not bend." The negation marker μή has also been inserted by the Origen recension. The vocalization אַל is further confirmed by T, if the edition of Sperber is taken as the textual base, and by V and S.

Concerning וְאֶל at the beginning of the second sentence, the *seghol* vocalization is again typical of the classical Tiberian text. Versional support, however, is questionable here as well. The absence of a corresponding item in G could possibly be explained in the same way as above. M would only have the support of T: ולה, if the Sperber edition is followed. The Hebrew manuscripts mentioned above and the Soncino edition read the *paṭaḥ* vocalization וְאַל, and this negation is again found in the Origen recension, V, and S and in the reading ולא of the Oxford and Urbinates manuscripts of T. Finally, it should be noted that in both sentence-initial positions, many Greek manuscripts read ἐπ' αὐτῇ, "against her," which corresponds to a *sevir* (a reading avoiding a difficulty in the text) אֵלֶיהָ in Ginsburg manuscript 3 and Oxford manuscript 69.

The third textual problem relates to the *ketiv* reading יִדְרֹךְ. The *ketiv* does not have any versional support, and the *qere* which omits the repetition of the verbal form as a dittography, has the support of all the versions.

In the first case, M's reading אַל received a B rating as the more difficult reading, the *paṭaḥ* vocalization being considered an assimilation to וְאַל in verse 3c. In the second case, half of the committee voted D for the *seghol* vocalization and the other half voted D in favor of the *paṭaḥ* reading. In the last instance, the *ketiv* vocalized as יִדְרֹךְ obtained a C rating, the omission in the versions being regarded as due to haplography.

Evaluation of Problems

From Houbigant to Holladay (2.396) many scholars preferred to read the double negation and to omit ידרך as dittography. Most modern versions (RSV, NRSV, NJB, NIV, RL, NAV, GNB) do the same. So, for example, NJB: "Let no archer bend his bow! // Let no man swagger in his breastplate!" Even the rhetorical questions in NEB and REB: "How will the archer then string his bow // or put on his coat of mail?" are simple transformations of a double negative in English (Brockington, 216).

On the other hand, a few recent translations (NAB, C) follow G in what is called (Textual Notes on the NAB, 424) the omission of the negatives: "Let the bowman draw his bow // and flaunt his coat of mail."

Possibly the whole textual discussion is translationally rather irrelevant, since the matter of vocalization largely depends on the answer to the question: who is the addressee? As stated by Holladay (2.396): "If the bowman is attacking Babylon, then a negative is wrong (so G); if the bowman is Babylonian, then a negative is called for (so V, S, and T)."

The interpretation proposed by the committee presupposes the ellipsis of a relative; אֶל־יִדְרֹךְ stands for אֶל אֲשֶׁר יִדְרֹךְ, "at he who is to shoot," "Let the archer bend his bow at the person who is about to shoot at him." Such an ellipsis is difficult, but not impossible.

Translation Proposals

GN is the only translation to present a model for the last-mentioned interpretation: *Ich gebe seinen Feinden den Befehl: Schießt die Bogenschützen nieder und all die stolzen gepfanzerten Krieger!* "I order his enemies: Shoot the bowmen and all the proud, armored soldiers."

51.11

Textual Decisions

In this verse as well as in verse 28, M speaks of מַלְכֵי, "the kings (of the Medes)," and this plural reading is attested by V and T in both verses. In verse 11 the plural is also confirmed by Josephus.

However, in both verses S renders the singular: "the king of the Medes," although it should be noted that the only difference between the singular and plural in Syriac consists in the absence or presence of a *seyame*, two dots above the noun.

In verse 28, all the witnesses of G (28.28) have the singular τὸν βασιλέα. The same is the case in verse 11 (28.11): βασιλέως (Μήδων), "of the king (of the Medes)," with the important exception of the first hand of Codex Sinaiticus, which has the plural.

The committee considered it unlikely that the latter rendering would be due to a recension against M and that therefore the first hand of Sinaiticus in verse 11 most likely represents the Old Greek. The singular in all other witnesses of G in verse 11 would then have to be ascribed to an assimilation to G in verse 28. Since the singular represents an attractive facilitation and the change to plural would be less plausible, M received a B evaluation in both cases.

Evaluation of Problems

From Duhm to McKane (1305) and Holladay (2.397), the singular reading was occasionally defended, but the proposals did not have an important impact on translation. Among older translations Moffatt, and among more recent translations NEB, REB, C, and W are the only versions to adopt the singular (NEB and REB basing their decision on G).

It is noteworthy that the plural in "the kings of the Medes" is the standard formula of the Hebrew Bible (compare Jer 25.25; Esth 10.2; Dan 8.20). Probably one needs to think of a coalition of vassal kings or even army commanders.

Translation Proposals

GNB is a possible model for translation: "The Lord has stirred up the kings of Media." A note as given in CEV: "Probably kings of smaller kingdoms that were part of the Median empire," may be useful.

51.13

Textual Decisions

This verse in M ends with the difficult expression אַמַּת בִּצְעֵךְ, literally: "the yard (measure) of your being-cut-off." The problem presented by the first word, אַמַּת, has especially been analyzed.

M is confirmed by Sym with certainty. According to the Barberini manuscript, Sym would read πῆχυς τὸ κτῆμά σου, "the cubit (measure) your possession." However, both Field and Ziegler correct κτῆμά with τμῆμα, "the portion cut off." This correction and the restoration of the genetive construction are established by the rendering of Sym according to the Syro-Hexapla ܐܪܟܐ ܕܩܛܝܥܘܬܟ which justifies the back translation πῆχυς τοῦ τμημάτος σου, "the measure of your portion cut off." M should also be considered to be the basis for the rendering of V: *pedalis praecisionis tuae*, "the foot (measure) of your cutting off." Finally, Aq could be based on M if the rendering ascribed to Aq in the Syro-Hexapla is taken as norm for the first word: ܐܪܟܐ which would yield: πῆχυς (πλεονεξίας σου), "the measure (of your greed)," with "greed" rendering another meaning of the noun בֶּצַע.

G (28.13) renders the expression with ἀληθῶς εἰς τὰ σπλάγχνα, "(an end has come) truly to your inward parts," which would be based on a different Hebrew Vorlage, אֱמֶת בְּמֵעֶךְ. The same vocalization for the first word is attested by Aq if the rendering according to the Barberini manuscript is taken as criterion: ἀλήθεια πλεονεξίας σου, "the truth of your greed."

It is impossible to reconstruct the textual basis of S: ܣܓܝܐܬ ܚܫܟ, "your affliction has increased," unless the first word reflects a Hebrew Vorlage פִּצְעֵךְ, "your wounding," and a paraphrase of T: "the time of the visitation of your wickedness."

M received a B evaluation, the committee being of the opinion that none of the possible variants could be preferred to it.

Evaluation of Problems

The vocalization אֱמֶת of G has only been defended by Houbigant and Ehrlich (369), and it is the basis for the rendering found in NEB and REB: "your destiny is certain," where apparently M בְּצַעֵךְ is used for "your destiny" and G ἀληθῶς for "certain." However, the variant vocalization of G for the first word depends on the variant consonantal reading of the second, and one is not allowed to be eclectic with regard to textual bases while translating.

Volz (432) proposed the emendation וְתַם, "and finished is," for the first word, and although his proposal found little approval, it has nevertheless been adopted by NJB: "the finish of your pillaging," the last word rendering one of the meanings of the noun בֶּצַע. Other translations, such as C and GN, also prefer to read the noun instead of the infinitive of the verb בצע, "to cut off."

There is little doubt, however, that M has to be rendered and that the weaver's metaphor must be maintained. The measure indicates that the weaver has completed the required length of the piece of cloth and that the moment has come to sever the warp threads which attach it to the loom. The imagery therefore denotes that the thread of life is cut off. If possible, the metaphor should be transferred in translation or replaced by an equivalent metaphor.

Translation Proposals

NRSV: "your end has come, // the thread of your life is cut," is an example of a transfer of metaphor.

51.19

Textual Decisions

This verse is identical to Jer 10.16, apart from the fact that in M the second half-line of 10.16 reads וְיִשְׂרָאֵל שֵׁבֶט נַחֲלָתוֹ, "and Israel is the tribe of his inheritance," whereas in 51.19 the same half-line reads וְשֵׁבֶט נַחֲלָתוֹ, "and the tribe of his inheritance."

In this verse M has the support of the Origen recension of G (28.19): καὶ ῥάβδος, "and the rod" (the other meaning of the Hebrew noun), of S: ܫܒܛܐ, "the tribe" or "the rod," and, as far as T is concerned, the rendering of manuscript Urbinates 1.

Approximately 30 Hebrew manuscripts, including the first hand of Kennicott manuscripts 30 and 150 (HUB), have the reading וְיִשְׂרָאֵל שֵׁבֶט which is an apparent assimilation to the text of 10.16. The same assimilation is found in the Lucianic recension of G: καὶ Ισραηλ ῥάβδος, "and Israel is the rod," in V: *et Israhel sceptrum* (same), and in all the manuscripts of the Sperber edition of T: וישראל שבטא, "and Israel is the tribe (of his inheritance)."

G (28.19), however, renders the half-line in question with (αὐτὸς) κληρονομία αὐτοῦ, "(he—that is, he who formed all things) is his inheritance," in both 10.16 and 51.19. In other words, ושבט in 15.19 and וישראל שבט in 10.16 were lacking in the Vorlage of G.

The committee considered it not impossible that M 51.19 was at the origin of an abbreviation in G in both verses and of an explicit statement in M 10.16. Without taking a position in the matter of literary development, it judged that no assimilation to the parallel or to the reading of G should be made. M was preferred with a B vote.

Evaluation of Problems

From Kennicott (1765, 422–23) to Holladay (2.397), the reading of M 10.16 was adopted for 51.19 on text-critical grounds. As in NAB: "Israel is his very own tribe," the same has been done for identical reasons in many modern translations: NEB, REB, NJB, C, FC, etc.

In fact, the possible implicit grammatical subject of 51.19 seems to be explicitly mentioned in 10.16. Some modern versions (NJV, RSV, NRSV, GNB, CEV, RL, etc.) create the impression that they follow 10.16 in 51.19 for the sake of meaningful translation.

With the exception of daughter-versions of G and some older translations, such as LV, G has not found any supporters.

NIV is the only translation to render M and not consider "Israel" the implicit grammatical subject: "(for he is the Maker of all things,) including the tribe of his inheritance." This rendering, however, puts too much constraint on Hebrew syntax.

Translation Proposals

NJV (but without the use of square brackets): "And Israel is His very own tribe," and CEV: "and he chose Israel // to be his very own," are examples of an explicit translational treatment.

51.39

Textual Decisions

In the second sentence of the verse, according to M, the purpose of "making them drunk" is that they יַעֲלֹזוּ, "may become merry." This reading is only confirmed with certainty by the rendering of Aq: ἀγαλλιάσονται, "that they may rejoice exceedingly."

G (28.39) renders (ὅπως) καρωθῶσι, "that they may swoon away," which according to Grotius would presuppose a Hebrew Vorlage with יְעֻלְּפוּ. It should be observed, however, that the Hebrew root עלף is never rendered in the Septuagint with the root καρο. Spohn may therefore be right in his assumption that G has provided a translation which fits into the context. The same type of gloss is found in V: *ut sopiantur*, "that they may be put to sleep," in S: ܘܢܬܬܢܝܚܘܢ (same), and in T's paraphrase: דלא יהון תקיפין, "so that they shall not be strong."

Sym presents a particular problem with his rendering ܢܬܪܘܙܘܢ, according to the Syro-Hexapla. Ziegler furnishes the back-translation γαυριάσουσιν, "that they may exult," which would make Sym a witness to M. Others have seen in the Syriac a derivation of the root ܪܟܟ with a meaning "that they may become weak," which would correspond to the gloss of the other versions. As the extensive note in Field (732) shows, the interpretation of Sym remains very uncertain.

Considering the reading of the versions to be interpretational and not due to a difference of Hebrew Vorlage, the committee gave M a B evaluation.

Evaluation of Problems

The hypothetical Vorlage of Grotius has been adopted more recently by Ehrlich (370), Rudolph (312), and Holladay (2.399), and it has been dictated by the apparatus of BHS. It is the basis for NAB: "that they may be overcome," whereas RSV appeals to G and V for its translation: "till they swoon away." The same versions may have been at the origin of other modern translations, such as as RL, EÜ, and C. It is not advisable, however, to adopt this versional evidence.

Both NEB and REB translate M "that they will writhe and toss." This interpretation, based on an Arabic homonym, was already embraced by Abulwalid (1875, 528.9–28) and many others, and this indication of *delirium tremens* could very well be adopted in translation (so also McKane, 1330–31).

However, with the majority of modern versions (NRSV, NJV, NJB, NIV, GNB, NAV, FC), the classical interpretation of M with its outstanding irony could be preferred.

Translation Proposals

For the latter choice above, NJB can be quoted: "and make them drink until they are tipsy," and for the first, REB: "and make them so drunk that they will writhe and toss."

51.49

Textual Decisions

The first half line of this verse, גַּם־בָּבֶל לִנְפֹּל חַלְלֵי יִשְׂרָאֵל contains in M the syntactically difficult expression חַלְלֵי יִשְׂרָאֵל, "slain of Israel," which could be considered vocative: "(Babylon, too, is to fall), O slain of Israel."

The ancient versions all tried to cope with this syntactical difficulty. Verses 44b–49a are lacking in G (28), but the Greek recensions of Origen and Lucian have adopted the rendering of Th: ἐν Βαβυλῶνι τοῦ πεσεῖν τραυματίας Ισραηλ, "in Babylon of falling the wounded man Israel." V provides this translation: *et quomodo fecit Babylon ut caderunt occisi in Israhel*, "and so did Babylon that the slain would fall in Israel," S: ܘܐܦ ܒܒܒܠ ܢܦܠܘܢ ܩܛܝܠܐ ܕܐܝܣܪܐܝܠ, "and also in Babylon will fall the slain of Israel," and T: אַף בבבל אתרמיאו קטילי ישראל, "also in Babylon were cast out the slain of Israel." Therefore, Th, S, and T have made a preposition explicit before בָּבֶל whereas V shows the absence of a preposition in its Vorlage. On the other side, V, S,

and T have rendered the verb as a third-person plural, whereas Th demonstrates that he read an infinitive preceded by a *lamed*.

Because all the versions presuppose M, M received an A rating.

Evaluation of Problems

Oort suggested that, before חַלְלֵי, a *lamed* dropped out due to haplography
(see the preceding לִנְפֹּל). It is true that a restoration of לְחַלְלֵי would give excellent sense to the whole verse: "Babylon has to fall for (the sake of) the
slain of Israel, as the slain of all the earth have fallen because of Babylon."
This is probably the reason for its adoption by almost all commentators (except for Giesebrecht, Ehrlich, and Holladay), and by nearly all translations
(apart from NAB, NJB, BR, and Chouraqui). Rare are the modern versions
that even provide a textual note (so only NEB, REB, FC, and GN), although
this is the least one might expect.

In spite of the satisfactory sense produced by the conjecture, the textual
situation hardly allows this manipulation. Only the rendering of M remains
justified. The vocative interpretation proposed from Michaelis to, recently,
Holladay (2.400) is the most acceptable solution, although a rendering according to S is not impossible.

Translation Proposals

NJB can be quoted as an example: "Babylon in her turn must fall, // you
slaughtered ones of Israel, // just as through Babylon there fell // men slaughtered all over the world."

51.58

Textual Decisions

The last line of this verse starts with the statement: "The peoples exhaust
themselves for nothing," after which M adds the parallel: וּלְאֻמִּים בְּדֵי־אֵשׁ וְיָעֵפוּ,
"and the nations for fire, and they are weary." The last two expressions have
presented textual and translation problems.

In regard to בְּדֵי־אֵשׁ, M was literally, though not meaningfully, rendered
by Th: ἐν ἱκανῷ πυρί, "with sufficient fire," Aq: ἐν ἱκανῷ πυρός, "in sufficiency (one of the possible meanings of בְּדֵי) of fire"; and Sym: εἰς ἱκανὸν
πυρός, "to sufficiency of fire," correctly by V: *in ignem*, and S: ܒܢܘܪܐ, both
"for fire." It is the basis for T's paraphrase: "and the fire shall consume the
kingdom."

G (28.58), however, renders ἐν ἀρχῇ, "in the beginning," or "during
(their) rule," which, as Cappel (1684, 539a) already saw, presupposes a Hebrew Vorlage בְּרֹאשׁ.

With regard to וְיָעֵפוּ, "and they are weary," the conjunction is attested by Aq and Sym: καὶ ἐκλυθήσονται, "and they will be weakened," V: *et disperibunt*, "and they will perish," and T: וישתלהון, "and they will be exhausted." G, Th, and S, on the other hand, did not render the conjunction.

Considering the rendering of G in the first case, בְּדֵי־אֵשׁ, as due to a graphical error, the committee attributed a B rating to M. The same evaluation was given to M for the last word, וְיָעֵפוּ, since the reading without the conjunction was regarded as a syntactical facilitation and a harmonization to the parallel text of Hab 2.13b.

Evaluation of Problems

An entirely deviating modern translation is presented by NEB and REB: "nations wore themselves out for a mere nothing." This rendering seems to be based on a vocalization of אֹשׁ, the meaning of which is, according to DCH: "foundation." This correction probably stems from a conjecture made by Perles (1895, I. 50). G. R. Driver (1959, 148) proposed the same on the basis of Arabic *'assu* / *'issu* / *'ussu*. It is not clear, however, how one can come from the meaning "foundation" in Arabic to "a mere nothing." Therefore, in spite of the convincing parallel with the first half-line, this conjecture will have to be disregarded.

As to the absence of the conjunction, only NAB and NRSV justify their respective translations by appealing to G, S, and Th: "for the flames the peoples weary themselves" / "and the nations weary themselves only for fire." All the others take translational liberty without citing textual evidence.

In fact, from the KJV on, it is hard to find any translation that has followed M literally; and translational freedom to delete the conjunction or even the whole verb, because of what in most languages is felt to be tiresome repetition of information (so NIV), should be granted.

Translation Proposals

NIV is one example among others to deal satisfactorily with the problems: "the peoples exhaust themselves for nothing, \\ the nations' labor is only fuel for the flames."

52.7

Textual Decisions

In the parallel text, Jer 39.4, the common information וְכֹל אַנְשֵׁי הַמִּלְחָמָה, "and all the soldiers," was preceded by וַיְהִי כַּאֲשֶׁר רָאָם צִדְקִיָּהוּ מֶלֶךְ־יְהוּדָה, "when King Zedekiah of Judah saw them." In the parallel text, 2 Kgs 25.4, the same king is implicitly referred to by a third-person singular masculine verb form. In M 52.7, however, no reference at all is made to the king. The same applies to all the ancient textual witnesses.

Wanting to protect M against a conjectural assimilation, the committee attributed an A rating to it.

Evaluation of Problems

From Thenius to McKane (1363) and Holladay (2.436), conjectures mentioning the king were proposed, but the variety of the proposals strongly underlines their conjectural character. NJB has adopted the minimum information "the king," as an addition. NEB, REB, and EÜ reproduce a slight variant form of Jer 39.4 in the text of their translations: "When King Zedekiah of Judah saw this, he and all his armed escort left the city by night." They signal this text as a probable reading in a footnote.

Although textual arguments are not valid here, it should be noted that King Zedekiah is mentioned in the next verse and that therefore, in some type of translations, it may be necessary to introduce him at an earlier stage for translational reasons (so CEV, GN).

Translation Proposals

An inclusive type of translation, such as "Then the city wall was broken through, and the whole army fled" (NIV), can be recommended.

52.13

Textual Decisions

After having mentioned the house of the Lord, the house of the king, and all the houses of Jerusalem, M finally speaks of וְאֶת־כָּל־בֵּית הַגָּדוֹל, "the house of every notable person."

This reading of M is confirmed by S: ܘܟܠ ܒܬܐ ܕܪܘܪܒܢܐ, "and all the houses of the princes," and T: וית כל בתי דרברביא (the same).

G, however, renders πᾶσαν οἰκίαν μεγάλην, "every great house," which seems to presuppose the absolute state vocalization of בַּיִת and an adjective interpretation of גָּדוֹל. V seems to have done the same, in view of its identical translation: *omnem domum magnam*.

The committee considered the construct vocalization בֵּית followed by a noun more likely to be correct, especially since גָּדוֹל is preceded by the definite article. Therefore, M received a B rating.

Evaluation of Problems

NJB does not render the last sentence of M, no doubt judging it to be superfluous after the reference to "all the houses of Jerusalem." In a footnote it states that here and in 2 Kgs 25.9, the parallel text, a gloss adds: "he also burnt the house of every important person." Here NJB has adopted the proposal of Giesebrecht (257–58), repeated by Rudolph (320) and Holladay (II, 437). There are no textual reasons for doing so, however.

NEB has the peculiar translation: "including the mansion of Gedaliah," which not only implies an interchange of characters and the deletion of *yod* but also an omission of כָּל (not mentioned by Brockington). Such speculations should be avoided.

A number of recent versions (RSV, NRSV, NAB, NIV, RL, EÜ) seem to interpret M in the sense of "important buildings," since they do not make any textual statement. As seen above, "houses of important people" is the more likely meaning, to be preferred, with NJV, REB, GNB, FC, and GrN. The other interpretation could be footnoted, however, especially in projects with Orthodox participation.

Translation Proposals

REB can be quoted as an example for translators: "every notable person's house was burnt down."

52.15

Textual Decisions

In addition to the people being deported in the parallel text, 2 Kgs 25.11, M mentions at the beginning of Jer 52:15 וּמִדַּלּוֹת הָעָם, "and (some) of the poor elements of the population."

The presence of this last category is confirmed by Aq: ἀπὸ δὲ τῶν πενή-των τοῦ λαοῦ, "of the poor of the people," adopted by the Greek recensions of Origen and Lucian, by V: *de pauperibus autem populi*, "of the poor of the people, on the other hand," by S: ܘܡܢ ܕܠܬ ܩܪܒܢ ܕܥܡܐ, and T: וּמֵחֲשִׁיכֵי עַמָּא, both: "and of the poor of the people."

On the other hand, the two words are lacking in Kennicott manuscript 84, dated by Kennicott (1780, 78) in 1136, a date queried by de Rossi (I, LXIII). The words are also missing in G. In the editions of the Greek text, the whole verse is lacking. It should be noted, however, that the third, fourth, and fifth words of the verse: וְאֶת־יֶתֶר הָעָם, "and the rest of the people," are present in G at the beginning of verse 16.

In view of the uniformity of the proto-Masoretic witnesses, M received a majority B vote.

Evaluation of Problems

From Châteillon's Latin Bible edition of 1697 to McKane (1368), the omission of the two words in M was regularly proposed. This proposal has also been followed in quite a number of recent translations (NAB, NEB, REB, GNB, NJB, EÜ, GN). Only NJB and GN correctly note that the words may have come from verse 16.

In fact, verses 15 and 16 start with the same word, וּמִדַּלּוֹת, "and (some) of the poor elements." This *homoioarcton* may even have been the reason for an accidental omission of verse 15 in G.

The additional category of the poor strata of the population in M does not make much sense, however, and the wrong insertion of a marginal variant is also a possibility.

Therefore, translators may follow the option of omitting the two words, but only if they duly annotate the decision, as in NJB and GN. If, however, they want to stay with M (as in RSV, NRSV, NIV, RL, NAV), they should do so in the most neutral way, without introducing a distinction between "the poor people" in verse 15 and the "very poorest" in verse 16 (CEV), a distinction which is certainly not implied in the text. NJV ingeniously combines the beginning of verse 15 with the beginning of verse 16, which does, however, lead to some degree of redundancy.

Translation Proposals

For the first approach, see REB: "Nebuzaradan, captain of the guard, deported the rest of the people left in the city, those who had defected to the king of Babylon, and the remaining artisans. (16) He left behind only the poorest class of people. . . ." For the second approach, see NRSV: "Nebuzaradan the captain of the guard carried into exile some of the poorest of the people and the rest of the people who where left in the city and the deserters who had defected to the king of Babylon, together with the rest of the artisans. (16) But Nebuzaradan the captain of the guard left some of the poorest people of the land. . . ."

52.22

Textual Decisions

After having given a description of the capital and decorations of one pillar, the last sentence of the verse in M states that it was the same for the second pillar, adding finally: וְרִמּוֹנִים, "and pomegranates." S and T confirm M literally.

G has a whole sentence, however, instead of this one word: ὀκτὼ ῥόαι τῷ πήχει τοῖς δώδεκα πήχεσι, "eight pomegranates to a cubit for the twelve cubits." According to the Barberini manuscript, Aq and Sym would have had the rendering καὶ ῥόαι, "and pomegranates," then: τῷ πηχυ (*sic*), and finally, attributed to Th as well: τοῖς δέκα, "for the ten" (instead of "for the twelve cubits" of G).

V has a lacuna due to *homoioteleuton*, the eye of the translator having shifted from the first occurrence of the word ורמונים in verse 22 to the first occurrence of הרמנים in verse 23. The committee expressed doubts about the authenticity of the fragmentary readings of "the three," and it considered it unlikely that G, in view of its idiomatic character, would represent a different Hebrew Vorlage. G was instead judged to be a gloss, developed to complete a lacuna. It might have taken its inspiration from the number 96 in the next sentence. M therefore received a C rating.

Evaluation of Problems

On the basis of the parallel text, 2 Kgs 25.17, Giesebrecht (258) omits the word in question, considering it to be redundant. He has been followed by several scholars and one translation: NJB with its brief rendering, "So also for the second pillar," and equally brief footnote, "Hebr. adds 'and the pomegranates.'"

Most scholars since Cappel (1684, 539b) estimate, however, that this word is all that remains of a mutilated sentence and, taking G as a model, they try to reconstruct the content of this sentence (see Holladay II, 438). With the exception of Septuagint-based translations, this practice is not followed in recent versions. NAB presents an unfinished sentence: "The pomegranates . . . ," without attempting to reconstruct.

However, it is not necessary to consider the word an erroneous repetition or the remains of a mutilated sentence. It may reflect a particular focus which must be respected (so RSV, NRSV, NJV, NIV, GNB, NEB, REB, RL, FC) or it could be seen as redundant information which can be left implicit (C, GrN).

In projects with Orthodox participation, it will be helpful to footnote the translation of G.

Translation Proposals

REB could present a model for the reproduction of M: "The other pillar, with its pomegranates, was exactly like it."